Contents

To my parents

Lift High the Cross

Lift High

the Cross

Where White Supremacy and the Christian Right Converge

Ann Burlein

Duke University Press

Durham & London

2002

© 2002 Duke University Press

All rights reserved

Printed in the United States of America

on acid-free paper ∞

Designed by C. H. Westmoreland

Typeset by Keystone Typesetting, Inc.

Library of Congress Cataloging-in-

Publication Data appear on the

last printed page of this book.

Acknowledgments

This book began as my dissertation. In this connection, I would like to thank my professors: Wesley Kort, for asking me to think broadly about how this project changed my assumptions regarding violence; Jean O'Barr, for letting me know how much she valued the type of insight I have about the world in a context that did not value it; Regina Schwartz, for the interest and support that she has shown my work; Ken Surin, for introducing me to the world of theory without dismissing my criticisms and resistance; and Grant Wacker, for a careful and candid reading that helped me think about how this text might be read by people who stand in a very different place than I do. Last, but certainly not least, I thank my dissertation advisor, Bruce Lawrence. At those times when the complexity of my sentence structure would lead me to despair of communicating what I saw, Bruce would simplify my sentences, but he would never let me sacrifice the complexity of my ideas, not even when I was ready to.

For giving me free range in their research library as I was starting this project, I thank Political Research Associates in Cambridge, Massachusetts; Citizen's Project in Colorado Springs; Equality Colorado in Denver; and the Center for Democratic Renewal in Atlanta. Special thanks to Jan and Jim Diers for opening their home to me in Colorado Springs and to Wenda Bauchspies for finding me housing amid her Peace Corps friends and traveling with me.

I was fortunate to go through graduate school with a group of colleagues—Karla Bohmbach, Sandie Gravett, Volker Greifenhagen, Kelly Jarrett, and Randy Styers—whose support and intelligence continue to sustain me. In particular, Kelly and Randy are the readers to whom I turn when I feel most insecure; this book is so much better for your conversations and insights, encouragement and commitment.

I have been blessed with an extraordinary array of other readers as well. Thanks to Stan Holt, for the enthusiasm with which he read, coming over to my house on his way to work, coffee in hand and comments in mind; Zemo Trevathan, for helping me find ways (and the courage) to write what I know in the way that I know it, however many rules I felt I was breaking; Garry Walton, for continually encouraging me to do the hard thing that needed doing but that I feared; and an anonymous reviewer for chapter-by-chapter comments that spurred me to get closer to the heart of this book. I am also grateful to Eloise Grathwohl, who was always ready with words of support when they were most needed. I thank Valerie Faulkner, who was my partner during this book's most difficult incarnation as a dissertation. I am also grateful to Kelly Cross; the work we did together allowed this book. Thanks, too, to Lou Sawyer, for innumerable conversations about writing, which expanded and deepened my sense of what is possible. Finally and crucially, I thank Maggie Tucker for the careful and thoughtful attention with which she prepared this manuscript for the Press.

Preface

My interest in studying the Right grew out of relocating to North Carolina to do graduate work in religious studies. Moving to North Carolina meant leaving Oakland, California, a city I loved. In Oakland I lived full and open within the spaces a cultural politics of identity promises: the power people produce when they identify to make common cause; the sense of self made possible by seeing so many others who identified "like me." Born in 1963, feminist at twelve, from a white working-class family, I practiced micro-politics as the only kind of politics I knew.

Yet, identity politics has its limits. Although power arises when people reclaim identities that culture scorns, focusing only on identity does violence to differences even as it reinforces unconscious attachments to places of wounding—which are, for all the ways we hate them, also the terms by which we were first brought into social being.[1] Such attachments block the long-term political work that seeks to go beyond fixing the hurting.

In the cultural feminism in which I moved during the mid-1980s, religion in its many forms (feminist spiritualities, Native American traditions, Vodou, Buddhism, Hinduism, Sufism) was a primary discourse through which issues of identity and difference were addressed and denied. The Left can harbor its own fundamentalist fantasies of religion as a return to innocence—a return that too often legitimates the reassertion of power. Yet, unlike those who dismiss such hybrid religious identification as flaky California irresponsibility, for me popular practices of hyphenated religious identity raised disturbing yet productive questions. How do we learn from other traditions, cultures, and people in ways that dismantle the complex histories of oppression, appropriation, and consumption encoded within our attempts to cross boundaries? How do we learn from others when we have so many ways of opening that are really about closing?

Graduate work in religious studies confronted me with how complex it can be to use knowledge as a way of opening when our ways of knowing encode histories and relations of domination. Academic disciplines act out complex relations of dependence with the culture within which they arise, a culture that positions knowledge as a form of power. Consider how the study of religion emerged amid colonialism, so that "other" religions were seen through an evolutionary lens, sometimes as "primitive" and other times as the ancient spiritual wisdom of a great but now dead civilization that was destined to be surpassed by Western scientific progress. Similarly, the dominance of white middle-class forms of Protestantism has led scholars to identify "true" religion with belief (often in The Word) and to discount as "superstition" or "magic" religions that focus on ritual practices, the body, and materiality more generally.[2] Whereas power relations can be overtly articulated, more often they form a silent curriculum: those lessons teachers inculcate without needing to save a special day on the syllabus. But if academics reiterate such structures of power, we also have the power to dismantle the violence at work in the tools we use. Accessing this power requires us to disidentify from the histories that inform us by confronting the curious, paradoxical, and often just plain old painful ways that the structures of power we oppose "out there" are also "inside" ourselves—and usually in ways that make them difficult to recognize as structures of power. Instead, such structures are often encoded as ideals of academic objectivity, as defenses that cocoon around a correct perception of the world, or even as the lived counterpoint of conflicting identities. For example, in graduate school, the privileges of being white worked against identifying with my working-class background. Both these identifications stand in contradictory and tense relationship with being a woman and being queer. How to disentangle this snarl?

The multiple and conflicting layers of this silent curriculum (popular and academic, personal and collective) were sharpened further for me by living in North Carolina, a state with a long history of religiously inflected supremacist organizing. Perhaps the most well-known incident was the murder of Communist Party activists by Klansmen in Greensboro in 1979. The other thing about North Carolina that most out-of-staters know is that for two decades North Carolinians elected Jesse Helms senator, helped in 1992 by Christian Coalition voter surveys distributed at churches as well as a race-baiting ad about affirmative action that would have made David Duke proud. North Carolina is a state where students tell me they encounter Christians who promise them that if they can just pray hard enough, Jesus will cure them of being gay or lesbian. In North Carolina, the high-tech wealth of the new sun belt South lives next door to entrenched rural poverty that is strongly marked (albeit not simply) by race.

As a graduate student, I worked with two organizations devoted to combating hate crimes. Attending Klan marches and listening to people who had been targeted by harassment, I learned anew the strange materiality of discourse: how words can wound. And I learned again the shocking ease with which one stereotype slips into another: when race or gender or class or sexuality is present, the others are not far behind. The result is uncanny: hate violence most often is located in the cultural spaces between violent deeds and free thought, inciteful speech and loaded silence, agency and submission, reality and fantasy.

The combination of graduate school and community work brought home how remaining silent in the face of supremacist cultural logics can constitute collusion. This "bringing home" often felt quite literal: my parents were born in Germany during WWII. Like many of their generation, my parents were shaped by a culture of spoken silences surrounding the war, National Socialism, the Holocaust, anti-Semitism.[3] This history speaks: 25 percent of hate group leaders in the States are of German origin.[4] Working against hate violence offered a productive way to undo and move through this history: disidentification can be a practice of faithfulness.

So suggests Minnie Bruce Pratt, who writes of remaining true to her father (who opposed the civil rights movement when she was a teen) by "striving to change much of what he believed in . . . acknowledging that I saw him caught in the grip of racial, sexual, cultural fears that I am still trying to understand in myself."[5] Pratt's reference to the civil rights movement is not accidental, for a key strategy within this movement involved mobilizing grief. Today this strategy remains apt, given how much grief there is to politics: from AIDS, to the dismantling of social programs in the name of empowering the poor, to female students who take for granted their right to equal pay but do not identify with feminist politics (the "I'm not a feminist, but . . ." phenomenon), to the whitening of colleges and universities in the name of racial equality, to the ways we act without a clear sense of how our work contributes to the whole and makes change. But there is also a politics to grief: how we remain true to the people and places we leave behind by fighting against the structures that position us to lose what we love. Not surprisingly, grief is also at the heart of right-wing conspiracy theories, whose appeal has much to do with managing loss, enabling people to acknowledge, and to refuse loss at one and the same time.

In tracing the concrete places out of which my investigation comes, in which this work remains rooted, and into which it seeks to branch out, I do not seek to take away this project's fundamental ambiguity. Indeed, I cannot. Insisting that hate violence not be ignored involves repeating and recirculating that which I oppose: making you read the words of white supremacists and the Christian right, for instance, and thereby giving their ideas wider audience. Representations of violence—even critical ones—can deepen our cultural fascination with violence. Opposition to the Right entangles me in it inexorably, inextricably. Was I not already so? The hope of a project like this one is that attending to this entanglement can create a way forward.

This ambiguity dogs not only me as author but also you as reader. For to read a text is in a sense to write it. Listening to words that are filled with fear and prejudice, the mind reaches so quickly—I am amazed at the speed—for answers, answers by which to close the questioning down: Who wants to live *these* questions? Who wants to see how cruel ideals can be? Who wants to open to the violence, suffering, and sheer ugliness involved in hating and being hated? Instead, we refuse: *Not going there.* The task of this book, then, is to go there in productive and creative ways that clarify commitments, engender determination, and open spaces wherein undreamed of possibilities can emerge. The task is to create political agency—rather than paralysis or voyeuristic fascination—out of this entangled encounter with forms of violence most people would rather not see.

Tracing the Moving Track of Violence (and Desire)

Many years ago I heard Toni Morrison read from her novel *Beloved,* which tells the story of Sethe, a young woman who escapes from slavery and who, when the slave catchers find her, kills her daughter rather than have her Beloved endure what she had known as a woman enslaved: horrors regarding which most slave narratives preferred to drop a veil.[6] Morrison prefaced her reading by asserting that the telling of Sethe's deed occurs at several points in the novel and yet never really quite occurs. In the scene where Sethe is confronted with her past by her lover, Paul D, Sethe wheels around the kitchen—just as her memories wheel around this deed that she says but cannot say straight on, just as the novel wheels around this trauma that it says again and again but cannot say straight on.

Like Sethe, this book, too, turns around an absence—not because something is suppressed and cannot be said, but more because such circling movement simply is the nature of trauma and violence, power and desire. The pages that follow trace the contoured shape of violence that shifts its shadow through memory and in so doing shape-shifts us. For ultimately, what I am analyzing is resistance: something you can't cut through, because behind the tangled memories there is nothing to "get." There is no "there" there, only this empty space wheeling one around and keeping one moving. In the hope of lessening the affective charge so that this empty space does not turn us around quite so much and we become free to put this energy to different use, this book traces how the Right's counter-memories move and move people.

When I first began thinking about the Right as a project for research, I found myself fascinated and infuriated at the way the Right uses religion to commit (what I saw as) sacrilege: to touch people's minds and hearts, their love for their families and worlds, those tender spaces of intimacy and trust that are so sacred in the fragility of their power—only to turn this openness into violence, into supremacy, into hatred. My interest in writing about the Right grew from my desire to put language around this turn, and the double-cross it enacts. For while this turn had captured my attention from the outset, I did not know how to capture its movement in words, and still haven't quite, despite the many chapters that follow in which I use different methodological approaches and in which I explore different contexts, all in an attempt to close a circle around this "turn."

Part of the difficulty is that this turning was also what I desired most to dismiss, something I sought to contain in words because I wanted no part of it. Yet, for me, the desire for distancing and the desire that is writing undid one another. After all, if the answers are really so clear and known, why write (or read) a book about the Right? Dismissal will do. I wanted something more: to use words (and critical reflection) not to close questioning down, but to open into learning something new. Yet how to resist the comfort of false clarity without falling into the opposite trap of excusing the violence I did see?

What my fascination with this turning recognized was the way the Right plays with power by using religion to access the ambiguous spaces that power creates and to render their ambiguity productive. This kind of play with power is something I hold very dear in my life. As teacher, partner, friend, lover, writer, I find myself drawn to and compelled by spaces whose strength derives from vulnerability, from the multiple ways in which I and others are exposed to risk. If power is a relation, then power works, and can be, the most tender interface. When you walk its line, familiarity others you, opens you beyond what you already know into spaces unforeseen and ambiguous: spaces where someone or something has power over you because you give it to them, where you open another by stripping yourself to the heart. To stand in such spaces renders you vulnerable, because there is no standing here, no way to get ground under your feet when the point is the slippage, the movement, the turning.

Thus this project, like any hope, walks a thin line between contradictory fears. Who hasn't had the experience of attacking something by hardening against it, by denying the intimate web of interlocking projections that link adversaries—only to find that you ended up making what you oppose all the stronger? The dynamics of projection can give one's adversaries a power they did not originally have. Yet, who has not had also the opposite experience of becoming complicit by withdrawing, keeping silent, or ignoring—and in so doing making what you oppose even stronger?

Seeking to negotiate a way between these two counterproductive responses, much of this text works to complicate our picture of the Right. I have deliberately chosen materials that shut the door to easy answers that insist that "they" are only in it for the money, that "they" just want to hate, or that "they" are merely using religion without being truly religious. The goal is to "understand" the Right, if you will, by putting aside the tendency to "other" or distance in favor of "seeing with" the Right in ways that challenge and broaden one's vision. Yet, I do not extend "seeing with" to "seeing through" the Right's eyes (a task I consider both impossible and simply disingenuous).[7] In drawing a line between "seeing with" and "seeing through," I seek to balance a different concern: to avoid having my attempts at "understanding" the Right translate into a kind of relativism that argues for excusing or tolerating violence. Just as it is possible to understand another without agreeing with him or her, so it is possible— and I think necessary—to practice a politics that can oppose without demonizing or excusing.

For the point of studying the Right, of going to the places that such words can send you, is to imagine new possibilities. Politics so often polarizes. The Right says x; we countermove with y. We say q; they countermove with p. This sort of political discourse has a lot of answers. Yet, insofar as these answers keep us fixated on the Right, they fail to think and dream big enough. My analysis of the Right is driven by my belief that there is more to the power and violence of culture than is dreamed of in such a narrowly choreographed "culture war."

In keeping with this belief, my text moves back and forth among different academic disciplines: using one discipline (for example, religion or media studies) to amplify another (such as sociology or political science), using theory to amplify politics and vice versa. My goal in moving among disciplines is to illuminate blind spots, those aspects of a phenomenon that a lens cannot see precisely because of what it does see. These intellectual shifts are accompanied by shifts in my voice as author, which ask you as reader to leave a comfort zone and take up a language with which you might feel less at home.

This sense of not being at home can become particularly powerful when I talk theory. Critical theory speaks a technical language that can intimidate those whose skills are located in other areas. Chapter 1 introduces the theoretical frameworks I use to analyze the Right (with definitions of critical terms noted in the index). I suggest that less theoretically inclined readers let go of worrying about the various undercurrents of theoretical conversation that inform my use of these terms and read for the main drift: What can these critical terms help you see about those aspects of everyday life that you take for granted, those aspects of which you are vaguely aware but that you can usually manage to avoid seeing fully?

Lift High the Cross

The Violence of Culture:

Countermemory and Niche Marketed Masculinity

1 Countermemory, Children, and Ignorance-Power

Religion as Countermemory:
The Source of the Right's Popular Appeal

One day in September 1992, I find myself sitting in the city plaza in the North Carolina town of Goldsboro (east of Raleigh). The sun bakes the cement and burns the back of my neck red as I take notes. I am listening to Virgil Griffin, Wizard of the Christian Knights of the Ku Klux Klan, as he shouts:

> And they want to talk about equal rights. I'd love to have some equal rights, ladies and gentlemen. I'd love to get a welfare check, drive a Cadillac, get food stamps, and get a check to pay me every month to live in a cute brick apartment like they're getting. . . . What's happened to our schools? They took parents out, thanks to Madelyn O'Hare the Bible [was] took out, they put the niggers in, and our schools they became jungles, ladies and gentlemen. And the only way we gonna straighten our school systems out is to put the niggers back in Niggersville, the whites in Whitesville, the Klan Bible back in . . . throw the faggots out and you will see our schools straighten out. They teaching your children today in school to be ashamed of theirselves cause of slavery. I tell you one thing, if you are a working person you are a slave today, a slave to the welfare system and their give-away programs. . . . I'm not in this organization for Virgil Griffin. I don't fight the courts in Washington, D.C. and other states to win my rights; I want to win rights for that little boy right there. . . . If you don't stand up and demand your rights, and get in the streets and fight for 'em, they will have no rights. Your children, your grandchildren, nor mine will have no rights! . . . There's people in North Carolina they

want a coon dog; they go out and buy one. Won't let 'em do it with any other dog; buy a thousand dollar pen, put that dog in and protect that dog. . . . But they'll take their little six-year-old daughter to the gate Monday morning, kick her out that gate, put her on a bus with forty damn niggers and don't care how much she's mixed, how much she's mongrelized![1]

This was the first Klan march I ever saw and it shocked me. I'd heard many protest speeches that use religion as an alternative way of remembering history and empowering people to stand up. Theorist Michel Foucault called this kind of alternative history a countermemory.[2] African American Christians read the Bible in ways that resisted slavery; black churches today continue to read the Bible in ways that reject racial discrimination and exploitation. Rastafarians blend biblical traditions celebrating Ethiopia with images of Zion, narrating countermemories that protest the unequal power relations implied in naming certain sections of the globe Third World. The American Indian movement invokes traditional beliefs to counter the dismissal of Native ways of living as obsolete and to denounce greed for Indian lands. Feminist forms of spirituality protest the denigration of women by celebrating forgotten foremothers. Greens use spirituality to craft a less exploitive relationship between humans and the environment.

In such countermemories, religion does more than provide beliefs to which people give intellectual agreement, professing "I believe in x"—as if "I" and "x" were somehow separate. Instead, religious symbols and rituals, texts and practices, institutions and moods help form identity and subjectivity—the very existence of that I—by shaping how people remember their histories, orient themselves within particular identities, and invest in their world. Used as a countermemory, religion can empower people to reframe their histories, identities, and worlds by reversing mainstream perspectives in ways that counter existing power relations.

Countermemories effect such reversals by working the in-between spaces, or interstices, where individuals are not separate from either the beliefs they hold or the contexts (cultural and political, historical and economic) in which they come to hold these beliefs. Listening to Virgil Griffin, one can hear the concrete grain of the multiple contexts from which he comes and to which his voice speaks: the regions and generations in which his Southern accent is spoken; the class-inflected grammar; the nostalgic and almost physical comfort offered by a world where the events of life—its joys and sorrows, births and losses—are always already written amid the well-thumbed pages of a family Bible whose weight can be held, solid, in the palm of your hand.

Listening to Griffin today, in my home, I hear the paradox of human agency, its double-cross: how vulnerable people are to the contexts that produce them. Vulnerable, and yet therefore ultimately how responsible. No one is a sovereign subject: clear in motivation and intention, free because undetermined by the sheer contingencies of particular life circumstances. Children are born into a world they do not make and whose power relations shape them without their say. Indeed, it is through submitting to relations of power that a child becomes a subject capable of having a say. Think, for instance, of the technologies of power at work in being given a name. What's in a name? A veritable world: gender and sex, race or ethnicity, patrilineage and property as well as national identity—all are assigned when swaddling a babe in language.

Yet, vulnerability is only one side of human agency. For the contexts wherein we emerge as people do not determine us *so fully* that we escape responsibility for the beliefs to which (and with which) we commit our lives. To the contrary: it is our vulnerability, the way we both root in and branch out into specific contexts, that makes us capable of determination, of acting in and on the world. Picking up whatever tools they have been given, people put them to use—and thereby transform the partial, tangled, and contradictory connections they have inherited. Such is the positive performative power, the promise and the hope, of countermemory; shaped within the crucible of power relations that no individual controls, people can perform power relations in different directions and in the service of different commitments.[3]

Countermemory on the Right

Scholars have tended to emphasize the positive aspects of countermemories, as if all countermemories were by definition opposed to oppression.[4] In contrast, Griffin's speech reveals how countermemories can be crosscut, undermined, by conflicting currents. For although Griffin's countermemory sought to reject the pain wrought by economic globalization, he did so by calling white folks to stand up for white rights in the name of a Klan Bible and that little white boy right there.

Viewed in retrospect, Griffin's countermemory tangled together all the major themes that would emerge later, when I researched the Right. Imagining civil (or equal) rights as "special rights" to a Cadillac and a cute brick apartment. Tracing national decline to Supreme Court decisions prohibiting mandatory school prayer. Decrying a federal government whose plans for a "new world order" are not framed with working people in mind. Sentimentalizing parental authority by insisting on the need to protect little white boys from gay teachers and little white girls from black boys. Romanticizing the home as the place where all our deepest needs are met, where each man takes care of his own.

Right-wing countermemories string these themes together by means of biblical plotlines. Liberation stories that portray God as political: listening to people when they cry out in bondage and siding with the oppressed. Images of Zion that identify the nation as God's holy temple, promising plenty and peace. Nationalistic stories of a rebellious generation that took its prosperity for granted and scorned its fathers' ways, bringing curses on the nation as a whole, including loss of sovereignty. Erotic symbols that depict disobedience in sexual terms, embodied in women. Traumatic memories that portray God's people as forgetting their identity whenever they come into contact with foreigners. Ideologies that cast historical relations between peoples as a transcendent duel between the one true God who is jealous and the many false foreign idols whose promises prove empty.

These biblical memories and plotlines have not "stayed put" in the ancient contexts in which they arose and to which they first spoke. Precisely by being included in the Bible, these themes take on a life of their own. Unmoored to move through time and across space, biblical stories and symbols have been remembered, which means reinterpreted for new times and spaces, often in ways that have little or no relation to the ancient contexts wherein they first took root. Consider how the Puritans who came to this continent identified themselves as Israel wandering in the desert, and how African American slaves who were forcibly brought to this land identified themselves as Israel enslaved. Such multivalent and contesting overlays, which circulate through and around biblical texts, are how the Bible "speaks" to people today, and therefore are how biblical authority is produced, performed, and perceived. Griffin's speech derives its power from engaging with these tangled cultural resonances, which he attempts to harness through the signifier of biblical authority.

Whereas most observers analyze today's Right in terms of legal issues, political parties, or public policies, in *Lift High the Cross* I argue that the Right engenders popular appeal by using religion as a countermemory that enables people to protest the present. These conservative counter-memories use the symbolic space of the Bible to provide the cultural crossing point for tying (or articulating) these diverse themes to one another. The point of articulation is rearticulation: taking memories apart and reassembling their bits and pieces to mean something completely different.[5] Countermemories work less by freezing meaning and more by producing movement, slipping multiple (and often conflicting) memories into, between, and through one another to reaccent and even reverse popular memories.

Yet, movement works both ways. As the prefix implies, if countermemories take shape inside the mainstream, drawing on mainstream currents to redirect their flow, then such memories are, by definition, always open to being *themselves* redirected, respun, *reversed*. As I listened that hot September day in the Goldsboro town square, Imperial Wizard Virgil Griffin redeployed rhetoric, symbolism, and practices of protest associated with the 1960s as tools for a white supremacist resistance that empowers white Christians to get up, stand up for their rights.

In the chapters that follow I explore the performative power of such reversals, trying to make sense of their popular appeal as well as their claim to truth. Although my focus is on the contemporary Right, using religion to perform reversals is nothing new. Indeed, right-wing discourses are astoundingly repetitive; names and places might change, but the plots and conclusions remain numbingly the same. Earlier I noted the positive power created when people pick up the tools they have been given and use them for different ends; right-wing countermemories like the one spun by Griffin highlight the negative side of religion's performative power.

Attending to the negative side of countermemory is particularly important because it is not just the Virgil Griffins of the world who get caught in

Ignorance-Power / 7

the underside of these interstices. As Audre Lorde reminded, the tools that lie ready to hand are most often the master's tools.[6] As such, both those tools and our relation to them (the manner in which we reach for them, the way their weight shifts in the palm) are embedded in and obscured by vulnerability and loss, by deeply held fantasies of power as well as by passionate attachments to the terms of our subjection. Investigating the popular appeal of today's Right testifies to how hard it is to pick up the tools we have been given and use them differently—*and how necessary.*

Consider how Griffin produces an empowering sense of agency by representing white Christians as a victimized minority fighting for the survival of its endangered young. "I'm not in this organization for Virgil Griffin," he proclaimed. To which I promptly respond: Methinks the gentleman protests too much. Yet Griffin continued, "I want to win rights for that little boy right there." I would be the last to deny that Griffin invokes children to gain political points, but *these words* rang true.

Children Are the Crossing Point

Rather than dismiss this claim of care for children as "mere" rhetoric, I contend that Griffin's claim illustrates the key characteristic of contemporary conservative countermemories. The first part of my argument asserts that the Right's popular appeal hinges on its use of religion to construct countermemories; the second part of my argument suggests that these conservative countermemories hinge on children, or, more exactly, adult images of children.

From xenophobic narratives about a rebellious generation that forgets its forefathers to liberatory visions of Zion, children are the hook whereby the Right's memory-work hits home with sufficient power to reorient people's identities, histories, and worlds. Children act as affective magnets, attracting fears about sexuality and gender, race, class, and nationhood in ways that move people into the Right's orbit without requiring them actually to agree with its philosophical, doctrinal, or political positions.[7] Conservative countermemories use children as the crossing point by which to reverse the direction of people's affective investments.

For adults, children embody the possibility of a future. Paradoxically, however, seeing children as the very hope of futurity means that children also become a site onto which people project individual and cultural fears. For just as there is no hope without fear, so there is no idealizing anything (including children) without casting something into the domain of the unideal or abject.[8] This backhanded gesture is how ideals are produced: through an ongoing (yet disowned) relationship with an "outside" where unideal people, bodies, or things are stigmatized, which is to say held at bay—close, but not too close. Thus, the abject can never be banished to a complete remove because its presence is required, even if only as an absence.

This interactive production between hopes and fears, idealization and abjectification, love and hate is what makes the popular appeal of counter-memories like Griffin's so difficult to analyze and confront. A politics of fear engenders its attractiveness, not simply by playing on how vulnerable (and violent) people can be when they are at their worst (although it does that too), but also, and even more powerfully, by playing on how vulnerable (and violent) people can be when they are trying to do "what's best." I contend that it is not so much an explicit commitment to (or attraction for) hatred, prejudice, and bigotry that hooks people into the Right's politics of fear. Rather, what renders people susceptible to, indeed, already implicated in, right-wing countermemories is their hopes for their children.

Recall the words spoken that hot September day in the Goldsboro town square: "I'm not in this organization for Virgil Griffin. . . . I want to win rights for that little boy right there." From this hope, Griffin spins out a series of fears: black rapists violating little six-year-old white schoolgirls, gay teachers recruiting children in public schools, welfare mothers having babies as a way to scam taxpayers and avoid working. Each of these images engenders its popular appeal by addressing, and constituting, its audience as *parents*. Griffin's speech engenders popular appeal by playing on these interlocking fears, which are embedded in, and therefore are constitutive of, the nation's most cherished hopes.

When Griffin talks of race he imagines fathers protecting little white six-year-old schoolgirls from riding big yellow schoolbuses with big black boys. His words are harsh, overtly foregrounding a history in which white men raped black women while white leaders, in North as well as South, sanctioned lynching through disseminating counterfantasies of black men raping white women.[9] Most white people are taught such lessons in softer tones and more intimate settings. Reflecting on the racial apartheid of Jim Crow, Lillian Smith writes:

> It began so long ago, not only in the history books but in our childhood. . . . I do not think our mothers were aware they were teaching us lessons. It was as if they were revolving mirrors, reflecting life outside the home, inside their memory, outside the home, and we were spectators entranced by the bright and terrible images we saw there. . . . We were taught in this way to love God, to love our white skin, and to believe in the sanctity of both. We learned at the same time to fear God and to think of Him as having complete power over our lives. As we were beginning to feel this power and to see it reflected in our parents, we were learning also to fear a power that was in our body and to fear dark people who were everywhere around us, though the ones who came into our homes we were taught to love [a contradiction that, Smith says later, produced a dual relationship with two mothers, one white and one black, that made the Oedipus complex seem almost a simple adjustment by comparison]. . . . Therefore when we as small children crept over the race line and ate and played with Negroes or broke other segregation customs known to us, we felt the same dread fear of consequences, the same overwhelming guilt we felt when we crept over the sex line and played with our body, or thought thoughts about God or our parents that we knew we must not think. Each was a "sin," each "deserved punishment," each would receive it in this world or the next. Each was tied up with the other and all were tied close to God. These were our first lessons. Wrapped together they were taught us by our mother's voice, memorized with her love, patted into our lives as she rocked us to sleep or fed us.[10]

Today children learn a postmodern version of these lessons, one fit for the global village of the 1990s, while being no less visceral. Noting how Nike has elevated the bodies of Michael Jordan and Tiger Woods to the status of international icons, Hazel Carby reminds us that while "there has been a stark reversal in the nature of the visibility of the black male body," sincere popular affection for athletes like Jordan coexists alongside "hundreds of thousands of black male bodies languishing out of sight of the media in the North American penal system. . . . If the spectacle of the lynched black body haunts the modern age, then the slow disintegration of black bodies and souls in jail, urban ghettos, and beleaguered schools haunts our postmodern times."[11] This postmodern version of these lessons requires all children, but particularly children of color, to regulate how their bodies and energies are perceived and not perceived. In the case of young black men, for instance, this training requires regulating one's body and energies so as not to be perceived as threatening—no easy task in a world where black bodies are always already framed by a racial lens.

Such lessons are reproduced by training children in familiarity. As Lillian Smith observed about her own white girlhood, this training takes place first and foremost on the domestic front, more through raised eyebrows, withdrawn bodies, and long silences than through public speeches like Griffin's.[12] Indeed, Griffin's speech depends on white children having received this intimate training in familiarity to pack its punch. Thus Linda Kintz argues that right-wing women play a seminal role in the movement: "It is only with women's help that the public-policy concerns of conservative economic theory and its attacks on government have been so powerfully collapsed into people's feelings about the family. . . . Though conservative women have been involved in the more obvious political activities of monitoring school boards, circulating initiative petitions, distributing voters' guides to support political candidates, and running for office, their most important political contribution may well be their role in the construction of feelings of sacred intimacy."[13] Everyday practices that predicate bonding on "same-as-me-ness" produce our very perceptions of intimacy and connection as threatened by difference rather than strengthened by it.

Hence the Right both idealizes and seeks to control a mother's tie with her child.[14] For, as is soon discovered by anyone who has ever tried to raise children in feminist or antiracist ways, children are born into, and trained by, contexts that exceed the nuclear family. By idealizing mother-infant bonding as the sole source of the sacred human capacity for intimacy, the Right engenders desire for a technology that disciplines both parents and children, relentlessly reconfining people's vision of what is possible within the horizon of the private family. Insofar as this domestic training orients people toward perceiving familiarity as the precondition of intimate connection, such affective discipline provides a crucial condition of possibility for a right-wing politics that seeks to reproduce a national body politic that perceives homogeneity as the precondition for entering into the imagined community we call the nation. Yet, as Smith's lessons indicate, this familiarity is a fiction, built on denying the ways that such lines are always already crossed—and therefore built on denying the double-cross this intimate training means for children.

Today, most segments of society, including much of the Right, would distance themselves from the overt racism on which Griffin's appeals to "save the children" turn. Although racial fears, particularly as articulated through economics and sexuality, are clearly still with us, their in-your-face profession is less so. Today, overt professions of stigmatization and threat tend to be articulated—and organized—more often by picking up a different thread of the supremacy tangle: fears regarding homosexuality.

Griffin's fear-filled image of gay teachers infiltrating public schools to seduce children speaks to his audience as parents who hope their children will one day have families just as they did. Precisely by holding up families as an ideal, "the family" is produced as something people are, or want to have, by producing homosexuality as something you (or your children) must not be or want: something unthinkable, impossible, even monstrous. This does not mean that stigmatizing gay people necessarily characterizes all straight people. Nor does it mean that stigmatizing homosexuality necessarily characterizes all forms of heterosexuality. It does mean, however, that stigmatization characterizes *normative* heterosexuality; indeed, stigmatizing homosexuality is how heterosexuality is produced and enforced as a norm, as something people *want* for their children.[15]

This stigmatization derives not from personal prejudice against gays and lesbians, but from cultural idealizations of "the family." So, for example, Edward Steichen's 1950s *Family of Man* exhibit (which juxtaposed pictures of people from around the world in an attempt to communicate their common humanity by showing that all people have a family) captioned a series of pictures of heterosexual couples with the words: "We two form a multitude."[16]

The cultural power of this logic (as distinguished from the power of individual prejudice) extends well beyond the Right, as indicated by its frequent reiteration within some gay-affirmative discourses. Think, for example, of gay discourses that represent homosexuality as something no one would willingly be if one had a choice. Or consider gay discourses that celebrate same-sex nuclear couples as alternative families that are not substantially different from "the family" but for their being gay. This celebration of the "but for" gay family excludes more extended and collective understandings of family (such as families of friends) that are not based on sexual coupling. These latter arrangements require mainstream definitions of family not simply to widen but, even more, to learn a new language of relation and community. Learning a new language, however, hinges on seeing that all kinship is fictional, that the biogenetic connection celebrated in "We two form a multitude" is "a peculiarly Western mode of demarcating a certain set of social ties, a culturally specific way to signify belonging."[17]

Said differently, learning new affectional languages requires imagining human community in terms other than the genealogies of Genesis, where all the people of the world descend from a primordial pair. For there are not a whole lot of steps—although there are some!—between Steichen's celebration "We two form a multitude" and the right-wing protest slogan "God made Adam and Eve, not Adam and Steve."

One of the intervening steps is a particular understanding of gender. The idealization of heterosexuality encoded in "We two form a multitude," for example, stigmatizes homosexuality by dichotomizing gender: "Male and female created He them" (Genesis 1:27). The force of this gender dichotomy extends beyond that segment of the population that reads the Bible literally.[18]

To be recognizable to others as a subject, one must be either a man or a woman—not both, neither, or some creative inflection of the two. This either/or dichotomy constructs femininity, for example, as a cultural ideal that women must be schooled to "be," and therefore with respect to which women will always fall short. For femininity, precisely as an ideal, is something no woman ever is but rather something that women imitate, strive after, or refuse (a lack whose impossible fulfillment generates revenue for companies that market commodities to women and men). Here too, gender ideals are a form of discipline: one way that power produces its effects.[19]

In proportion to the height of a culture's hopes in femininity stand its fears. When Griffin invokes interracial sex, welfare queens sucking the country dry, and faggots in the schools, at the root of all these evil threats he envisions a godless woman, Madelyn Murray O'Hare, whose suit before the Supreme Court forced on the nation her own perverse refusal of the great chain of being that sutures family to country and God. In conservative countermemories that are even more explicitly antifeminist than Griffin's, this figure is often envisioned as the woman whose independent thinking marks her even further beyond the pale of family, church, and nation: the femiNazi lesbian.[20]

Thus, ideals of femininity are a double-edged sword. On the one hand, idealizing Woman effaces the murky middle spaces wherein women are both genders, neither gender, or just something else altogether. On the other hand, elevating Femininity as one pole sets up Masculinity as its complement: an ideal that is equally unattainable. For no man has a penis that is The Phallus, that symbol of absolute authority, knowledge, and power. Insofar as no man is a real Man, all men are marked by a falling short. One way popular culture attempts to manage this crisis is the masculine romance. Consider how action-adventure films and men's pulp fiction project male lack onto women: men do not fall short, it is women who lack strength and need protection.[21] By keeping women safe, men keep themselves from falling into the stigmatized domain of those who lack manhood.[22] If the heart of the family arises from bonds of sentiment between husband and wife, then hopes for familial happiness require Men to protect the purity of Women's capacity to form those intimate bonds of sacred sentiment that give rise to the world: "We two form a multitude."

At stake in protecting the family through policing lines of familiality is property. Here, property means more than economic capital. Kintz suggests that American national ideology entails an emotional attachment to property that is expressed politically as populism. "I'd love to have some equal rights . . . if you are a working person you are a slave today"; statements like these ally working people with multinational corporations by situating them in the same structural position: opposing big government.[23] As Griffin concludes: "If you are a working person you are a slave today to the welfare system and its give-away programs." The Right erases the reality of class divisions while speaking a democratic rhetoric of class rights: the dream that those who live in America, or buy its products, can make themselves new, pull themselves up by their own bootstraps onto the next rung of the class ladder. And if not in their lives, then in their children's—a hope that disregards the tendency of upward mobility to sever kinship ties. Speaking about his own encounter with this dream when his parents fled to the United States from Argentina to escape oppression by Peron, Ariel Dorfman writes:

> The friendly story the United States told me about myself . . . was the story America had already told itself, had already used to convert to nationhood the teeming millions that had come to its shores in hopes of a better life, the story that had treated those huddled masses of foreign adults from underdeveloped lands as if they were children and needed to grow up. It was the story of modernization and virtue and zest, the get-up-and-go story that the United States [tells] the world. . . . The story that tells every human being to be like America itself and the problem will be solved. . . . You can re-invent yourself. . . . America appeared on its shining horse and turned on me the full force of its power, the very power it was unleashing on the globe, and with the same energy and the same cheap and accessible and cheerful culture, convinced me, as it was right then trying to convince the world, that tomorrow is another day, tomorrow will always be better. . . . America, made of immigrants and pioneers and entrepreneurs, told me that I was free, that I should not let others determine my life. America told me I could be innocent again.[24]

Knotting these themes of sexuality, gender, race/ethnicity, and property together is a notion of the individual as God's child and therefore as possessed of certain inalienable rights—a notion that, as Dorfman's reflections indicate, idealizes innocence in ways that can be quite aggressive. As a representation of futurity, the child's body, with its endearing smallness, gives physical embodiment to the national body politic that is a community we imagine rather than live concretely. By securing concrete embodiment in children's future, the nation is proclaimed *in retrospect* as God-given and God-destined, as innocent as the children we wish we were and in whose name we claim to act. By speaking in the name of children, we represent our exercise of power and our assertion of rights as legitimate, untouched by the uncertainty that characterizes intentionality and untainted by moral ambivalence. In the words of historian William Chafe, "Americans have tended to see themselves as a chosen people with a distinctive mission to impart their faith and values to the rest of mankind," starting first and foremost with their children. As a result, Chafe continues, "Although all countries attempt to put the best face possible on their military and diplomatic actions, Americans have seemed more committed than most to describing their involvement in the world as pure and altruistic."[25] Given this commitment to narrating the nation through protestations of innocence, acknowledging the nation as imperfect and its history as less than ideal becomes tantamount to betrayal: "They are teaching your children to be ashamed of themselves because of slavery."

Training children not in familiarity but in critical distance could, however, represent this acknowledgment not as blasphemy but as a different kind of loyalty. In this way of thinking, people keep faith with their heritage by undoing the fears that haunt, trap, and limit the tradition, elders, and history they love. Such critical distance, however, requires us to craft different ways of relating inside and outside than familiarity and stigmatization.

Innocence and Ignore-ance Power

Yet, when it comes to children, we often prefer ideals and resist new ways. For resistance is rooted in the very notion of childhood, a notion that has not always been with us, but was invented at a specific moment in time. Analyzing the historical emergence of "the child" in eighteenth-century British portraiture (before then, children were represented as miniature adults), art historian Anne Higonnet argues that "the modern child is always the sign of a bygone era, of a past which is necessarily the past of adults, yet which, being so distinct, so sheltered, so innocent, is also inevitably a lost past, and therefore understood through the kind of memory we call nostalgia." Higonnet suggests that Romantic images of children as innocent became so powerfully hegemonic in Western culture because these images enable adults to deny the painful and unideal aspects of human experience and society that mark us as "adult" by idealizing childhood, an idealization accomplished above all, according to Higonnet, through depicting children's bodies as innocent of sexuality. This nostalgic vision of the innocent child provides adults with an experience of transcendence that acknowledges loss only in order to refuse it more fully.[26]

It is the duality of this gesture that produces its appeal. Suppressing all acknowledgment of the wrenching pain of loss is too saccharine, too artificial, and therefore too frustrating. Yet no one wants to see this wrenching pain either, not really and certainly not fully—better to turn away in favor of sacralizing the duty to protect an innocence that is always already going, going, gone. Held up in this way, images of the innocent child enable adults to acknowledge that life, history, and the world are less than ideal. Yet this adult acknowledgment is posited in such a way that it defends against what it sees: in America, you can be innocent again. The pull of images of children, then, has much to do with the attractions of ignorance: the appeal of a gesture whereby one hand cannot know what the other is doing; the seduction of seeing and not seeing at the same time.

Focusing on the way the Right manipulates our cultural idealization of children suggests that the problem posed by the Right's popularity is not that Virgil Griffin and his followers, for instance, simply need to be educated, that truth merely need be spoken to power. Rather than a lack in need of being filled, ignorance can be an act that people perform: *ignore-ance.*[27] Foucault coined the phrase knowledge-power to denote the ability of words and facts, disciplines and institutions to produce subjects who perform certain relations of power simply as a condition of becoming a subject who speaks and knows. Playing off Foucault, I use the term ignorance-power to denote the ability of the Right's countermemories to produce subjects who perform supremacist relations of power not just through what people say and know, but also and primarily through what people need not say and can afford not to know: the fears and aggressions, silences and desires that circulate through what is best in people, their highest ideals and deepest hopes. The power of such ignore-ance stems less from individual prejudices and more from its structural placement. Ignorance haunts culture because it inhabits the structures of everyday life so deeply that it need not speak its name in order to take effect.

The Violence of Culture:
Rethinking Hate Speech and Hate Crime

In contrast to this use of the term, when most people call the Right ignorant they seek to separate the Right from mainstream culture by denormalizing it, above all by representing individual leaders as ignorantly misusing religion for ideological or political ends rather than being sincerely religious. This strategy locates the power of hate speech and hate violence within the individual who speaks the slur. The appeal of this strategy derives from the desire to hold perpetrators accountable before the law. Yet therein lies its problem. For the peculiar power of hate speech stems primarily not from the individual who says the slur, but from the cultural history that congeals in the spoken sounds. We hear not just Virgil Griffin saying these words at this particular moment on the steps of the Goldsboro town hall, but the history that lives in and acts through his present words. Hate speech wounds because of a social "power accrued through time which is concealed at the moment [a slur is uttered] through a single subject who utters injurious terms."[28] Confining our understanding of (and opposition to) hate speech within legal terms can inadvertently *further* the concealment of this social power, insofar as focusing on the individual can enable people to ignore the structural nature of such violence. This ignorance comes at a price. How, then, are we to work free of this history that is "fundamentally unprosecutable"?[29]

At the heart of this question lies the claim that the paranoid Right is always with us (as historian Richard Hofstadter argued so famously years ago) not as a backward survival from some preceding time (as Hofstadter himself seems to have thought), but rather as modernity's constitutive outside, its other face.[30] In *Prophesy Deliverance!,* Cornel West argues that the internal dynamics of modern Enlightenment discourse "secrete" white supremacy as their underside. West analyzes white supremacy as

> a particular logical consequence of the quest for truth and knowledge in the modern West.... The creative fusion of scientific investigation, Cartesian epistemology, and classical ideals [of beauty] produced forms of rationality, scientificity, and objectivity which, though efficacious in the quest for truth and knowledge, prohibited the intelligibility and legitimacy of the idea of black equality in beauty, culture, and intellectual capacity. In fact, to "think" such an idea was to be deemed irrational, barbaric, or mad. . . . The concrete effects of this exclusion and the intellectual traces of this silence continue to haunt the modern West: on the nondiscursive level in ghetto streets, and on the discursive level, in methodological assumptions in the disciplines of the humanities.[31]

Or consider how Hitler's "final solution" depended on the very technologies of knowledge and progress through which modernity identified itself as enlightened. Similarly, the words of Klan Wizard Virgil Griffin wound not because the Klan is so powerful today in North Carolina, but because the violence of exclusion, ignorance, and hatred that empower Griffin's words are enacted everyday *as culture*. The violence that lies at the heart of Griffin's speech is not the violence that civilization conquers. The violence that lies at the heart of Griffin's countermemory is the cultural violence through which society enables, civilizes, and socializes: the intimate training in familiarity linking race, sex, and God that Lillian Smith learned at her mother's knee through arched eyebrows, withdrawn bodies, and overlong silences. Such violence happens in the murky spaces where subjectivity and agency emerge, where the familiar cadences of biblical countermemories function as crossing points that turn hope for children into support for a politics of fear.

The problem of the Right, then, is the problem of how we tackle the power of ignorance: in others, in ourselves, in culture. To take up the power of this history and wield it to different ends, we need to see its present effects and production, the traces of its presence: how supremacy is articulated, supported, and produced by mainstream structures and relations of power.[32] Such vision requires attending to the ways that we are never who we think we are. For who we are emerges in invisible and immeasurable dependency on the relations of power that shape and inform us, on the interstices in which our identities and capacity for agency simultaneously root and branch out. The worlds we inhabit are haunted by the histories through which they/we came to be. We cross into our contexts and they cross into us. This is the double-cross of agency. The most abstract structures of power take effect through, as, and in the embodied memories and unconscious fantasies through which we feel at home in the world; the everyday perceptions by which we recognize and feel intimacy, trust, and connection; the gestures by which we instinctively reach out to touch others and to construct possibilities for hope.

Understanding how power is performed in the microspaces of everyday psychic life does not mean that people are nothing more than power's puppets or brainwashed automatons. It does mean, however, that what we tend to regard as our most private psychic life is also power's "vanishing point," where objective (or public) structures of social power cross over and produce—become, and therefore disappear into—our subjective sense of "internality" or interiority. In other words, power works not only along a unidirectional line (when stone crushes bug), but also and perhaps most effectively along circuitous feedback loops of idealization/ab-

Ignorance-Power / 19

jectification. Writes Judith Butler: "Figured within the workings of the psyche is the power of the state to preempt an insurrectionary rage.... The process of forming the subject is a process of rendering the territorializing power of the state invisible—and effective—as the ideality of conscience," whereby society "regulate[s] the losses that will and will not be grieved." In this view, structures of power determine the psyche through, according to, and as circuitous loops of disallowed—censored—love and loss that wheel us around the empty space of loss and abjection in complex vectors of approach/avoidance, knowledge/ignorance, self-accusation/righteous judgment, hope/fear.[33]

In keeping with Butler's insight, I have named this book after a Protestant hymn in whose phrases and cadences the religious imperative "Lift high the cross, the love of Christ proclaim" crosses into the violence of lifting high the cross as a "triumphant sign [behind which] the hosts of God in conquering ranks combine."[34] I cite this hymn to highlight how the reversals that drive conservative countermemories, exemplified in this chapter by Griffin's claim to have joined the Klan "to win rights for that little boy right there," derive their appeal and force from mainstream structures of power that have always already vanished into/as our deepest commitments and innermost ideals: the hopes and fears people harbor for their children.

Although we say that only love can conquer hate, such a statement can be true only if we do not hold onto its truth in ways that obscure the double-cross between social power and our most personal hopes and dreams in which agency originates. My point here is not just that love, lofty religious ideals, and popular hopes can rationalize or mask aggressions and fears, exclusion and meanness. If that were all, then the task would be simply to separate substance from mask. To the contrary: there is a point—and in contemporary culture, children are often it—where people's love for others, their highest religious ideals and deepest hopes cross into a politics of aggression, exclusion, and fear. And vice versa: there is a point where a politics of aggression, exclusion, and indifference vanishes into religious ideals, love for one's family, and identification with the nation. To the extent that we refuse to see this double-cross, much less take it up in the service of other commitments, the Right's countermemories turn our ignorance into its power.

2 Converging Case Studies

Body Politics as Brand Recognition

My analysis takes the form of two case studies, each of which focuses on a particular right-wing organization. I do this through close readings of primary materials that include radio, shortwave, and cable broadcasts; sermons; books and pamphlets; Web sites; and newsletters. The first case study explores white supremacy by way of Christian Identity minister Pete Peters and his Scriptures for America outreach program, which is thought to be one of the largest white supremacist radio ministries in the United States. Christian Identity is a white supremacist religion that believes that the Anglo-Saxon-Celtic-Germanic-Scandinavian and kindred peoples who founded this nation are the literal descendants of the Ten Tribes of Israel, so that white Christians, and not Jews, are God's chosen people and the Promised Land is not Israel but Jerusalem. Peters uses this counter-memory to reframe rural economic crisis as conspiracy. The nation, Peters claims, has been conquered by Jews who are using the media to seduce the nation into forgetting its destiny: to be a white theocracy where Jesus is king, the Bible is law, and each man is head of his own household.

The second case study explores the Christian right by way of an organization with a significantly larger and relatively more mainstream constituency. James Dobson's Focus on the Family ministry has an annual operating budget that tops $100 million and a mailing list that exceeds 3.5 million names. The ministry represents itself as fighting to preserve the Bible-based family (represented in its logo as a Victorian mother and father with child), which Dobson alleges is threatened by a secular humanist conspiracy that has been seeking since the 1960s to erase all memory of the nation's Christian heritage by brainwashing its children through sex education, multiculturalism, and pop culture.

In choosing the case study approach and focusing on these two ministries, I do *not* imply that either organization or its leader (separately or in tandem) is primarily responsible for the current prominence of the Right. The turn to the Right in U.S. culture runs deeper than specific leaders, organizations, or even movements.[1] My goal in focusing on the Right's memory-work, and especially in comparing and contrasting these two different versions, is to foreground the larger conjunction of cultural forces of which these ministries are symptomatic and with which they interact.

Terminology

"The Right" is no stable united force but a conglomeration of formations that emerged through the coming together of shifting alliances. Analysts range these alliances along a continuum. Groups located toward the white *supremacist* end of the spectrum include National Socialists (such as Aryan Nations and Church of the Creator), skinheads, Klans, Christian Identity believers, and Holocaust revisionists. Groups located toward the new right end of the spectrum include Republican regulars (such as Jesse Helms), neoconservatives, corporate conservatives and big business PACs, think tanks (such as the Heritage Foundation), conservative philanthropies (such as the Scaife Foundation), the "political" right (groups such as the Council for National Policy), as well as the self-declared "Christian" right (including such groups as the Christian Coalition). Calling one pole white supremacist does not mean that the other end of the spectrum is free of racial supremacy. Likewise, although many white supremacists identify as religious and although Peters is Christian, neither would be included in the "religious" or "Christian" right.

These problems in terminology reflect the politics that lies within names. As I show in chapter 4, Peters proudly proclaims himself a white supremacist. Yet he labels himself a white separatist when seeking to portray Christian Identity as "simply" a white people's version of civil rights.[2] Because I challenge this identification, I use the term white supremacy when discussing Peters.

Similarly, Dobson and Focus on the Family eschew the term Christian right, alleging that it places them outside the mainstream. They also rarely use the term fundamentalism, preferring "conservative Christian." Yet not all conservatives, much less most Christians, would agree with Dobson's religious or political beliefs. Behind the welter of conflicting terms lies a complex history in the process of being remapped. For example, fundamentalist refers to a particular subset of white Bible-believing Protestants who in the early 1900s identified themselves as militantly antimodern. But fundamentalist is also commonly used to refer to Bible-believing Christians more generally who would not identify their religious belief with an antimodern ideology (although their devotional and supernatural reading strategies retain tensions with modern biblical scholarship). Likewise, although evangelical refers to a particular subset of Bible-believing Christians who in the 1940s and 1950s distinguished themselves from militantly antimodern fundamentalists, the term is also quite commonly used more generally to refer to Protestants who actively attempt to convert people of other religious persuasions to (a certain version of) Christianity. In the case studies, I most often use the phrase Christian right when describing the movement out of which Focus on the Family arose because this term refuses Dobson's identification of his brand of Christianity with all Christians or with the mainstream, preserving the political edge that characterizes the re-formation of born-again Christianity at the close of the past century.[3]

Although these designations are flawed, categorizing the Right in terms of a continuum preserves sociological distinctions. For instance, David Duke, with his history of Klan and Nazi activity, is not just another born-again Christian—despite his attempts to present himself as such when seeking election and despite the support he received in doing so from Billy McCormack, Baptist minister and director of the Louisiana Christian Coalition.[4] Likewise, in the beginning of his ministry, Peters often represented Christian Identity as no more extreme or un-American than Mormon beliefs about the Ten Tribes of ancient Israel.[5] When Peters became involved in antigay campaigns during the late 1980s, he portrayed himself as no different from any other conservative pastor with religious objections to homosexuality.

Peters speaks a rhetoric of rural producer radicalism to a predominantly lower-middle-class audience with *rural* identifications (if not roots), whose traditional middle-class status is being shaken by postindustrialization. Peters's rhetoric highlights working people while encouraging identifications with small property. In contrast, Dobson speaks a more genteel, professional-knowledge class vernacular. Although Dobson's countermemory also stresses the traditional Western homestead, the key issue for his constituency is their *suburban* identification.

Exploring the specifics of each countermemory demonstrates that, whereas the "culture wars" are a form of class warfare with complex relations to the emerging global economy, this warfare is being waged through nostalgic appeals to "the Bible-based family," whose sentimentalism sets into motion a whole chain of social silences. To capture the way the Right has taken its stand in the space between economics and culture (and therefore cannot be reduced to one or the other), I use the generalizing term supremacy (or supremacist religion) to denote the feedback loops whereby race slips into gender, which slips into sexuality, which slips into class, which slips into concerns for national supremacy. These mobile loops of personal and communal identity are a primary way that economic relations are lived in a postindustrial economy.

Converging Countermemories: The Production of Supremacist Desire

Despite their different sociological placements vis-à-vis the global economy (to which I turn momentarily), Peters and Dobson disseminate countermemories that converge through reading the national present within biblical narratives of cultural trauma. Again and again, ancient Israel finds that blessings turn to curses when a disobedient generation arises that takes prosperity for granted, forgets the covenant, and scorns its fathers' ways in order to worship other gods and enjoy deviant sexual relations with foreign women. Likewise, Peters and Dobson spin generational narratives that trace shifts in national prosperity and power to the forgetfulness of God allegedly induced by 1960s social movements.

Setting these generational memories within an apocalyptic framework, both men warn that the time for memory-work is running out. Each imagines the nation to be caught in an invisible—culture—war: "For we are not contending against flesh and blood, but against the principalities, against the powers, against the world rulers of this present darkness" (Ephesians 6:12, RSV). Although Peters and Dobson identify the world rulers somewhat differently, both identify memory as the terrain of spiritual warfare and the strategy by which the nation will be won. Both ministries dream a land made holy by popular remembrance: the rebirth of a nation.

In *The History of Sexuality,* Foucault argued that power in modern societies works less by forbidding desire ("Thou shalt not") and more by producing desire ("Go for the gusto").[6] In keeping with Foucault's insight, the case studies explore how the memory-work of media ministries like those founded by Peters and Dobson takes effect less by prohibiting what can be said or cared about and more by determining what seems worth saying or caring about at all. Both Peters and Dobson disseminate countermemories that act less by prohibiting the pleasures of the modern world and more by engendering desire for "the Bible-based family," which both ministries envision as the nation's sole defense against a communist-inspired "enemy within" that seeks to destroy the national soul by re-programming the sexual and gender mores of its young. The result is a paradoxical postmodern politics that appropriates pop cultural genres to empower people . . . to submit. By producing affective possibilities that punctuate the flow of information overload, the Right constructs sites where people can stop, install themselves, and take some control of their lives by taking up a perspective on the world. In so doing, the Right rearticulates mainstream institutions and histories, ways of thinking and structures of feeling to access the language of "the popular" and to speak in its name. After all, hegemonies are constructed not by making other people speak your language, but by speaking someone else's language even better than they do, reaccenting its words and silences. Yet these affective possibilities are produced in such a way that the very investments from which people derive empowerment end up furthering popular apathy and passivity vis-à-vis the shifting socioeconomic structures that determine their own lives and their children's future.[7]

Diverging Styles:
Nichemarketing

Converging countermemories do not, however, signal identification. Con-flating the white supremacist right with the Christian right obscures how they interact. Differentiating himself from the overt intolerance of hate groups such as Peters's Scriptures for America, Dobson speaks not as a minister but as a behavioral psychologist. His public policy division has gradually come to eschew overt calls for theocracy. Instead, Dobson likens the Bible to an internal "gyroscope" that guided the Puritans and the framers of the U.S. Constitution and that "still operate[s] deep within the spirits of the American people,"[8] as the shared consensus of most— although not all—citizens. Identifying "the Bible-based family" as the nation's *cultural* heritage enables Dobson to domesticate difference: differentiating "assimilable" feminists from "radical" feminists, for example, or "good" homosexuals who decline to express their homoerotic desires from unrepentant homosexual militants who insist on being actively queer.

In contrast, Peters castigates the desire to be tolerant, to love the sinner but hate the sin, as "effeminate" and "lukewarm." Peters calls the nation to resist the temptation of becoming "politically correct" in favor of establishing a white theocracy that is "biblically correct." Accusing leaders such as Dobson of proclaiming the Christian roots of the nation but fearing to name their racial nature, Peters represents militias as the logical extension of a politics of family values: Bible-believing men who keep their promise to defend their family from a federal government that even Dobson describes as controlled by an "alien force."[9]

Chapter 5 argues that the antithetical strategies adopted by ministries like Peters's and Dobson's are best conceptualized as differences in marketing style that stimulate desire through brand recognition. "If the three keys to selling real estate are location, location, location," quips Coca-Cola in its 1994 *Annual Report,* "then the three keys to selling consumer products are differentiation, differentiation, differentiation."[10] Peters adopts the confrontational style of the early Clint Eastwood, identifying with violence as his public image. In contrast, Dobson sounds more like Arnold Schwartzenegger in *Kindergarten Cop* learning that a real man would rather be a father than a paramilitary warrior.

Yet the cross-over figure of Schwartzenegger reveals the situation as one of nichemarketing. Both Peters and Dobson rearticulate a more mainstream sensibility regarding masculinity: the romance of masculine protectionism (epitomized by movies like *Rambo* and technofiction writers like Tom Clancy) that emerged in popular culture in response to challenges to national supremacy, the most pivotal of which was Vietnam (about which I speak more in chapter 5). While each ministry speaks an idiom appropriate to its constituents, both produce desire for action-adventure heroism. Each dreams of this land made holy by white Christian men who rise from the ashes of victimization like a phoenix, poised to take a stand and take this country back.

Moreover, both ministries engender this desire through nostalgic appeals to a golden age, a time when the nation had not yet lost its faith in that Old Time Religion. Yet the fact that both Peters and Dobson have pioneered the use of mass communications technologies reveals that the Right's nostalgia for a golden age does not arise from the desire to return to its bygone sociohistorical arrangements (à la the Amish). Instead, the Right's calls for "religious return" have more in common with Coca-Cola's decision to return to its contour bottle (originally introduced in 1916 to differentiate Coke from its competition) to cash in on the cultural capital of its contour shape, "recognizable the world over without even a trace of brand identification."[11] Much like romantic images of children as innocent, right-wing appeals to traditional religion invoke religion as an image by which to "unleash the power" of nostalgia (as Coke puts it), and thereby clear some space from which people can protest the present and invest themselves in the world on a gut (or affective) level.

This is why pointing out contradictions—how "creation science" clothes the Bible in scientific drag; how fundamentalists pioneer postmodern media to communicate an antimodern message—does not bring the Right tumbling down like a house of cards. Who really believes that eating Mrs. Smith's pies will make us feel as unconditionally loved as we wish our mothers had loved us? Or that driving a certain car will win the woman of our dreams? Yet we buy nevertheless.[12]

This blur of contradictions is how postindustrial societies work: imagination shifts into the realm of direct economic production so that what matters most is not producing material things from nature (as in industrial societies) but producing images.[13] This is true of images in the psychoanalytic sense: fantasy and desire, ego ideals and identifications. Subjectivity is style—less something we are than something we do—and the stage for this performance is the market. Our primary identities—what we think of as most uniquely, deeply, and really us—are formed on the basis of consumer and taste preferences.[14] This is also true for collective images: the nation as an imagined community, the alternative communities afforded by new social movements, as well as religious identity.[15]

In such a world, communities are products, commodities that capitalism makes. Difference is just one more way to produce a marketing niche. And bodies—well, in a context that proliferates prostheses of all kinds, bodies are just not what they used to be, and perhaps never really were. Pop culture targets the intersection between the body and the emotions; that is the key to its popularity, why it moves people and matters so much to them.[16] The so-called populism of the Right is mostly about this: insofar as the Right fights a culture war on the level of pop culture, it stages its countermemories as a right-wing body politics that performs religion as the possibility of protest and passion.

Hence the Right's penchant for a politics of scandal in which political concerns are represented as "gut issues." No issue is intrinsically a gut issue; it must be constructed as such by eviscerating, or "gutting," the issue of its political import, "reducing the complexity of the debates, the various interpretations and contradictions that surround it, to a matter of affective investment."[17] In such politics, what matters is less the particular issue around which people mobilize and more the masculine sensibility (or "gut") produced by shuttling people through an oscillating series of moral panics. By this means, the Right remasculinizes the national body politic.

In chapter 1 I suggested that Virgil Griffin's countermemory invokes the innocence of children to disavow the violence at the origin of this nation and thereby righteously to resanctify power. This disavowal works not only within particular countermemories but also across the right-wing continuum, linking its disparate sections in a relay or feedback loop, so that groups that sincerely disdain one another can nevertheless feed off each other. If at one pole the white supremacist right promotes itself by explicitly scapegoating race, at the other pole the Christian right promotes itself most explicitly as organizing around gender and sexuality. Although the specific issue that each pole deploys is important (particularly to those scapegoated), even more important is the conspiratorial sensibility—or gut—(re)produced as adherents construct links among a shifting series of enemies and thereby engender a stance of embattled victimization from which to reassert power. Analyzing Peters alongside Dobson deconstructs the opposition between "hard" and "soft" Right: both Peters and Dobson draw on biblical narratives that imagine the body and the nation as God's Temple in need of cleansing in order to manipulate the murky ground where race, gender, and sexuality intersect alongside fears concerning class, region, and nationalism.

As noted earlier, the result is paradoxical: the Right calls people to have the guts to take a stand (no mean feat), yet does so by means of conspiratorial countermemories that construct passivity as a new form of political activism. For apocalyptic conspiracy theories are empty at their heart. No individual, corporation, or nation controls a change such as economic globalization. Instead, such changes happen, mostly in a depersonalized, contingent, and even purposeless way—and *then* get crisis-managed. Although globalization is currently managed by multinationals in complex (and unequal) partnership with First World national governments, societies could shape these changes differently. To date, we have not, in part because framing these issues as "gut issues" reduces what matters to "only two possibilities: either fanaticism or sentimentality."[18] However empowering, neither possibility equips people to confront the complex changes that are rendering too many people's lives so deeply unlivable. Mobilizing people through a politics that protests the loss of a past that is already going, going, gone works less to help people assert power over the abstract structures that shape their lives and their children's futures and more to help people live with the structures they protest. Always Coca-Cola indeed.

Thus, the key to these right-wing invocations of religious memory—and the convergences between white supremacy and the Christian right that they make possible—lies in the power fantasy through which identification with an ideal produces an imaginary body. My use of imaginary as a technical term (which denotes the level of identification) draws on feminist appropriations of psychoanalyst Jacques Lacan. In his essay "The Mirror Stage," Lacan argued that you can recognize "Oh, that's me!" only if you are not the figure in the mirror to which you point. The point of such identification is to take on the fullness of that ideal as that which you really are (and never mind the ways you really aren't). Insofar as this recognition enacts a prior but ignored misrecognition, such dreams of fullness rest on holding loss at bay. Such fantasies of realness are empty— but are all the more powerful for that emptiness, by virtue of this double gesture through which such fantasies hold loss close but not too close.[19]

This is where gender enters the stage. Judith Butler suggests that gender is ungrieved loss: a performance whereby one declares allegiance to those loves that constitute the prior, but disavowed, misrecognition that enables identification with social norms and ideals.[20] Butler's analysis helps make sense of the knot at the heart of the Right's memory-work. By narrating the nation through a plotline of religious return, Peters and Dobson revivify the present assertion of power through projecting an imaginary masculine body whose ego boundaries fuse with the boundaries of the national body politic through narratives of apocalypse. The following chapters investigate male protectionism as the place where the positive and negative dimensions of religion's performative power cross: having the guts to take a stand, take action, and take control in the name of the Bible and that little white boy right there.

Each of the following case studies adheres to the same structure. Each opening chapter recounts a brief history and sociology of the organization in question. Each middle chapter explores the countermemory that lies at the heart of how the organization rearticulates popular hopes and fears regarding children and thereby engenders its appeal. Each concluding chapter explores the politics of such memory-work, and in so doing investigates the mechanisms through which these two sociologically distinct segments of the Right are beginning to converge: both ministries use popular culture to issue nostalgic calls for religious return and thereby to project an idealized masculine body whose protectionism resanctifies the present assertion of power: personal power, social power, and the crossing-point—ignorance-power—where each vanishes into the other.

Christian Identity,

Scriptures for America, and Pete Peters

3 Mainstream Roots

Until the Oklahoma City bombing brought it to the fore, Christian Identity was little studied. When I began researching in 1993, printed materials were limited to one full-length academic book, a few academic articles published in the 1993 issue of the journal *Terrorism and Political Violence,* a smattering of journalistic accounts describing the story behind sensational acts of terrorism, and a pamphlet written by activist Leonard Zeskind and published by the National Council of Churches that warned about the potential of Christian Identity to bind together formerly feuding sections of the white supremacist constellation (particularly neo-Nazis and Klansmen).[1]

Now, when I tell people I am writing about Christian Identity, many have heard something, albeit vague. Most often, they remember the flurry of media speculation about Christian Identity's connection with the bombing of the Murrah Federal Building in Oklahoma City.[2] At other times, they recall Eric Rudolph, who has been charged with the 1988 bombing of a Birmingham abortion clinic and is wanted in connection with the 1996 Olympic Park bombing as well as the bombing of a gay bar. Moreover, the subject of this study has been mentioned on national news. During the 1996 Republican primaries, Patrick Buchanan demoted one of his top aides, Larry Pratt, head of Gunowners of America, when reporters disclosed that Pratt had attended meetings and made common cause with a white supremacist minister. That minister was Pete Peters.

Most discussion of Christian Identity positions the movement on the extreme margins of society, without problematizing this notion of margin. This lack of problematization results, in part, from the fact that most public and scholarly attention to the Christian Identity movement arises out of concern for its possible criminal violence. While analysts adopt a variety of positions (from sounding the alarm to downplaying connections with violence), discussion of Christian Identity remains framed within legal and public policy questions, whose constraints subtly dictate the terms of the debate. Yet, framing analysis exclusively within the legal-illegal binary plays too easily into the desire to dismiss Christian Identity (and white supremacy more generally) as extremists: not us, but them. In his study of the old Protestant right, historian Leo Ribuffo has argued powerfully against dismissing the Far Right as extremist without problematizing the underlying conceptualization that opposes extreme to mainstream, margin to center, and criminal to normal. Ribuffo argues that "the theory segregating the Far Right from the mainstream obscures the source of [its] indecency."[3] Christian Identity did not come from nowhere, even if that is the way it appears on our TV screens.

A Sociology of Christian Identity

Sociologically, Christian Identity is not a centralized denomination but a fluid movement. Groups and individuals with diverse ideological and religious beliefs come together (and just as frequently fall apart) through shifting alliances. The movement holds together primarily through media networks (periodicals, newsletters, radio broadcasts, computer bulletin boards) sponsored by independent congregations. Congregations are frequently built around a charismatic leader who fills a variety of roles: pastor, writer, theologian, TV and radio personality, as well as movement activist and circuit rider.[4]

Estimates place the number of Christian Identity believers in the United States anywhere from 10,000 to 30,000.[5] In *The Politics of Righteousness,* sociologist James Aho suggests that today's adherents tend to be white and middle class.[6] They also tend to be college-educated, although primarily in applied fields with degrees from state universities rather than in liberal arts with degrees from Ivy League schools. Moreover, they tend to be located in or have relocated to rural areas and small towns.[7]

The decisive factor in converting to Christian Identity is familiarity, just as it is for someone joining a "new religious movement" like Krishna Consciousness. Most of Aho's respondents encountered Christian Identity in their everyday lives: at Bible studies, on coffee breaks, around kitchen tables. Most frequently, they were introduced to Christian Identity by an admired family member (usually a father, older brother, spouse, or fiancé). In the midst of discussing other things, the family member loaned a cassette tape or pamphlet or (less often) invited them to a speech or workshop.

This picture of how people join Christian Identity contradicts the common assumption that converts join extremist movements because they are socially isolated, psychologically alienated, and lacking friends or family— as if a subculture is the best such misfits can do. Underlying this assumption is the view that no one would choose to join an extremist movement under "normal" circumstances. In contrast, Aho observes, "My research indicates that the most important of those community ties is membership in independent fundamentalist, Baptist or Presbyterian congregations."[8] The most powerful statistical predictor of Christian Identity membership is religious background. Aho surmises, "The majority . . . were taught as youngsters what today they express in their righteous politics."[9]

Although Aho's findings suggest that fundamentalism is an important predisposer to Christian Identity belief, not all fundamentalists become Christian Identity believers. Not only do some come from other—or no— religious traditions, but more important, there is considerable hostility between Christian Identity and fundamentalism (as the following two chapters show). There is so much hostility, in fact, that political scientist Michael Barkun points to Christian Identity's break with fundamentalism as what makes right-wing groups since the 1970s so distinctive.[10]

Pete Peters and Scriptures for America

In many ways, Pete Peters exemplifies this sociological profile. By his own account, Peters was born in 1946 in Ogallalah, Nebraska, and raised on a western Nebraska ranch. He received a B.S. from Colorado State University in ag-business and economics, and an additional degree from the University of Nebraska School of Agriculture. In college during the 1960s, Peters claims to have been a member of the John Birch Society and Young Americans for Freedom, opposing the antiwar movement.[11]

Peters attributes his ministerial vocation to his wife, Cheri Peters, who, until her death from cancer in 1999, was often the catalyst for changes throughout Peters's ministerial career. Peters studied for three years at the Church of Christ Bible Training School in Gehring, Nebraska, where he received a bachelor's degree in Sacred Literature of the Bible.[12] He began preaching at age twenty-nine as a minister for the Church of Christ.[13] In 1977, he went to the LaPorte Church of Christ at the request of the congregation. (LaPorte, Colorado, is a small town north of Denver, located outside the university town of Fort Collins.) Because the church could not support him full time, Peters also worked for the U.S. Department of Agriculture, including a stint as supervisor with the Farmers' Housing Administration.[14]

This position saw Peters making loans to farmers at the height of the farm crisis. As was the case in California with Proposition 13 (whose crucial role in the formation of the Christian right is examined in chapter 8), the farm crisis was preceded by rising land prices in the 1970s, which turned many farmers into paper millionaires. Encouraged to take out loans to enlarge their farms against this collateral, many farmers lost everything in the early 1980s, when food prices fell and interest rates rose to nearly 22 percent.[15] Writes historian Catherine McNichol Stock: "From North Dakota to Texas and Alabama to Colorado, farmland that had been held by families for more than a century was lost to foreclosures in less than half a decade. Children whose families grew food endured the humiliation of being unable to buy it themselves."[16]

In this climate, the white supremacist right staged a comeback in the mid-1980s. Peters converted to Christian Identity at this time, in the process losing all but five of his original church members.[17] (By the mid-1990s Peters had built Sunday attendance at his local church to about a hundred.)

Peters attributes his Christian Identity conversion to radio sermons broadcast by Christian Identity minister Sheldon Emry, whom Peters first heard in 1976 while attending Bible College.[18] Emry led the Lord's Covenant Church and its America's Promise Ministry in Phoenix, Arizona, from 1967 until his death in 1985. Author of texts (such as *Billions for Bankers*) which remain important in Christian Identity circles today, Emry built America's Promise into a tape and literature outlet as well as a radio ministry. He ordained Peters as a Christian Identity minister in October 1984.[19]

Upon converting to Christian Identity, Peters shifted to full-time ministerial work. Following the example of his mentor Emry, Peters's first task was to develop extensive communication networks as an alternative to mainstream media. Beginning in 1984, Peters has taped his Sunday sermons, distributing them free (until 1999, when he began charging a nominal fee). He also distributes a free monthly newsletter (the idea for which came from Cheri Peters, who often provided the necessary labor). Peters acquired a printing press and publishes his own pamphlets and books. He broadcasts on radio. Just before the Oklahoma bombing, he had amassed sufficient funds to broadcast on two shortwave frequencies seven days a week, as well as nine AM and FM stations. He had even begun a TV program on the "family values–oriented" Keystone Inspirational Network, which interspersed his program with standard fundamentalist fare such as Falwell's *Old Time Gospel Hour* and Robertson's *700 Club*. (The network took Peters's program off the air after the Oklahoma City bombing.) Peters was an early pioneer on the Internet, establishing a Web page and compiling a repository of Christian Identity materials for downloading.[20] As a result of his pioneering work with new information technologies, his outreach program, Scriptures for America, is considered to be one of the country's largest and most active, attracting "a following of the more militant of Identity adherents."[21]

In these efforts, Peters worked closely with his wife, Cheri Peters, who had her own column in the monthly newsletter entitled "For Women Only." Her column usually addressed issues of gender and family, most often in terms that evoked the ideology of Republican motherhood. Consider the following: "If mothers and fathers throughout the years had continued to teach their precious jewels the ways of God, their National Heritage, and written upon their hearts the laws God has established for us, maybe our nation wouldn't be in the darkness it is in today! . . . A Mother's heart is her child's schoolroom!"[22] Cheri's solution to this national crisis included "memory-work," by which she meant memorizing Bible passages. For adults, she also recommended sex education: "There is no place for sex outside the marriage bed, and again there is no place for frigidity within the marriage bed." In one early column, her remarks on child discipline were so close to James Dobson's book *Dare to Discipline* that they verged on plagiarism.[23] When Scriptures for America was taken off the air in 1987, Cheri aired her own radio program for about five months.[24]

Since 1984, Pete Peters has held his congregation together by annual Bible camps, one of his more effective evangelization strategies (and one that came from Cheri Peters). Attendance has grown to approximately five hundred from almost every state. Summer Bible camps are advertised as family fun; featured in 1996 were a talent night, Saxon games, a quilting bee, campfire singing and devotionals, a date night for marrieds only, Virginia reel for everyone, a mother-daughter tea, and paintball for the boys. Also in 1996, Pete and Cheri staged "The Marriage Zone," a take-off on *The Twilight Zone,* which humorously depicted the typical pitfalls of married life. In other years, Pete and Cheri reenacted the "Battle of the Ages," portraying "the age-old battle between parents and child." There is also a country market where Christian goods and services are sold (overseen by a market director who must approve each item).

Summer Bible camp trains adherents in Christian Identity. Sample workshop topics for the 1988 camp included marriage, child rearing, biblical law, victory over persecution, outreach ministries, kingdom dominion, anti-Christ tactics, baptism, and Bible health principles.[25]

Bible camp also provides access to Christian Identity leaders. In 1987, lawyer Kirk Lyons spoke to Peters's camp about how he got a jury to acquit Christian Identity adherent Doug Sheets, who had been charged with shooting five gay men in Shelby, North Carolina, killing three and wounding two. Peters passed a hat for donations to Lyons's legal efforts on behalf of white supremacists who get in trouble with the law, which Lyons models as a white supremacist ACLU.

A more frequent featured speaker is Richard Hoskins, whose book, *The Vigilantes of Christendom,* is made available by SFA. In this book, Hoskins envisions a secret line of avengers who mercilessly annihilate the enemies of God. Their lineage stretches from Doug Sheets, Robert Mathews, Jesse James, King Arthur, St. George, and Robin Hood all the way back in unbroken transmission to Phineas, the Israelite priest in Numbers 25 who stabbed an Israelite man and his foreign-born wife while the two were engaged in sexual intercourse. In keeping with their namesake, the task of these unbeatable avengers is to keep Christ's people pure by eliminating its black sheep.[26]

In addition to his annual Rocky Mountain Family Bible Camp, Peters hosts or cosponsors several weekend camps during the year and travels around the country speaking at various Christian Identity–friendly gatherings. Since 1989, Scriptures for America has run a "political prisoners" support group, giving financial and emotional assistance to imprisoned Christian Identity adherents and their families.[27]

History of the Christian Identity Movement

When Pete and Cheri Peters converted to Christian Identity, they circulated within a subcultural milieu whose roots extend into mainstream American life. Intellectually, Christian Identity descends from Anglo-Israelism (also called British Israelism), which developed in England during the second half of the nineteenth century.[28] Adherents believed Anglo-Saxons to be the biological descendants of ancient Israel's Ten Tribes, which scattered abroad in 722 B.C.E. when Assyria conquered Israel's Northern Kingdom. According to Barkun, Anglo-Israelism peaked during the 1920s, as Britain escalated its repression of India "in defense of the realm."[29] At this time, Anglo-Israelism boasted about five thousand members, drawn mostly from the middle class, with a few aristocrats and military officers providing high visibility and resources.

In North America, imagining the New World as a new Israel and speculating about the identity of the Ten Lost Tribes were common ways of thinking for many. Charles Fox Parham (influential in founding the Pentecostalist movement) and J. H. Allen (influential in founding the Church of God Holiness) "infused British-Israelism into the premillennial evangelical sects that were emerging out of midwestern Methodism" at the turn of the century (Barkun, *Racist Right,* 20–21).[30]

Anglo-Israelism in the United States remained within Bible circles until the 1930s, when it was linked to the political right by Howard Rand, a Massachusetts lawyer who had been raised in an Anglo-Israelite home and who founded the Anglo-Saxon Federation of America, and Federation President Will Cameron, a lay preacher best known to the public for his role as public relations agent for Henry Ford (Barkun, *Racist Right,* 33). Cameron's articles in Ford's *Dearborn Independent* linked the biblical hermeneutics of British Israelism to political notions of Jewish conspiracy for world domination popularized in the *Protocols of the Elders of Zion* (33–34).

Barkun finds it "ironical" that Ford, himself an agent of so many of the changes that modern industrialization brought to American life, "be-

Mainstream Roots / 39

came, along with the 1920s Ku Klux Klan, one of the voices of anti-Semitic resentment" (*Racist Right*, 34). To me, this contradiction suggests how power can work through disavowal. Fordism entailed creating a new kind of human being.[31] Such intense discipline engenders intense resistance. One need not blame popular anti-Semitism on the intentional cultivation of industrialists like Ford to see how Ford's populist image might profit— both in his eyes as well as the eyes of others—from displacing popular resentment against the deep personal and cultural changes wrought by Fordism.

Barkun reads Anglo-Israelism as no more anti-Semitic than evangelical Protestants of the time tended to be. Although anti-Semitic themes were present in Rand's Anglo-Saxon Federation, for example, anti-Semitism was not the focus of its public policies (Barkun, *Racist Right*, 48). Barkun attributes this backgrounding of anti-Semitism to the paternalistic belief that Jews could be made to repent of conspiracy, be converted to Christianity, and thus were "salvageable"—although only as future Christians and not as Jews (115–16). Yet, paternalism cuts two ways. When Zionists began demanding British withdrawal from Israel, a Vancouver-based group of British Israelites published the first statements identifying Jews as the literal offspring of Satan, prone to forms of social subversion such as communism, beginning the process whereby an explicitly anti-Semitic and racialist ideology would be grafted onto the implicit anti-Semitism of Anglo-Israelism (48–52).

Although the Vancouver connection was crucial, 1940s Los Angeles was the place where Anglo-Israelism morphed into the movement we know today as Christian Identity. From 1890 to 1930, Los Angeles was one of the fastest growing cities in the United States and a hotbed of religious experimentation. Not only did Anglo-Israelism impinge on many sides (from Pentecostalism and revivalism to Rand's Anglo-Saxon Federation), but it became part of a cultic milieu where it circulated among a host of diverse beliefs, including pseudo-science and the occult (Barkun, *Racist Right*, 63). The resulting "bizarre mixture," Barkun suggests, was less akin to the political anti-Semitism of Europe in the late 1800s than to "the folk religion of the Middle Ages, re-theologizing anti-Semitism as the center of a dualist vision in which the powers of light and darkness confront one another in a battle whose implications will be both universal and everlasting."[32]

Many of these strands came together in the figure of Gerald Smith. A fundamentalist minister, Smith joined William Pelley's Silver Shirts, which Pelley modeled after Hitler's Brown Shirts, and worked as a national organizer for Huey Long's "Save Our Wealth" campaign, after which he moved to Detroit and met Henry Ford, who convinced him that "Communism is Jewish."[33] Smith built a coherent Christian Identity network on the West Coast (Barkun, *Racist Right*, 49), training the next two generations of Christian Identity leaders in either his Christian Nationalist Crusade organization (founded in 1947) or in its youth wing. These two generations founded the organizations and projects that constitute the subculture that trained and mentored Pete Peters.

Early in his career, Peters associated himself with the survivalist Christian Patriots Defense League.[34] Along with the associated Citizens Emergency Defense System, the League was founded by Southern Illinois millionaire John Harrell after his release from jail for tax evasion. Harrell called for the preservation of a "mid-America Survival Zone" where white Christians could prevail over the "ruthless Communist dictatorship" that would rule America during the Tribulation. He gathered the faithful to paramilitary training in the Ozarks.[35] Peters connected to the Christian Patriots Defense League through his mentor Emry as well as through Jack Mohr. A former Baptist preacher and John Bircher as well as a former Korean prisoner of war, Mohr became minister of defense for the League after becoming convinced that "Communism is Jewish" when, while lecturing about the communist menace on the college lecture circuit in the 1960s, Mohr "discovered" that leaders of campus radicalism had been raised in Jewish families.[36]

It was Peters's association with Mohr that first brought Peters to local attention, although in relation to a section of the white supremacist constellation with which Peters usually experiences a theological and stylistic disconnect. In 1983, breakaway associates of Aryan Nations, several of whom met in Peters's Colorado congregation, formed The Order. Founder Robert Mathews is thought to have patterned the group after *The Turner Diaries*, a book that might also have influenced Timothy McVeigh. Written by neo-Nazi William Pierce, *The Turner Diaries* is a futuristic prophecy book that purports to narrate the race war that established white supremacy in the United States. Real-life Order members passed counterfeit money and held up armored vehicles to finance white revolution against "the Zionist Occupied Government" (or ZOG) of the United States.[37]

The rise and fall of The Order coincided with Peters's own emergence into the Christian Identity movement. On January 7 and 8, 1984, Peters hosted Mohr at the LaPorte Church of Christ, sparking a spate of denunciation in nearby Fort Collins that ranged from letters to the editor and protests by the Fort Collins Interfaith Council, to a group of Church of Christ pastors who visited Peters.[38] The controversy came to the attention of Alan Berg, a Denver talk show host who was Jewish. Berg hosted—and roasted—Peters and Mohr on the air on February 13, 1984. Several Order members heard the show; one called to debate Berg, who hung up on him (as was Berg's wont).[39] On June 18, 1984, The Order machine-gunned Berg to death. In 1985, the same year that Peters was officially ordained, 23 Order members and associates went on trial in Seattle; ten were convicted and given lengthy prison sentences.

No Typical Identity Leader

Despite the fact that he first came to public attention in connection with The Order, Peters styles himself as first and foremost a pastor and preacher. He has not become an alternative legal theoretician, a traveling paramilitary trainer, head of a survivalist community, or founder of alternative banking institutions (like those with which the Montana Freemen were reportedly involved). In choosing Peters to study, I do not mean to imply that all Christian Identity leaders and adherents share his focus on developing specifically religious forms of organizing. Christian Identity is too decentralized and mobile a movement to be summarized through one leader.

If Peters should not be read as a "typical" Christian Identity leader, what can be learned from studying the LaPorte Church of Christ and Scriptures for America? When this chapter began, I noted that most discussions of Christian Identity position the movement on the extreme margins of society without questioning the notion of margin, because most attention to this movement arises out of concern for criminal violence. In contrast, I contend that the challenge of understanding Christian Identity lies in comprehending, as Catherine McNichol Stock observes, how the roots of violence, racism and hatred can be and have been nourished in the same soil and from the same experiences that generated rural movements for democracy and equality. In many places and at many times in the American past, the best and the worst, the most forgiving and the most vengeful, the most egalitarian and the most authoritarian, the brightest and the darkest visions of American life were alive in the same men's souls, nurtured at the same dinner tables, learned in the same schools, preached in the same pulpits. Not two sets of beliefs, then, but two expressions of the same beliefs and circumstances bound Left and Right together in an unwavering, desperate, synthetic embrace. This interrelationship cannot and should not be ignored.[40]

In the following chapter, I focus on the specifics of Peters's white supremacist countermemory. What is its appeal? its dynamics? its power to transvalue biblical Christianity into a politics of white supremacy? Rather than refuting this countermemory by pointing out its contradictions, I explore the specific techniques of its production: the larger social, economic, and political conditions that it articulates, that it seeks to redeploy, and by which it is often used in turn. Above all, I trace the multiple trajectories along which the Bible (and cultural memories of the Bible) facilitate the production of a countermemory that imagines nationhood, history, bodies, and power in ways that engender a supremacist sensibility.

4 Biblical Memories and the Erotics of Domination

"Not Politically Correct but Biblically Correct"

Our deepest cultural assumptions are biblical and they are not always attractive.—Regina Schwartz, *The Curse of Cain*[1]

Although terrorism brought attention to Scriptures for America and Christian Identity, the significance of Peters's ministry lies more in his attempt to mainstream white supremacy by reading the Bible as a counter-memory. Anthropologist Susan Harding suggests that the Bible played a similar role in the antiabortion movement: "What made abortion a volcanic issue for born-agains—the only issue that spun them in large numbers into political organizations, support groups, public hearings, demonstrations, and, most recently, jails—was the Biblicization of anti-abortion rhetoric, carried out mostly by preachers."[2] Yet, such contemporary positions are not "in" the Bible in some straightforward way: they must be "biblicized," linked to narratives and images with deep cultural resonance.

As social psychologist Raphael Ezekiel observes, "The imagery employed in the [Christian Identity] movement is indeed ancient."[3] Jews as serpents. Whites as warriors. African Americans as apes. Mexicans as aliens consuming the land. Women as harlots. The land as karmic Zion bearing fruit for those who follow its laws while vomiting up those who disobey. Yet this imagery is equally postmodern, proliferated by the Internet, shortwave, and fax, stylized through cartoons and talk shows.

The power of biblicization lies in linking the ancient past to this postmodern present. Links create media memories that are difficult to distinguish from the personal memories people construct about their own experiences. Consider how media images that featured federal tanks advancing on Waco exerted a greater truth/reality effect for some Americans than the federal subsidies they received to keep their farms going. It is no longer easy to remember what was "live" and what was Memorex.[4]

Read in this environment, the Bible changes. By the Bible, we usually mean a book confined within covers. Yet no one reads the Bible in abstraction from the concrete ways this book has been told and not told, cited and refuted, intentionally meditated on and unconsciously enacted. Information technologies accelerated this ability of words and books, and thus of The Word and The Book, to speak to new contexts in unintended ways.[5] Communication technologies work not by promoting sustained reflection, but by moving information.[6] In this environment, the Bible functions less like the self-contained book it appears to be (although never really was) and more like hypertext: connecting disparate discourses and histories, practices and fantasies through paths that need not be linear.

Hyperlinks happen because words signify in ways that escape control. Peters reads the same words in the Bible as you and I, but he reverses their evaluative accent. According to linguist V. N. Volosinov, "In actual fact, each living ideological sign has two faces, like Janus. Any current curse word can become a word of praise, any current truth must inevitably sound to many other people as the greatest lie."[7] Peters spins (or rearticulates) praises as curses and truths as lies by manipulating not only what we *say* about religion, family, and nation, but also what we leave *unsaid:* the unspoken and often unspeakable hopes and fears concerning race, class, gender, and sexuality that shadow American dreams.

As these silences multiply, they become mobile. Slipping into one another until we cannot keep track of their movements, such silences produce an epistemic murk in which what people know becomes radically uncertain and "up for grabs."[8] According to Peters, Israel is not Israel, Jews are not the Jews, and the federal government is a Zionist Occupied Government or U.S.S.A. When nothing is what it seems, black and white divisions separating agents from victims blur. Such floating causality can produce terror.[9]

It can also be pleasurable. Rather than avoiding scandalizing listeners, Peters deploys shock strategically. He knows that overt proclamations of hatred can turn off potential converts. In pamphlets such as *Will the Real Hate Group Stand Up?*, Peters respins this shock. Did not Paul proclaim Christianity a stumbling block? Christian Identity, Peters says proudly, is not politically correct (p.c.), but biblically correct (b.c.). Being "b.c. not p.c." differentiates him, Peters proclaims, from televangelists who seek to please their audience. This logic of scandal turns the incredibility of his claims into their proof: nobody would talk about a Jewish conspiracy to win friends and influence people, therefore Peters must be "the real thing"!

Studying Peters has often felt like plunging into epistemic murk. When I first started reading his books and newsletters and listening to his sermons and radio broadcasts, the most surprising thing to me was that Peters can be right—although in a profoundly wrong way. Peters sees that working people have the deck stacked against them, an injustice that NAFTA and GATT never intended to change. And he is right that the liberation envisioned in the Bible is not personal or spiritual in ways that exclude the public and political. Disillusioned with "the system," Peters turns to the Bible in protest.

Studying Christian Identity as a cultural phenomenon entails exploring how Peters can be right in such a profoundly wrong way, how he can see some things so clearly while ignoring other things so completely. For Peters does not use the Bible to turn his disillusionment into a door that opens him to others. Instead, he warns: "I believe the first resource that ever got away from America was not the arms race or any of these things, but the baby-boom generation. My generation. All the propaganda back then was 'Go to college, young man, you have to go to college.' . . . And when my generation got out of college they could hardly get a job in a filling station. Why did they want me to go to college? Because we sent our most valuable resource, the baby-boom generation, and let an anti-Christ philosophy fill their minds. It never dawned on us that the enemies would want to *teach*."[10] Peters exhorts listeners to read their Bible to recover the lost memory of America's identity as a Christian nation before it dies along with the generation that is carrying it.

In the Hebrew Bible, after the twelve tribes of Israel leave Egypt and enter the Promised Land, they become a nation with their own king. After King David dies, his son Solomon rules. At Solomon's death, the nation splits: ten tribes form the Northern Kingdom, and the remaining two tribes form the Southern Kingdom. The Northern Kingdom is defeated by Assyria in 722 B.C.E., and the South is conquered by Babylon around 586 B.C.E. Most historians consider the Ten Tribes to have become part of Assyria. That might be what is written in the history books, Peters acknowledges, but history is written by the winners. Here Peters appropriates a style of narrating history that grew out of 1960s social movements to open the door for an invented tradition about the "hidden" identity of these lost tribes: how they made their way over the Caucasus mountains to settle Europe, after which they pushed into the British Isles until they finally set sail, Pilgrims to the Promised Land.[11]

The thesis of this chapter is that Peters produces the appeal and truth of a white supremacist countermemory—for both racism's appeal as well as its ability to seem true must be produced: neither are "natural" or "given"—by setting into motion the swirl of cultural silences that link race and class to gender and sexuality. By slipping from one to another, Peters converts hope into fear, love into hate, submission to God into supremacist politics—actively producing desire for a white supremacist theocracy.

This desire hinges on how Peters links two dimensions of the sacred. He relies on mainstream memories of the United States as a Christian nation founded on the Bible. These public memories stand within a diverse tradition that scholars call "civil religion." The United States has been imagined as an errand in the wilderness, a city on a hill, the apostle of democracy, a crucible where black Americans forged a redemptive message for all humanity.[12]

Yet Peters could not engender desire for white supremacy if the Bible did not also access personal memories, particularly popular traditions of a family Bible. Such practices revere the Bible as sacred not only because of its spiritual and moral wisdom, but also because the Bible is a material object that creates, stores, and activates family memories, like a family photo album.[13]

Consider how a photographer brings a family photo into focus through mental images of what a family should look like. Likewise, family members pose for the camera, composing features and bodies to conform to their understanding of these genre conventions. Theorist Marianne Hirsch argues that when we look at family photos, we say "Look how much I look like grandmother!" less because we discover physical resemblances that are "in there" than because the context of family photos engenders an "affiliative gaze."[14] Looking at family pictures means looking for likeness and ignoring difference.

Likewise, the Bible acts less as a record of past events than as a stimulus for present acts of memory. Reading through an affiliative gaze, readers "find" their situation (and therefore themselves) in the biblical text and thus also in the family of God: "Look how much this present situation resembles David's!"[15] Just as we bring family pictures into focus by projecting ideal images, so we bring the "family of God" (or the secular "family of humanity") into focus by projecting ideal images of authority and submission, belonging and trust. When read *only* through such an affiliative lens, the Bible constructs memories focused on belonging that ignore the violence that circulates in, through, and around biblical memories. The result is a screen: religion (God's family) is created as a space of pure goodness, a space of innocence.

This screen effect is not an inevitable result of reading the Bible for spiritual comfort and insight. Part of keeping faith with a tradition involves undoing those aspects of its history that limit the liberatory power of its vision. Theologian Sharon Welch argues that when we refuse this task, we run the risk of participating in an erotics of domination. She uses this term to describe how people who exercise power can take pleasure in imagining themselves as victims who are simply carrying out orders, as good and faithful servants who keep the terms of their contract/covenant by submitting to authority—even to the point of doing what they would otherwise not do, of doing what they do not wish to do.[16] More than simple hypocrisy, such contradictions reveal power as a relation that is (re)created and (re)produced through feedback loops linking authority and submission, the pleasures of rebellion and the enjoyments of obedience, the empowerment of clarity and the terror of epistemic murk.[17]

In *Nationalism and Sexuality,* historian George Mosse demonstrates how nineteenth-century Europeans embraced race to negotiate this feedback loop between authority and submission, public and private—loops that had become quite problematic during the transition to modern life and society:

> The consciousness of change, of the new speed of time, of the possible loss of control over one's life, were basic issues to which racism addressed itself. Through its appeal to history and nature it attempted to make time stand still, to provide [some] men and women not only with a usable racial past but also with a piece of eternity that would give them support. The outsider filled a crucial function as the anti-type [of the ideal national

Man]—a warning of what the future might hold if society relaxed its controls and abandoned its quest for respectability. . . .

Normality required keeping in touch with the immutable and genuine forces of nature. The quest for rootedness which informed the bourgeoisie set it against its place of origin. Its members feared the impersonal monster they themselves had created: the monumental streets and buildings [that characterized the city], the anonymous mass.[18]

Race was embraced as a piece of nature/eternity that held at bay the fears produced by modern life—close, but not too close. "Racism," concludes Mosse, "is heightened nationalism."[19]

We've seen racism function as a modernist disavowal strategy before. In chapter 3, I noted that the populist image of archindustrialist Henry Ford profited, in his own eyes and in others', from articulating popular resentment against the changes wrought by Fordism through the racial imaginary of Christian Identity. As a third-generation leader, Peters grapples not with the onset of modernization but with its transformation. The global economy has rendered the middle-class status of Peters's rural-identified constituency radically uncertain. As the borders of nations become explicitly recognized as permeable membranes, the racialized, sexualized, and gendered imagery that helped birth the nation as an "imagined community" seems equally uncertain.[20] In response, Peters engages in a "quest for rootedness" that sets him against the globality implicit in the post–World War II American supremacy for which he waxes nostalgic, against the capitalism in which he places a sacred trust, and against the information technologies and accompanying postmodern sensibilities without which his ministry simply could not be. These are not just contradictions. Peters renders these gaps productive by offering race as a technology of transcendence. Race endows the nation with a numinous mission. And race offers a discipline that enables mystical union with God. Racism here is spiritual and erotic, the consummate tool of power. By its means, Peters offers the pleasures of submission alongside the pleasures of supremacy, enabling listeners to taste both while owning neither.

Nineteenth-century Europe enabled people to inhabit both positions—exercising domination while professing submission—by framing racism as science.[21] Likewise, Peters frames white supremacy not as a power fantasy but as biblical science, a.k.a. biblical literalism. Peters's brand of biblical literalism derives from a philosophical system popular in antebellum America as Baconianism. Baconianism influenced the mainstream Church of Christ, the denomination wherein Peters was ordained before converting to Christian Identity, and was especially influential for one of its key founders, Alexander Campbell (1788–1866).[22] Campbell read the Bible as that ancestor of modern science, Francis Bacon, read the world, as "a book of facts, not of opinions, [or] theories."[23] As its name indicates, this brand of biblical literalism is a modern way to read. Although biblical texts (once canonized) were regarded as "true," it was not until the rise of modernity that the Bible began to be read as true in the same way that science is thought true.[24]

Trained in this Baconian tradition, Peters promotes Christian Identity as a brand of biblical literalism that offers a superior "science" to that of his primary target group: Christian fundamentalists. For instance, at an October 1992 meeting convened to strategize a movementwide response to the armed encounter between the Weaver family and government agents at Ruby Ridge, Peters delivered the opening address not as an overview of the facts, but as a traditional Bible study. He led 160 Patriot activists in turning the pages of their Bibles, explaining: "Our Creator did not package this creation and give it to us without an instruction manual. He knew some things would go haywire at times and he told us how to correct them. It's just a matter of trying to figure out what the answer is."[25] Although Peters acknowledges that he has to figure out the answer, this figuring does not qualify the obviousness of the answer.

To read letters on a page, one refers to other letters ("cat," not "bat" nor "can" nor "cut") and to the negative space out of which each letter's shape emerges. Likewise, biblical literalism must constantly go "beyond the letter." Peters treats the Bible as a puzzle whose truth must be assembled by highlighting certain verses, hunting different occurrences of a word, using multiple translations and scholarly aids, supplementing one biblical story with another as well as with books like *The Protocols of the Elders of Zion* and *The Light and the Glory* (a history of the United States written by Christian right author Peter Marshall).[26]

One might wonder, though, what kind of literalism or empiricism, however supplemented, could "find" the United States as the biblical Promised Land or the Anglo-Saxon-Celtic-Germanic peoples as Israel. To explain, Peters sets readers counting the FS in the phrase "Finished files are the result of years of scientific study combined with the experience of many years." Reading the Bible is like counting the FS. Everything is "in there," but people count different numbers. Why? Most people were taught to read phonetically; therefore, Peters argues, "even though they see 'of' as 'of' they believe it is 'ov' and thus cannot see the 'f.' So it is with people who have been made to believe that the Jews are God's chosen people. They will fail to make the discovery even though Jesus said [in John 10:25–32, for example] they [the Judeans to whom he was speaking] were not his sheep."[27] Peters styles Christian Identity as an exercise in unlearning the conventional ways people are taught to see, as a hypothesis that recruits can test "for themselves" by reading the Bible. Scientific method requires a scientist to adopt a particular set of conditions and a particular sort of viewing to be able to confirm scientific truths. Similarly, biblical literalism requires readers to adopt a particular set of conditions and a particular sort of viewing to "look and see."

Such scientific realism ignores the agency of the representer who makes something present for people to see. We reenact this disavowal whenever we read a map. Although maps are abstract simplifications, they help us find our way because we read them as if they were "the real thing."[28] Peters maps the Bible much as a cartographer who covers over his role in drawing the map. As Peters puts it, "We want a Christian America and nothing else. We don't want a Judeo-Christian America. Call it bigotry, call it hatred, call it racism, but don't say it's not in the Bible."[29] Or, as the Christian right quips, "Facts don't hate. They just are." In this way, Peters seeks to shift Christian Identity from the unprotected realm of inciteful speech to the legally protected realm of intellectual inquiry.

Yet the racialized maps that Peters produces are not "in there" as "givens" that absolve readers of responsibility for the interpretations they construct. Although Peters claims merely to say aloud what others fear to speak, this claim is double-edged. We tend to imagine white supremacists as embittered individuals eaten up with hatred, but interviews paint a portrait of political organizers who are enjoying the power of leadership.[30]

Likewise, studying Peters confronted me with how *familiar* the racism, anti-Semitism, misogyny, and homophobia were. Reflecting on the maps she found in the back of the Bible her parents gave her when she was a little girl growing up in the segregated South, feminist poet and essayist Minnie

Bruce Pratt observes that these maps inscribed a particular Christian conceptualization of "the Holy Land"—one in which Jews did not appear.[31]

What sets white supremacists apart from the mainstream is less how they "hate" and more how they articulate cultural silences and erasures—like the ones Pratt found in the maps at the back of her Bible—into a countermemory, one they then articulate as a mechanism for leadership. *These articulations matter.* When Peters reads the Bible, he does not simply express what is already inside the Bible, inside Christianity, or inside people. Speaking silences is not "simple." If you can "do things with words" (as Austin quipped), you can do things with silences.[32] Peters does: he builds cultural silences into maps that produce people as certain sorts of supremacist subjects by endowing them with a repertoire of interpretive desires and practical strategies for perceiving the world. This is the power of maps. The rest of this chapter explores the power of white supremacist belief by asking: What are the maps in Peters's Bible?

Capitalism and Creation: The Genesis of (Re)Production

The Bible opens with two creation accounts, which have long been read in racial terms. During the 1800s, the United States became the primary locus for debates between polygenesis (God created many races) and monogenesis (God created one race, with all humans descending from one pair of primordial parents).[33] Peters represents these traditions through the rationalist rhetoric of biblical literalism. Not only do Genesis 1 and 2 use different terminology, they disagree about what God created on which days. Biblical scholarship interprets these differences as evidence that these stories originated in different historical communities. In contrast, Peters argues, "Things which are unequal cannot be equal to each other"; thus, neither the chapters, nor the people created within them, can be the same.

When Peters reads Genesis 1, he identifies "the most basic law" of creation as God's command that the earth produce everything "according to its kind" (plants, v. 11–12; sea creatures, v. 21; animals, v. 24–25). For Peters, this law proves that interracial sex is against God's creation order: "Just as white-tailed deer mate only with white-tailed deer, and mule deer mate only with mule deer, so black people should mate only with blacks and white with whites."[34] Peters's reading smooths over a gap in the biblical text. When God creates humans in Genesis 1, the phrase "according to its kind" is missing. Peters fills the phrase in, but not without precedent. Nineteenth-century debates over whether humans were one or many species revolved around this same issue. Did interracial sex produce fertile young? Or did interracial sex produce offspring unable to reproduce according to their kind, like mules? Writes cultural theorist Robert Young: "It has often been suggested that there are intrinsic links between racism and sexuality. What has not been emphasized is that debates about theories of race in the nineteenth century, by settling on the possibility or impossibility of hybridity, focused explicitly on the issue of sexuality and the issue of sexual unions between whites and blacks."[35]

Embedded in these "intrinsic links" among race, sex, and reproduction lie fears regarding (economic) production. Reading Genesis 1 and 2 sequentially, Peters finds a God who judges the first people as lacking, for "there was no one to till the ground" (Genesis 2:5). Thus God creates a second time: breathing into the dust a soul, creating Adam, father of the white race, to care for the garden. Repeating the racial hierarchy of Victorian anthropology, Peters reads Adam as a culture-bearer who brings agricultural technology and civilization to "primitives."[36]

In keeping with his rural identifications, Peters emphasizes Adam's bond to the ground: "His heart is in the land because his heart was made out of the land." Much as Israel told stories about Abraham and Sarah to claim a land inhabited by other people, so Peters tells this creation story to claim North America for white Christians. At a 1996 Patriot meeting, Peters claimed that other races "do not have the same dream about the land that you and I do. We just want a piece of *terra firma,* do we not? We don't want to rent a condo in New York City! . . . We want our own vine under which to sit, do we not? What are the chances of our children getting to rent a condo, much less own a piece of land, if we continue as we are?"[37] For Peters, the Bible is a book whose covenant promises mandate private ownership of land.[38]

Peters's reading biblicizes a historically powerful American self-conception regarding democracy: the populist ethic of rural producerism. Historian Catherine McNichol Stock argues that this ethic animated a series of struggles: from fights by the North Carolina Regulators and Ethan Allen's Mountain Boys, which protested feudal relations between landowners and tenants; to Shay's Rebellion, which sought to stop farm foreclosures in Massachusetts during the 1780s; to the Whiskey Rebellion, in which Appalachian frontiersmen protested federal plans to repay the national debt by taxing the frontier.[39] Stock demonstrates how these rural protest movements articulated working-class rebellion by distinguishing the productivity of small frontier farmers and settlers from the parasitical profiteering of Eastern merchants, lawyers, businessmen, and large land-owners who lived off the former's labor. Yet this class radicalism was expressed through, and deflected by, stereotypes regarding religion and race—to the detriment of Native Americans, Chinese and Mexican la-borers, African Americans, Jews, and Catholics.[40]

Likewise, Peters distinguishes the productive capitalism of white Chris-tians, whom he believes own private property out of a desire "to till the ground and care for it" (Genesis 2:15), from the parasitical capitalism of Jews, who Peters believes cannot make the land produce on their own and therefore must appropriate others' productive labor. Like earlier forms of rural producerism, Peters articulates class conflict but pulls back from seeing how capitalism betrays its producing classes. Instead, he blames Jews for contaminating capitalism by practices such as credit, loans, interest, and printing paper money without gold or silver to back it up. As Peters tells it, once Jews began these practices, everyone had to do likewise just to compete. As standards lowered, the government began regulating business and created "big government" at the expense of "the little man."

Sex in the Garden:
Biology and Culture (Genesis 3)

Peters's reading of the creation stories departs from a common belief in the Christian Identity movement. This belief, which developed (in part) in the North American South circa 1900, reads the Garden of Eden story (Genesis 3) as narrating the creation of two seedlines.[41] According to this reading, Eve was sexually seduced in the garden by Satan (masquerading as a serpent). From their sexual union, Eve conceived Cain. Cain's geneal-ogy or seedline runs to Ham to the Canaanites to Ahab to Judas Iscariot to the Jews. Cain's seed is the seed of all evil. The other seedline descends from Eve's union with Adam, from whose seed descends all good. This seedline stretches from Adam to Abel and his brother Seth to Abraham to David to the Israelite tribes to the Anglo-Saxon-Germanic-Celtic-Scandinavian and kindred peoples of Europe to the Pilgrims to their white Christian remnant in the United States. The two seedlines are locked in a murderous rivalry, as were the original two brothers, Cain and Abel.

In *Religion and the Racist Right,* Michael Barkun identifies this theory of two seedlines as the essential Christian Identity belief. For Barkun, belief in two seedlines distinguishes the anti-Semitism and racism of Christian Identity from the philo-Semitism of its intellectual predecessor, Anglo-Israelism (which also believed that Anglo-Saxons were the Ten Lost Tribes). Although Peters is a Christian Identity minister, he does not preach the two-seedlines theory.[42]

In *Arguing the Apocalypse,* Stephen O'Leary notes that the book of Revelation can be read as a comedy: God wins.[43] Yet, most readers fixate on the terrifying violence that precedes this "happily ever after." By rejecting seedline theory, Peters counters this tendency to read apocalypticism as tragedy. Instead, he characterizes seedline theory as "a Jewish fable," propaganda that the enemy disseminates to weaken people by fostering fear.[44] As a pastor who seeks to motivate people to fight for the kingdom, Peters imagines Israel's enemies not as Satan's seed, but as God's tools. God gave Israel's enemies the power to punish Israel, but the power behind the hammer lies in the hand that wields it. Here, there is hope: what God has given, God can take away.

Rejecting the biological fantasy of two seedlines, Peters calls Judaism a culture, a way of thinking and acting. Yet this rejection has more to do with marketing Christian Identity for the post-1960s era than with rejecting racism. Today, people talk less about biological differences between races and more about welfare dependency, inner-city ghettos, gangsta rappers, and cultures of entitlement. Comments Young: "The close relation between the developments of the concepts of culture and race in the nineteenth century means that an implicit racism lies powerfully hidden but repeatedly propagated within Western notions of culture."[45]

Peters imagines race less as the biological fantasy of two seedlines in favor of emphasizing the cultural fantasy of covenant; for Peters, the distinguishing mark of Adamic peoples is that God wrote his law on their hearts. He cites Hebrews 8:10: "For the covenant I will make with the house of Israel after those days, says the Lord, is this: I will set my laws in their understanding and write them in their hearts." And only *their* hearts.

If God had meant to include all races, Peters asserts, he would have said so. Peters reads this positive statement as an argument about absence, so that what defines other peoples is lack of culture: "Other races do not have the law of God written on their hearts."[46]

Yet Peters pulls biology back in to "guarantee" the eternality of this cultural covenant. Much as science envisioned the world as a book written by the hand of God in the language of eternal laws, so Peters translates the biblical image of God writing his law on Israelite hearts into a scientific idiom. White Israel, Peters proclaims, carries the law of God's covenant "genetically written by the Great Geneticist, our Creator."[47] Thus Peters positions Christian Identity within the murky area where biological forms of racism slip into cultural forms and then slip back into biological determinism. What lets him do this is sex.

Sex and the Law of the Father:
Homosexuality and the Story of Ham (Genesis 9)

Although Peters rejects the idea of one satanic seedline, he embraces the racial reading of the curse of Ham once used to justify slavery. In this story, Noah gets drunk and falls asleep naked. Ham, one of Noah's sons and the father of Canaan, sees "his father's nakedness" and tells his two brothers, who help him cover their father. When Noah wakes up, he proclaims, "Cursed be Canaan, slave of slaves shall he be to his brothers" (Genesis 9:25).

Peters reads the biblical phrase alleging that Ham saw "his father's nakedness" as a euphemism for Ham having sex with his mother. For Peters, incest explains why Noah curses not Ham but Ham's son Canaan: "God doesn't sit up there and say, 'Ahah! That was wrong—I'm gonna curse you!' It doesn't work that way. If you want to sum up God in one word that word would be LAW. When you violate the law there are natural consequences. One thing leads to another, to another, to another. It wasn't that God said to Ham, 'OK, you did this. Now I'm going to curse Canaan.' It was a result of violated genetic law."[48]

When literary critic Regina Schwartz reads this story, she, too, reads a story that upholds the Law of the Father. Unlike Peters, for whom the thought of biblical ancestors engaging in homosexuality seems best left unthought, Schwartz reads Ham's sin as homosexual incest. For Schwartz, fears regarding homosexuality explain why Noah directs his curse against Ham's son Canaan, thereby forcing the brothers into rivalry. Underneath the sibling rivalry that dogs the biblical family, Schwartz finds the "palpable fear that when men love one another they will overthrow their father."[49] She concludes: "As Noah's terrible curse of his son belies and as the general biblical hysteria about homosexuality suggests, the son's desire for the father is also primary in biblical traditions. Only this desire—denied, repressed, suppressed and punished—explains both the ferocity of biblical injunctions against homosexuality and the ferocity of the deity's determination to punish his children, to stomp out their desire with its threat of parricidal displacement."[50] Unlike the heroes in Greek myths, men in the Bible forge their identity by slaying the Other, not the father. In Schwartz's reading, the Bible forms identity through a circular process in which Israel comes to know itself through violently repudiating its Other—from whom Israel can then hold itself apart as holy. This process secures the father's authority by demonizing other peoples who function as Israel's rivalrous doubles.[51]

Likewise, Peters holds homosexuality at bay—close, but not too close—by finding a biblical master plot that prescribes racial apartheid: "The curse was in his descendants in the form of spiritual and moral deformity, and Canaan's descendants were a cursed people. They were an idolatrous, incestuous, immoral, depraved, ungodly lot, thinking and acting much differently from the others. These were the sinful people living in the Promised Land when the Israelites entered it. In Deuteronomy 7, God's people were to destroy them and not intermarry with them, but Israel disobeyed and consequently these people were always trouble in the land, acting as pricks and thorns (Numbers 33:55)."[52] In this scenario, danger is sexual: pricks and thorns. Although Peters reaches to biology to secure the eternity of the covenant, even biological traces written by the Great Geneticist can be forgotten due to deviant sex. Here we see how modern Peters's maps are. For Peters, sex is your truest truth, powerful enough to erase an eternal law. The connection here between sex and loss is profound and absolute. Deviant sex can induce a forgetting so powerful that one loses everything: self, God, family, heritage, nation. When racism is heightened nationalism, gender and sexuality become the primary imaginaries through which fears regarding race and the nation are made visible, controlled, and managed.

Biblical Memories / 57

Peters traces how the divine law that was written on Adam's heart was reinscribed in a covenant with Abraham in which God pledges that Abraham's seed will occupy the Promised Land and become a great nation.[53] The issue of how to understand covenant promises is a loaded one in Christianity. Debates about Hebrew prophecies that were not fulfilled (or New Testament prophecies that spoke of God's kingdom as if it would soon be realized) were part of the fundamentalist/modernist controversy at the beginning of the twentieth century. As a result of this controversy, the northern elites who led Protestant denominations split into two camps, liberals and fundamentalists, a division that still shapes U.S. Protestantism.[54] Peters promotes Christian Identity as a middle way between (what he sees as) liberal accommodation to culture and fundamentalist withdrawal from culture.

Peters's argument goes like this: In the Bible, God promises an everlasting covenant. How should today's world read these promises? Peters sees two traditional possibilities. First, perhaps God lied. Peters attributes this path to liberal Christians who finessed problems in interpretation by reading the Bible as imaginative narratives teaching values and spiritual insight. Second, perhaps God kept the spirit of his promise, but changed the letter. Peters attributes this option to fundamentalist and evangelical Christians who teach that Jesus transformed the old covenant of law (made with the nation of Israel) into a new covenant that includes all believers as Abraham's spiritual seed. Christians live under a new dispensation in which unfulfilled biblical prophecies refer to Jesus' return.

Declaring that liberals accuse God of lying and fundamentalists accuse God of changing his mind, Peters constructs a hyperliteral counter-memory that rejects any theology that incorporates loss as a contradiction in terms: God can never lose. Thus, the Ten Lost Tribes could never have been lost to Assyria; they must have been deliberately omitted from the history books in what Peters avers to be the biggest culture theft of all time: someone must have stolen the identity of white Israel as God's chosen people. And who else could the thieves be but those who today are called God's chosen? Herein lies the danger of idealizing God as absolute power: faced with loss, Peters substitutes conspiracy theory.

Peters finds this culture theft in the story of Jacob and Esau, twin sons of Abraham's heir, Isaac. When Isaac's wife Rebecca became pregnant, the twins struggled in her womb. Distressed, she cried to the Lord and received the following prophecy: "Two nations in your womb, two peoples, going their own ways from birth! One shall be stronger than the other; the older shall be servant to the younger" (Genesis 25:23). The firstborn twin was named Esau, the younger was named Jacob. In ancient Israel it was the custom that the firstborn son receive the family inheritance, but Jacob deliberately deceived both his older brother and his father to appropriate his brother's inheritance. Jacob's name was later changed to Israel and his descendants became the Twelve Tribes of Israel. According to Peters, Esau's sons intermarried with the Edomites and became "the Jews."

Biblical scholars read the story of Jacob and Esau (like the story of Ham and Canaan) as ancient Israelites making sense of their relationships with the other peoples with whom they lived. How do the Israelites and the Edomites relate? They fight. Why do they fight? They've always fought—they were fighting back in the womb! Building on this folkloric interpretation, biblical scholar Susan Niditch reads Jacob as a trickster figure, a hero who bucks the established order, not through merit or superior courage, but through trickery. Niditch's reading includes reflection on the ethical ambivalence of power as part of the story's moral.[55]

Peters also reads Jacob as an eponymous ancestor, but he refuses any consideration of the moral ambivalence of power. Instead, he reads the story as sanctioning an eternal enmity between Jacob's and Esau's descendants. He links the story to stereotypes of Jews as devious tricksters who are always trying to get the better of others through a shady deal. To do this, Peters must reverse the story: he reads Esau as the archdeceiver, not Jacob!

Faced with a projection that is counterfactual in many senses, nowhere does Peters's attempt to style the Christian Identity message within a rhetoric of rationality become more elaborate than in his word study of the term "Jew." In an early sermon entitled "The Most Confusing Word in Scripture: Jew," Peters invests significance in the fact that the Bible frequently calls the people who fill its pages "Israel" or "Hebrews," but rarely (and only in late texts) "Jews." Peters concludes that the contemporary meaning of the word Jew is a late addition that has been read back into the original Hebrew.

Scholars also acknowledge a distinction between the religion of biblical Israel and the religion we know today as Judaism (which developed out of the rabbis' response to Rome's destruction of the Jerusalem Temple in 70 C.E., an event which made it impossible for ancient Israel to keep the covenant in the same way as before). Peters seizes on this distinction as confirmation that rabbinic Jews, with their sacred book of the Talmud, are completely unrelated to biblical Israel, whose sacred book is the Bible. Thus he clears away space for an invented tradition regarding who the Jews "really" are.

Peters styles himself as a biblical scholar correcting the "original" meaning of an ancient word—at the same time that he brings his linguistic turn home by invoking homophobia. Words are not constant, Peters rightly declares; their meaning is affected by time and place. To prove his point, he cites the phrase "the gay nineties," which draws a laugh. The word "gay," he concludes, has changed its meaning over time. And over place: "If I go to England and order a pack of fags I will get one thing, but if I go to San Francisco and order a pack of fags I will get a different thing." After the laughter subsides, Peters notes that the word Jew is a Hellenization of the Hebrew word *Yehudi* (or Judahite). Originally referring to a member of the tribe of Judah, the term came to refer to the Southern Kingdom after the nation divided.

When Judah was conquered by Babylon in 586 B.C.E., some members of the southern tribe of Judah remained in the land and others were deported to Babylon. Peters argues that the space vacated by the deportees was filled by foreigners, especially Israel's age-old enemies, the Edomites (descendants of Esau) and the Canaanites (descendants of Ham). To complicate the picture further, Peters alleges that when in Babylon, some of the exiled Israelites assimilated, writing the Talmud and the Kabbalah (the "bad figs" of Jeremiah 24). When the Babylonian captivity ended, a portion of those exiled returned to Jerusalem. Therefore, Peters concludes, by the time Jesus was born, the people who would have been called Jews because they inhabited the geographic space designated by the term *Yehud* included Israelites, Babylonian turncoats, Edomites, and Canaanites.[56]

From this anthropology, Peters concludes that Judah, at the time of Jesus' birth, was a multiracial society. Drawing on the New Testament parable of the sower, Peters sees Jesus as having been sent into a mission field in which the good seed of white Israel was mixed among thorns and thistles. Hence, Peters claims, Jesus made distinctions regarding those for whom his message was intended. He cites Matthew 15, in which a Canaanite woman beseeches Jesus to heal her daughter, who is tormented by demons. Jesus refuses, saying, "I was sent to the lost sheep of the house of Israel, and to them alone.... It is not right to take the children's bread and throw it to dogs" (Matthew 15:24, 26). Peters comments: "Now we are beginning to get into some uncharted water for the present blinded Christian world. Not because the water or this scripture is that deep and hard to understand but because this passage of scripture does not fit the Christ that has been painted for them all their lives, a Christ sitting on a rock with a black child on one knee, a yellow child on the other, a white one holding his hand and a brown one touching his shoulder. The Jesus of this scripture made a distinction between races, specifically the Canaanite and the Israelite (the lost sheep of the house of Israel). Today the NAACP (the National Association for the Advancement of Canaanite People) would sue such a Savior."[57]

According to Peters, God discriminates because God is the God of Israel. "Does anyone have a translation that says God delivered all races? Or that says God is the God of all humankind?" Peters asks. No, he responds, because the Bible does not say that. "What's that you say?" he pretends. "You thought God loved everyone the same? The Bible does not say that either." Peters sends people paging through their Bibles to find Malachi 1:2–5, which reads: "I have loved you, says the Lord. But you say, 'How have you loved us?' Is not Esau Jacob's brother? says the Lord. Yet I have loved Jacob but I have hated Esau; I have made his hill country a desolation and his heritage a desert for jackals."[58]

When Gomer Meets the Antichrist, or, You Always Hurt the One You Love

How does Peters make his peace with believing in a God who hates other races—races that God himself created? One way is by reading the Bible as not only about race but also about conspiracy. Jesus' life began with conspiracy, when King Herod sought to kill him, and ended the same way, when the elders plotted his arrest (John 11:46–47, 53), stirred up the masses to demand his crucifixion (Mark 15:11–13), pressured Pilate to condemn him even though Pilate knew he was innocent (John 19:12, 16), and bribed the guards to suppress news of his resurrection (Matthew 28:12–15). Peters concludes: "A study of the Four Gospels and of the Book of Acts reveals cover-ups, pay-offs, conspiracy, intrigue, manipulation of public opinion, unrighteous law enforcement, a malicious media, and a behind-the-scenes establishment."[59]

Peters relates this conspiratorial reading of Jesus' sacrifice to biblical passages that warn of deceivers who do not confess Christ and of impostors who belong to "the synagogue of Satan."[60] He castigates Christians who are waiting for a supernatural Antichrist with a capital A, "little realizing that antichrists are all over the place": "those people, the plural, who do not confess Christ" in this world.[61] Thus, for Peters, what distinguishes Christian Identity is the belief that Jesus came not just to save souls, but also to rescue Israel from flesh-and-blood enemies. "To a person who is halfway honest and willing to sit down and look at the facts and history, archaeologically and biblically, it is not hard to prove that the Anglo-Saxon-Celtic-Scandinavian and kindred peoples are the Israel people of the Bible. There are other groups out there that teach that. They do not have any problem [with police and media] because they do not address verse 71 of Luke 1 ['He proclaimed that he would deliver us from our enemies, out of the hands of all those who hate us']. The real problem comes when you try to convince people today that there are enemies that hate them. Then all of a sudden, you are a radical!"[62] Just as Christ was crucified for being an "extremist" and the early Christians were persecuted for being enemies of Rome, so, Peters asserts, Christian Identity is persecuted today for being biblically correct rather than politically correct. Portraying white Christians as persecuted victims, Peters claims that being "anti-" the anti-Christ is not hatred.

Indeed, Peters frames white supremacy as Christian repentance. As he reads the situation: "Sometimes when the [Israelite] herd has gotten away from you and you cannot herd them up—then a [Canaanite] dog is valuable. . . . The dog was created in God's plan. Although it appears to curse God's people, it ultimately has a good end—to bring them back."[63] Thus, Peters will claim that Christian Identity actually solves racial strife because "it puts the blame where it belongs," teaching that whites "are just simply a supreme race of sinners that have never obeyed their God and have always fallen from his grace."[64]

When racism is repentance, supremacy becomes service: white Israel must shoulder the burden of its world-historical destiny. Citing God's promise that Israel will be a blessing to all peoples, Peters asks, "What race of people have witnessed to others by way of missionaries, printing Bibles, etc.?"[65] Elsewhere, Peters insists that only the white race helps others, citing U.S. overseas aid and development programs.[66] At this point, Peters often gets personal, declaring that anti-Semitism, far from attracting him, kept him from committing his life to Christian Identity for years.

Certainly, the maps Peters finds in his Bible are ambivalent when it comes to divine violence. After all, although God hates the anti-Christ forces, God also seems to hate Israel: has he not called in the dogs and said "Sic 'em!"? Peters manages this ambivalence by recasting violence from a racial to a gender imaginary.

As usual, Peters spins his views in conversation with a biblical text, in this case, Hosea. The prophecies collected in Hosea speak to the Northern Kingdom of ancient Israel as it faced Assyrian conquest. The prophecies interpret this trauma as punishment, charging Israel with forsaking its covenant obligations to its God. Hosea drives this message home by literalizing a metaphor: Just as Israel's God was bound through a covenant with the nation Israel, so Hosea enters into a marriage covenant with Gomer, a woman known to have sex with other men.[67]

Peters focuses on Hosea's metaphor in an extended series of sermons he titles "The Greatest Love Story Never Told" (first delivered in fall 1993). Although Peters's intention is to show that God's love for white Israel is as real as a man's love for his wife, what he dramatizes is male supremacy. For instance, he supplements Hosea with the story of a man, just married, who is driving away from the church in a carriage with his bride when the horse stumbles. The man pulls up the reins, says "Whoa! That's once." When the horse stumbles again, he pulls out a revolver, says "That's twice," and shoots the horse between the eyes. The bride yells, "What are you doing? Are you crazy!" The man replies, "That's once." After the church laughs and claps, Peters likens the man's warnings to the thunder, lightning, and thick cloud that made the people tremble when God came to Sinai to give them the covenant law and they pledged their troth to him (Exodus 19). He preaches, "He was teaching his bride to revere him, and that's the way it should be in a marriage . . . 'It's very simple honey, from this day forward I'm the boss.' That was to be the relationship. Where he leads, she follows."[68] Thus, when Peters retells Hosea, male vulnerability comes to mean that God can be so hurt his love becomes wrathful violence:

> Do we ever stop to think in America that we are offensive to God and had better make propitiation? Christ gave himself up to make God favorable, kind and merciful to us. Again, everything is so out of kilter. The world never thinks of an offended God who needs to be made merciful to us. . . . I once had coffee with a man who told me what it was like to find out his wife was unfaithful. He described his rage and anger when he found his wife with another man. He took a tool from the garage and destroyed every bit of furniture. He spent hours destroying every possession in the house. You say: "Well, I don't think that's the right thing to do." Listen, you don't want to get in his way. He was pouring out his rage. So he went through the house and emptied it out bit by bit, room by room. He was exhausted, but felt release.
>
> I thought about that in light of Christ who made propitiation for his people who had been unfaithful to their God. . . . Has it occurred to us that maybe God is striking at us in his anger and in his wrath? That there is anger and wrath behind the events taking place in the land today?[69]

Peters points to Malachi 1, where God professes his love for Israel by hating Esau: "Think about it. What kind of love story would it be if he did not love his bride about everything else? Suppose my wife comes to me and says, 'Do you love me more than any other woman?' And I say, 'Well, honey, I love you like I love all the other women.' "[70] Narrating Christian Identity as a romance, Peters renders violence acceptable by rooting it in the natural order: gender is how things just are.[71]

At the heart of Peters's strategy lies a historically specific understanding of gender rooted in the Victorian era. Victorians envisioned men and women as polar opposites and rooted this abstract dichotomy in the alleged biological obviousness of anatomical sex, epitomized by that origin moment when the doctor proclaims "It's a girl!" In contrast, scholars in women's studies have argued that statements such as "It's a girl!" are less declarative than performative, producing what they seem to find: girling the girl. The recent emergence of an intersexual movement has revealed the elaborate medical interventions to which babies born with ambiguous genitalia are often subjected. It takes work, medical and ideological, to sustain cultural beliefs in gender as a self-evident either/or proposition. Likewise, queer theorists have argued that being a biological woman (however determined) says nothing about gender roles: not all women become housewives and mothers, and of those who do, not all identify themselves solely as such. Nor does biological sex say anything about sexual desire: not all women desire men.[72] In contrast, when Peters retells the marriage metaphor, he ties gender to sex quite closely. This tie enables him to slide invisibly, and hence with the illusion of inevitability and necessity, from (1) heterosexuality as the only natural sexual order to (2) patriarchal gender relations as the only possible social order (heterosexual marriage clarifies paternity and thus secures male inheritance rights) to (3) white theocracy as the only possible governmental order of the nation.

For, ultimately, this love story is about the nation. When Peters tells the Greatest Love Story Never Told, he instructs listeners to visualize the events in their mind's eye as a TV miniseries, complete with detailed scenery and large crowds, country music theme songs and elaborate costumes. Even if they are not sitting face-to-face in Peters's church but are at home with the radio or mail-order tapes, listeners imagine their compatriots coming together week after week to cocreate this love story in which they, too, recognize themselves: "Oh, that's who I am!"[73] By making listeners imaginable to themselves, Peters's performance calls the nation into existence.

Peters's performance produces the nation in another locale as well. He visualizes the nation Israel on screen: "Oh, that's who we are!"[74] Yet the image that Peters proffers for identification is split. When he dramatizes the marriage metaphor, he looks—not through Gomer's eyes—but through the male gaze, thereby positioning Israel to identify with this all-powerful masculinity. Yet he also depicts Israel as the beloved object of this male gaze: not the agent who establishes racial theocracy but the beautiful virgin whose nature finds pleasure in submission ("I lead, you follow"). Through this split identification (the male God/the beloved seen by God), Peters makes white Israel visible to itself as a nation while making racial supremacy invisible: it is not power but God's passion for his people. This passion makes God vulnerable and his people moral. Romance is how Peters makes racism work.

For the story Peters performs when he dramatizes The Greatest Love Story Never Told is the romance of identity formation: the emergence of a subject. Its fascination recalls the pleasure children take in hearing how their parents got together: to produce them! As narcissistic narratives of ego formation, the very context engenders an affiliative gaze (much like family photos). By imagining the nation as a romance with which people can identify ("Look how much I look like my grandmother!"), Peters births the nation as a collective subject. And in so doing, he births individuals as the "sovereign" subjects they "know" they really are but rarely can be in the world.

In this romance, it is the imbrication of the collective and the individual that matters most. Etienne Balibar has argued that a social formation reproduces itself as a nation "through integrating the inculcation of political values into a more elementary process . . . [namely,] affects of love and hate and representations of the self." In this way, the external, territorial boundaries of the nation are lived "as a projection and protection of an internal collective personality, which each of us carries within ourselves and enables us to inhabit the space of the state as a place where we have always been—and always will be—at home."[75] This integration was accomplished for nineteenth-century Europeans, Mosse argues, through holding up ideals of respectability, morality, and conscience as the mark of the middle-class citizen: "That's who I am!" Yet, implicit in the ability to identify with ideals is the way that nineteenth-century Europe made the nation visible to itself by projecting its disorder, immorality, and incivility onto others who were classified as Other—outside the pale, originating beyond the nation's territory—through visual markers of class, sexuality, gender, and race/ethnicity: "I am not that!"

The national and the individual subject intertwine through splitting: on one hand, identifying with ideals; on the other hand, projecting anything less than ideal onto others. One of the privileges of becoming a sovereign subject is that one hand need not know what the other is doing: sovereign subjects can ignore both what they project as well as the violence of the process of identification and projection by which a subject becomes itself. A crucial mechanism for effecting this ignore-ance is the gaze: identifying with those like me by casting others as Others who, through the force of my glance, are marked by (and hence made to carry) the violence of my history.[76] This is why power is not short-circuited when we say "The oppressor is also oppressed" and "The oppressor also experiences violence," true though these statements be. Sometimes if you have power, you can hold that violence at bay. This is how white folks can live in a culture flooded with racism and not see it, even as racism operates with an in-your-face impunity that can take another's breath away.

Racism Is Heightened Nationalism: The Contamination of Pop Culture

The cover of Peters's first book, *The Greatest Discovery of Our Age*, depicts an open Bible on whose pages shimmers a map of North America—not the continental land mass, but the United States, complete with state boundaries. Light from the heavens illuminates the land, spilling over the Bible's open pages as the *Mayflower* sails underneath: Aryans following a promise revealed by the sun.

How does a biblical literalist find a U.S. map in the Bible? Peters rests his identification on covenant promises made not with the nomad Abraham, but with ancient Israel's "model" king, David. When David became king, he wanted to build God a house (i.e., a Temple). God refused, but agreed to bless David's house (i.e., his dynasty) and allow David's son Solomon to build the Jerusalem Temple, promising: "Your house and your kingdom shall endure before me forever; your throne shall be established forever" (2 Samuel 7:16). Once again, the Bible promises an everlasting covenant, one imagined through wordplay linking nation and family, that went unfulfilled. In this textual gap, Peters "finds" America. In *Awake, Awake, O America! You Are in the Bible!*, Peter writes:

> II Samuel 7:10 says, "I will also appoint a place for my people Israel and will plant them, that they may live in their own place and not be disturbed again, nor will the wicked afflict them anymore as formerly." To understand the meaning and significance of this prophecy we must consider the time and the place it was spoken in light of God's covenants with Abraham the father of the children of Israel. God had promised Abraham in Genesis 12:2 that He would make him a great nation and then in Genesis 17:1–7 that his seed would even form a multitude of nations. When

II Samuel 7:10 was spoken the Israel people had formed the old nation of Israel and were in the old land of Palestine with David as their King, but if they are to form a multitude of nations and a truly great nation called ZION, then there must be more land.

The great and rich geographic land mass called the North American Continent was and is that land and was so recognized by Puritans and Pilgrims.[77]

Citing Peter Marshall's *The Light and the Glory,* Peters finds it no coincidence that the text John Cotton chose for his sermon as one thousand Puritans departed for North America was 2 Samuel 7:10.

Peters also points to other unfulfilled prophesies. The world has never beaten its swords into plowshares, as prophesied in Isaiah 2. Because God does not lie, Isaiah's prophecy must presage an Israel yet to come. And is it not interesting, Peter continues, that America very quickly became the richest nation, where most of the people in the world long to live, as prophesied in Isaiah 2:2? Likewise, has any other nation sent out more missionaries and printed more Bibles (as per Isaiah 2:3)? And was not America founded by outcasts called immigrants, as prophesied in Micah 4:6–7?

Rhetorical questions like these assume what they claim to prove. Peters deploys them as dividing lines: one either recognizes the code or one does not.[78] Thus, Christian Identity often uses wordplays. Peters's favorite is JerusAlem: at the heart of the Promised Land is the good ol' U.S.A. Wordplays function as circular affirmations, combining the shock of plunging into an inverted world with the pleasure of confirming what one suspected all along.

The key to Peters's code, the assumption underlying the self-evidence of these "proofs," is the identity that Peters "just sees" between unfulfilled biblical promises and his nostalgic sense that the United States was a land of great promise and will be so again. In other words, Peters's biblical literalism is less about the Bible and more about America. For Peters did not begin by searching the Bible for clues regarding the identity of God's chosen. To the contrary, his exegetical search was motivated by a reading of the American present. Thus, when he sets out to convince people that the United States is the Promised Land, he uses the mainstream narrative called the American jeremiad, reciting story after story in which citizens lament "What went wrong?"[79] Peters knows: "What has happened has simply been a people repeating the history of their Israel race!"[80] Peters reads popular laments as signs by which generations who have forgotten the covenant can compare their present situation with biblical Israel and "see" their Christian Identity, like explorers seeking a continent or scientists seeking universal laws. As a covenant people, Israel has a repetition compulsion.

The primal scene that set the stage for this repetition compulsion is Deuteronomy 28. After the Hebrews fled from slavery in Egypt, wandered through the desert, and were about to enter the Promised Land—perched on the boundary between bondage and nationhood—Moses reminded them again of the covenant they pledged at Sinai. Deuteronomy 28 enumerates the blessings that God will bestow if Israel obeys "her man": children, rain, crops, victory in war, enough wealth to lend to other nations without ever borrowing. Yet four-fifths of this chapter recounts how God will reverse these blessings if Israel does not obey: barren wives, dust instead of rain, starvation, disease, rule by foreign nations with no reverence for age or pity for the young, captivity for children after whom "your eyes will strain all day long but you will be powerless." The people's labor will profit their enemies: "A woman will be pledged to you, but another shall ravish her; you will build a house but not live in it; you will plant a vineyard but not enjoy its fruit" (Deuteronomy 28:30).

The cover of Peters's book *A Scriptural Justification of Racism* is dominated by a ring of people of color drawn as stereotypes: a Chinese man, a Russian Jew, an Indian, a black man, and a Mexican. Together, they tower over a little white man who has been pushed way off into the righthand corner. This figure throws nervous glances over his shoulder at the looming figures as he frantically reads in the Holy Bible the following verse: "The alien who is among you shall rise above you higher and higher, but you shall go down lower and lower" (Deuteronomy 28). That's once.

Several years later, Peters devoted an entire book, *America the Conquered,* to matching the curses of Deuteronomy 28 with America's current crisis. Page after page chronicles the plight of paradise lost. For Peters, who worked for the FHA during the farm crisis, the key sign that white America has been conquered is the power that "aliens" exercise over Israel's homes. Thus, he fills *America the Conquered* with reproductions of newspaper articles asserting that white people have been removed from farmland to

Biblical Memories / 69

cities and from houses to rentals, while "aliens" consume the fruit of white Israel's labor through government programs such as welfare and affirmative action.

Peters's title frames this book as an argument against militias that warn that the nation will be conquered unless citizens take up arms.[81] Instead, Peters proclaims that America has *already* been conquered—but by spiritual, not physical warfare. By invoking biblical language of "spiritual warfare," he can deny violence as he invokes it. He does this by framing conspiracy theory as generational memory: "Remember years ago how the people were enticed to buy on credit? It was so easy at first. Remember how wives and mothers were enticed to go out into the work world to earn that little extra, so they could buy a new sofa or automobile? Today, the father and mother both must work just to earn a living. Remember those government social welfare programs of the NEW DEAL looked so inviting and workable? Now, look what group of people does all the work and receives the least in benefits. . . . This is all part of an economic conquest."[82]

Just as the nation was created by promises linking David's dynastic house to the house of the Lord, so Peters warns that the nation can be uncreated by disorder in the home. Here Peters links pre-1960s Old Right themes to newer practices of tax protest and citizen militias that have proliferated across the Patriot movement, as well as mainstream affective epidemics about the national debt, which envision the federal government as a household that spends more than it takes in (perhaps because effeminate, bleeding-heart liberals put too much on credit). Peters biblicizes these links: white Americans have been enslaved by a Babylonian system whose practices of taxation, credit, and consumption violate the principles of rural producerism and private property that he finds in Genesis. Peters holds that Israel was conquered by economic practices that are culturally coded as feminine: consumption: Thus does he slip from identifying with Gomer to identifying with her male "protector." As a result, this nation will not stay female for long.

Having made his peace with a racist God through gender, Peters sets about identifying with the male gaze. He notes that Israel was warned that if it associated with the other people in the land, those nations would become "thorns and thistles" in its side (Joshua 23:13). Earlier, I observed that Peters associates these thorns and thistles with Jesus' parable of the sower, where the good seed is choked out of existence by the thorns and thistles in its midst. In the parable, the thistles symbolize worldly cares, wealth, illicit desires, and the pleasures of life—a lack of control that Peters associates with Jews and African Americans (a.k.a. Edomites and Canaanites). Here Peters biblicizes the racial undertones of 1950s critics who decried the "savage" and "sexual" rhythms of rock music as communist brainwashing (see, for instance, chapter 7's discussion of Dobson associate David Noebel). The cost of allowing "other peoples" to remain in the land is that white Israel becomes contaminated by their lack of control. And the primary pathway for contamination is women and sex. Peters's proof text is Numbers 25, the same text by which Richard Hoskins elaborated his Phineas Priesthood (see chapter 3).

In Numbers 25, the men of Israel become sexually involved with the daughters of Moab. Because they neglect Yahweh in favor of worshipping the local deity, Baal of Peor, Yahweh sends a plague (which Peters elsewhere likens to AIDS). The plague ends when Israel's high priest, Phineas, acting on the command of Yahweh, runs his spear through the bodies of an Israelite man and his Midianite wife while the couple are engaged in sexual intercourse.

Phineas is where the marriage metaphor ends up. Remember how it began: To know one's Christian—racial—identity is to know yourself beloved. The nation in relation to God is feminine. But the way you know yourself beloved is to find yourself inescapably held—judged guilty—in the hands of an angry God. Representing God in this way enables Peters to reframe the nation as masculine in relation to the world. For the victimized must be protected against future victimization. Thus, one embodies Christian Identity by shouldering one's burden, daring to take a stand in the world—not out of desire or hostility but because one must "take one's punishment like a man." Doing violence to others here is experienced as disciplining oneself. Aggression directed outward is lived as internal self-discipline, holding oneself, and one's own, to norms and ideals. Thus, the true Christian must dare to stand proxy for that angry hand by doing God's work in the world even when it breaks his heart.

To move from identifying the nation with Gomer as beloved object of the male gaze to identifying the nation with God pouring out his rage, Peters must go beyond the letter of the biblical story, reading between the lines and interpolating from external sources (most notably, a reading of Josephus). As usual, however, Peters bases his reading in the biblical text:

in this case, he reads Numbers 25 as amplifying Numbers 22–24. In these earlier chapters, the Midianites and the Moabites fear the Israelites, who are about to enter Canaan. They pay Balaam, a Baal priest, to curse Israel. Three times Balaam tries to curse Israel, but each time he ends up blessing Israel instead. In the Bible's version. Balaam tells Midian and Moab that they can pay him as much money as they want, but he cannot curse a nation that God has blessed. In Peters's version, when Balaam realizes he cannot curse Israel himself, he counsels the Midianites and Moabites to send their most beautiful daughters into the Israelite camp to seduce Israel's young men, thus forcing God to send a plague. This conspiracy is not "in there"; Peters explicitly goes to other sources and interpolates it in. It's as if he has to go beyond a text in which the men of Israel—not Gomer!—engage in deviant sex: the men must have been intentionally seduced.

For intentional seduction is what Peters "just sees" in the United States today. Comparing Balaam the Canaanite priest to today's media and citing *How the Jews Made Hollywood,* Peters charges that the "Jew-controlled" media promotes homosexuality, interracial sex, adultery, and premarital sex to trick Israel into erasing its genetic covenant. Demonstrating how his white supremacist countermemory relies on prejudices embedded in biblical scholarship, Peters notes: "In Haley's Bible Handbook, under *Religion of the Canaanites,* it says Baal was their principal God. Priestesses were Temple prostitutes. Sodomites were male Temple prostitutes. The worship of Baal consisted in orgies. Temples were centers of vice. Not only is this a war, it is also a promoting of religion. Whose God is going to prevail?"[83]

From this reference volume, Peters moves to reading the cover of the June 8 1992 issue of *Newsweek* entitled "Whose Values?", which he holds aloft as he proclaims:

> The WASP family it pictures with two tow-headed little children, looks just like Ozzie and Harriet where one wage earner could support a family— those days don't exist anymore do they? Why? Because we have been deceived and the wrath of God has been turned upon us. There is only one answer—repentance. And repentance is not just turning back to the laws of God. Repentance is running every stinking Canaanite out of this country. I long for the day that Madonna's little naked body can be chained to a stake and God's people can stone her. And anyone else who would bring

in such a filthy vile religion into this land. Anyone else who would wage war with us and try to exalt their God over ours. This is a battle—not an exotic playpen of sex. They've used the same tactic they've used on us before [at Peor].[84]

Peters moves from linking the prejudices of scholarship and popular culture to conservative countermemories propounded by the Christian right. He proceeds to quote from *The Institutes of Biblical Law,* a classic text not of Christian Identity but of a section of the Christian right known as Christian Reconstructionism. Authored by Rousas Rushdoony in 1973, *The Institutes* cites a favorite author of James Dobson's, Victorian anthropologist Joseph Daniel Unwin (1895–1936). Unwin argued that the mental and cultural development of a nation are directly dependent on its people developing a sexual code that confines sexuality to marital monogamy. Unwin asserted that any civilization that ceases to follow this sexual code will decline in three generations.[85] Three generations, Peters intones ominously. From the sexual revolution of the 1960s, America has but one generation left before all the memory traces of its Christian heritage are erased from its genes.

In the gap between Numbers 24 and 25 Peters finds the elders of Zion as his mirror image: biblical literalists pouring over the Bible searching for clues to that secret weapon by which the New World Order can bring Israel to its knees. For is not the Bible an instruction manual? This, Peters proclaims, is the true meaning of the Bible's talk of spiritual warfare: the anti-Christ forces use Israel's identity against it. Nay, they use Israel's God against it. Peters warns: "They know the word! They know the limitations of our God! . . . You say 'Blasphemy! My God has no limits.' Oh yes he does. He has told you he cannot lie. And they looked at this and said, 'You can't lie—We've got ministers all across the nation teaching Christians to love us who hate Jesus Christ. Now keep your word and bring on the curses!'"[86]

Peters reads the curses not as punishments over which God has control, but as a law to which God must submit. Sex is a truth to which even God must give way: the vulnerable and wounded lover, cut to the quick by his beloved's unfaithfulness, submits to cursing his people. Peters produces desire for a white supremacist countermemory by depicting God, too, as caught in the same erotics of domination that characterizes his followers, disavowing his power in the very act of its exercise. The figure of

Biblical Memories / 73

Phineas is where the marriage metaphor leads not just for Peters but for Peters's God.

Through this countermemory, Peters gives meaning to suffering and, more important, reveals how to end that suffering. In the summer Bible Camp that Peters held the year after the Oklahoma City bombing, he urged those in attendance to tap into the covenant law and use the blessings to reverse the curse onto their enemies. Through this racial countermemory, Peters turns despair into mystical grounds for future hope. In this chapter, I have shown how the key to this transvaluation is the way Peters links race and class to gender and sexuality. By setting these signifiers in motion, Peters engenders desire for an erotics of domination in which both white Israel and God himself are caught, transfixed. In the next chapter, I explore the overlaps between Christian Identity and the Christian right that have surfaced in connection with the haunting power of a violence that attracts at the same time—and to the extent that—it repels.

5 Nichemarketing the Apocalypse

Violence as Hard-Sell

Analysts see Christian Identity today as a movement shaped, and even divided, by two choices. Should adherents withdraw from a mainstream they see as hopelessly corrupt? Or should adherents selectively engage with the mainstream to create conditions appropriate for the kingdom?[1] Rather than being lived as abstract either/ors, such choices constitute crossroads where people find themselves again and again: Is this not how commitments are made, politicization happens, and a life is lived?

Much, then, depends on how leaders imagine this crossroads over time. When Christian Identity believers wage spiritual warfare against "the powers, principalities and world rulers of this present darkness" (Ephesians 6:12), to what extent do they envision their fight as literal and to what extent metaphorical? How do they imagine the human and the divine to connect? Do believers pledge themselves to act as the spark that ignites the cleansing fire of divine vengeance that will usher in the kingdom now? Or do believers pledge to preserve their identity, submitting to the powers that be to continue performing the truth of the remnant in the face of this darkening age?

These questions lie at the heart of Christian Identity. I find them unsettling. For when politics is war by other means (as Foucault argued), religion can become the ultimate power fantasy. In calling religion a power fantasy, I am not dismissing religion. Dismissal assumes a reductive understanding of both power and fantasy. My life has taught me the opposite: it matters how we imagine power. Such imaginings are part of why people do religion. How to keep hope alive in a world filled with suffering, suffering that is—let us have the courage to say it—unendurable? And when do hopes become your worst fear, a form of violence that you must let die? For what is it, really, to hold an elusive and invisible something as that which is most real in the face of a visible reality that does not see your ultimate concern?

Negotiating this gap lies at the heart of apocalypticism. I mean apocalypticism not just in the strict sense of Christians who believe in a literal end to time, but in the more secular sense, too, of an apocalyptic sensibility that dreams of a new and better world to be reborn at the end of this vale of tears, however these tears be caused.[2]

In negotiating this gap, desire emerges as a complicating factor. According to Lacan, what desire wants is to run, not complete, its course. The object of desire is deferred even as it is sought, precisely so that one can seek and reseek perpetually.[3] Thus, even such a movement as Christian Identity, which revels in overt expressions of hatred and openly desires to vanquish its enemies, does not, cannot, offer a straightforward economy of desire. Instead, violence operates in Christian Identity as a pole of attraction precisely because—and to the extent that—it is also denied.

I find such reflections unsettling because they locate Christian Identity in the terrain between reality and fantasy. Reality and fantasy are distinguishable: you can tell, sometimes, that what you are doing is fantasy if only because therein lies its appeal (think of day-dreaming). Yet, though distinct, reality and fantasy are not clearly so. The "real" world crosses into fantasy and fantasy crosses into the real, producing self-fulfilling prophecies of all sorts.

In this chapter, I explore these questions by focusing on Peters's life course as a Christian Identity minister. As noted in chapter 3, Pete and Cheri Peters embraced Christian Identity just when a significant minority of its leaders began advocating the use of force to effect revolutionary change—and just when Robert Mathews began The Order to walk that talk. Mathews's project ended in his death, as well as a federal crackdown that culminated in a movementwide sedition trial.[4] Emerging as leaders in this context, the Peterses began their career by engaging in various mainstreaming projects. This chapter focuses on the mainstreaming projects that Pete Peters set into motion in 1988. In the first two sections, I explore the power fantasies that informed these attempts. In the third section, I investigate how Peters's understanding of spiritual warfare changed through interacting with the mainstream. This change happened because Peters's commitment to mainstreaming arises from a power fantasy that has nothing to do with accommodating to the mainstream. When his main-streaming efforts do not effect the expected results, rather than question his belief in God as Law, he denounces mainstreaming—including his belief in the Constitution as a divinely authored text that links the human and the divine—as idolatry. Pushed to rework his understanding of spiritual warfare, Peters intensifies his identification with violence.

Peters's life course provides the chapter's overarching plotline. But his commitments do not take shape in a vacuum. Thus, the second section also explores how convergences have recently emerged between Christian Identity and the Christian right. Both ministries offer a politics of the body—both the individual body envisioned as a Temple of the Holy Spirit and the national body politic envisioned as God's Temple—in need of cleansing. Thus, both Peters and Dobson call Christians to articulate people's concern for their children into the romance of male protectionism by invoking the same biblical image. In this dangerous and deceitful age, the story goes, men must protect the innocence of their families by taking this country back from secular humanists, who have been surreptitiously re-programming the sexual and gender mores of young people through pop culture since the 1960s as part of a conspiracy to annihilate all memory of Christianity from the national body politic.

Along with imagining masculinity, the Right's body politics also imagines a social world: the boundaries of belonging that enable people to feel at home in that imagined community we call the nation. This late modern version of the masculine romance uses apocalypse as a crucible to fuse the boundaries of the masculine body with the boundaries of the national body politic, resurrecting masculinity, the morality of power, and national identity—and thereby closing the gap between what is and what ought to be.

At the Heart of Mainstreaming Lies a Body Fantasy:
Remnant Resolves

The text that best illustrates Peters's early efforts at mainstreaming is a pamphlet entitled *Remnant Resolves*. During Scriptures for America's (SFA's) July 1988 Family Bible Camp, members felt "spiritually burdened" by "the need and the desire to see Biblical principles of government once again established in our nation"; SFA wrote *Remnant Resolves* as a first step toward realizing this dream so that "the fight of our Forefathers against tyranny may not have been in vain."[5]

In its preamble, *Remnant Resolves* sets forth a classic creation mythology of religious nationalism. God made the United States as a nation whose nature IS the Bible and created its citizens as a people whose nature IS the First Amendment: "We recognize that our purpose on the earth is to worship God and enjoy Him forever, and that the highest form of worship is obedience to His Law" (*RR*, 3). This vision is illustrated on the pamphlet's cover, on which a large heavenly hand, surrounded by light, reaches down with a scroll entitled *Remnant Resolves* that spills over a tiny map of the North American continent. God's hand is big, the scroll is bigger, and the land mass is dwarfed by them both. Religious and political freedom are envisioned as a hierarchical chain of authority in which obedient submission to God's overpowering hand empowers Christians to be the visible representatives of that invisible hand: Phineas, the High Priest, who runs his spear through the coupling bodies of an interethnic pair. Given this vision, it is impossible to classify Peters's mainstreaming efforts as either religion or politics. When God is law and human freedom lies in religious obedience, spirituality requires execution in the world.

The first section of *Remnant Resolves* delineates what, then, one must do to build this vision. The most fundamental building block, according to the pamphlet, is self-government. Yet self-government does not mean democracy. According to *Remnant Resolves,* any government in which men *make* law enshrines human hubris as a collective King George. Instead, *Remnant Resolves* promotes biblically correct government in which (white Christian) men *administer* laws given by God (*RR*, 5–6).

Scriptures for America does not shrink from the corollary. Civil government that punishes good and protects evil is counterfeit authority, and "Christians have the right, indeed, the undeniable duty to resist this tyranny" in favor of executing biblical law. The text specifically enjoins substituting charity for welfare, preventing Jews from holding office, using a gun to defend "life, family, liberty and property," and repudiating sexual sins such as abortion, interracial marriage, and homosexuality (*RR*, 6).

Here *Remnant Resolves* reiterates an argument made earlier by Peters in *Authority: Resistance or Obedience? The Key to the Kingdom:* "The authority the scripture speaks of[6] comes from God, does His will, i.e. executes

His law, punishes evildoers, and gives no cause to fear to those who do good. IT IS NOT a governing authority that would protect homosexuals, forbid Bibles and Jesus in school, finance and promote the murder of babies in the womb, slaughter our youth in unconstitutional no-win wars [Vietnam], forbid Christian parents from giving their children a Christian education, forbid travel without a license, deny the first fruits of our labors [income tax], feed those who will not work, require a number to exist [Social Security], etc."[7]

Peters's pamphlet refutes a reconfiguration of the Christian Identity movement that arose after the 1985 sedition trials as Christian Identity leaders such as Dan Gayman pulled back from advocating violence, interpreting Romans 13 as mandating submission to the state in all but the most extreme emergencies.[8] In contrast, in a sermon entitled "Sedition and the Old Time Religion" (which echoed the analysis of Cheri Peters in her documentary on the sedition trials entitled *Sedition . . . U.S.S.A. Style*), Peters argued that Christians owe their deepest allegiance not to the state—that is communism—but to Christ their King as free men.[9] Peters calls this freedom "the Old Time Religion," which he defines by quoting James 1:27: "This is the true and undefiled religion in the sight of our God and Father, to visit orphans in their distress, and to keep oneself unstained by the world." Acknowledging that liberal churches interpret James as calling Christians to build orphanages, Peters castigates social Gospellers for refusing to address the cause of the orphan's plight. In Peters's view, it is the government that creates orphans and widows through no-win wars in foreign lands like Vietnam as well as through social programs like abortion and welfare. Obeying such ungodly authority, Peters declares, closes the door in God's face. In contrast, active resistance opens the door to God's kingdom now.[10] In this religious imaginary, the coming of the kingdom hinges on whether humans open or close the door.

In keeping with this view, Peters uses nostalgia (in this case, for the Old Time Religion) to represent a fundamentally antidemocratic stance as populist and empowering. Likewise, SFA models *Remnant Resolves* after resolutions made by colonial committees of correspondence. This nostalgic mimicry invents a transmission history in which *Remnant Resolves* forms the most recent link in a chain that extends from the Constitution to the Articles of Confederation, the Declaration of Independence, the Declaration of Rights drawn up by the First Continental Congress, the

Fairfax Resolves—all the way back to the early covenants made by the Puritans.

In so doing, SFA inserts *Remnant Resolves* into a wider political and hermeneutic sensibility called Christian Constitutionalism. This sensibility interprets the Bible alongside legal documents like the Constitution and the Declaration of Independence as equivalent Scriptures: the Bible is read as law and legal documents are read as God's inspired Word. Christian Constitutionalism includes not just white supremacists like Peters but also Christian Patriots, tax protestors, and militia members, most of whom would not identify with white supremacy. It also includes large segments of the Christian right, particularly those influenced by Christian Reconstructionism, a movement whose calls for reconstructing the United States according to biblical law have exerted influence far beyond its small number of card-carrying members.

Christian Constitutionalism fabricates an alternative legal tradition that is also a religious tradition of sacred texts. Yet, for all its nostalgia, this "invented tradition" is intensely antitraditionalist.[11] It rejects all traditions of hermeneutics as man-made systems that corrupt God's meaning. Constitutionalists "fundamentalize" historical documents as well as their authors, reading any and all references to the Bible or God as evidence that America's forefathers founded an explicitly Christian republic—even when these references are metaphorical and even when uttered by deists.

Constitutional fundamentalists invent traditions for their opponents as well. Sociologists Jeffrey Hadden and Anthony Schupe suggest that the whole notion of secular humanism hinges on a literalist reading of the 1961 Supreme Court case *Torcaso v. Watkins*.[12] This case declared it unconstitutional for a state (in this case, Maryland) to require citizens (here Torcaso, who was appointed public notary) to swear an oath affirming belief in God. Justice Hugo Black wrote a brief footnote in which he opined: "Among religions in this country which do not teach what would generally be considered a belief in the existence of God are Buddhism, Taoism, Ethical Culture, Secular Humanism, and others."[13] According to historian Martin Marty, "A new name for a non-existent denomination was born full-blown from the mind of one justice."[14] Decontextualized and repeated in newsletters, radio shows, and publishing houses, secular humanism became "real" by this re-citing.

Likewise, Constitutionalist claims that the income tax was unconstitutionally ratified, for example, are cited and re-cited in legal clinics, lectures, radio broadcasts, computer bulletin boards, and independently published books. Circular citation within these alternative communication networks produces a simulated web that endows such claims with the effects of truth for those who stand within these communities.

Radicalizing the Stream: May the Government Take Warning

Entering into and redirecting these circles of citation is why SFA wrote *Remnant Resolves.* The first half of the pamphlet delineates the building blocks for establishing Christ's Lordship over the nation; the second half formulates a plan for "mass distribution with the goal of getting them read into the Congressional record."[15] Urging individuals to file the pamphlet at their county courthouse (which many deem the highest level of legitimate government), SFA reasoned that once *Remnant Resolves* became a matter of public record, various Patriot groups across the country could appeal to it as precedent when filing liens or setting up common-law courts.[16]

Remnant Resolves was also intended to put federal authorities on notice. In March 1989, Peters and five other Christian Identity leaders took the pamphlet to Washington, D.C., where they claim to have lobbied sixty congressional officials, speaking in particular against gun control. The trip concluded on March 24 with a public reading of *Remnant Resolves* on the steps of the Capitol at high noon on Good Friday, the traditional day and time of Jesus' crucifixion.

Setting the public reading of *Remnant Resolves* in the context of sacred time indicates that Peters's mainstreaming attempts do not arise from a willingness to work within the system. Instead, when Peters sees the capital city, he remembers Acts 17:16–23, in which Paul points to an altar that the Greeks had dedicated "to an unknown God" and says, "What therefore you worship in ignorance, this I proclaim to you."[17] Peters goes to D.C. as a prophet who denounces the nation for mistaking these stone buildings and the state power they memorialize for the God whose mighty arm made America possible. He warns that war can be averted IF the government heeds *Remnant Resolves:* "The authorities in King George III's government, as well as the King himself, made a grave error in not listening to and taking seriously these resolves. It is our prayer the same tragic mistake will not occur again."[18] This prophetic proclamation is a relation of force. Peters delivers an ultimatum. Yet, a relation of force is a relation; it is conditional on the hearer's response. Peters focuses not on the fact that the only acceptable response to an ultimatum is capitulation, but on his vulnerability in this relation. Will they hear?

May Christians Take Warning: Trumping the Christian Right

How ought the nation to respond? Peters's model is biblical: cleanse the Temple. As noted earlier, this model is one that Peters shares with the Christian right: James Dobson explicitly patterned his Focus on the Family ministry after this biblical image (see chapter 8). The image of cleansing the nation as God's Temple appears in the Bible as a response to the threat posed by the Assyrian Empire, which destroyed the Northern Kingdom of Israel in 722 B.C.E. and which invaded the Southern Kingdom a few years later during Hezekiah's reign but was repulsed at its capital, Jerusalem. Like much in the Hebrew Bible, the image recurs. Its first appearance describes the reforms instituted by King Hezekiah; its second appearance describes similar reforms (re)instituted by King Josiah. Dobson models Focus on the Family on the reforms of Hezekiah (narrated in 2 Kings 18); SFA models its *Remnant Resolves* on the reforms of Josiah (narrated in 2 Kings 22–23 and 2 Chronicles 34–35).

Josiah became king as Assyria was disintegrating. Sensing a power vacuum, Josiah rejected his predecessors' pro-Assyrian policy of "cultural cosmopolitanism" and promoted nationalism by encouraging worship of Yahweh.[19] The Bible represents Josiah's policies as carrying out covenant promises that Israel had made long ago and forgotten. These promises were found in a mysterious "book of the law" (assumed since the time of Jerome to be some version of Deuteronomy) that was discovered in the Temple during Josiah's reign. Several biblical scholars have suggested that this mysterious book of the law was not so much found as planted—not an original text but a pretext for Josiah's reforms.[20]

Homi Bhabha has suggested that nations are narrations.[21] Here, the Bible (re)creates the nation of ancient Israel through narrating a story of religious return. The nation had forgotten its God, lost its book of the law. Its antidote was to remember. Thus, Josiah commanded the law book to be read publicly in a covenant ceremony that (re)committed the nation to Yahweh and to his house, the Jerusalem Temple. This commitment was (re)produced by removing "foreign" symbols from the Jerusalem Temple and destroying local places of worship (the high places that dotted the countryside) where the fertility deities of the populace and indigenous Canaanites were honored either in place of Yahweh or in a syncretistic form alongside Yahweh.

Josiah's reforms used religious remembrance as a technology of power to construct national identity at the level of bodily ego. According to philosopher Etienne Balibar, such embodied memories enable people to live the nation's political boundaries as "a projection and protection of an internal collective personality," and thereby inhabit the abstract entity of "Israel" as "home."[22] Yet there is a price for such empowerment: Josiah produces a sense of belonging inside the nation by casting indigenous religious practices as outside the nation.

Modeled after Josiah's reforms, *Remnant Resolves* rejects the cultural cosmopolitanism of the "New World Order." Instead, it warns that if Congress does not return to the nation's original creation order, Christian men are resolved to do it for them. Also like Josiah, Peters stages a public reading of *Remnant Resolves* on the Capitol steps at the moment of Christ's salvific death for the sins of his people. This staging reenacts the covenant: Jesus' death holds out the promise of forgiveness and redemption: if "my people who are called by my name humble themselves and pray and seek my face and turn from their wicked ways, then I will hear from heaven, will forgive their sin, and heal their land" (2 Chronicles 7:14). Thus, like Josiah, Peters positions religion as the vanishing point where state power crosses into the psyche to produce national identity—having been called by God's name. And Peters does so, like Josiah, by stigmatizing both "aliens" and his competitors.

In the newsletter describing sfa's D.C. trip, Peters distinguished sfa's "standing in the gates" (the gates were the public gathering places in walled biblical cities) from "Christians [who] have been playing church, saving souls, building fun parks, etc., allowing the gates (local, state and nation) to go to hell."[23] Peters castigates the Christian right for proclaiming, "If we make him the Lord and king of all, then he will heal this land" and yet defining the culture war as "a battle with a spiritual Satan. . . . It amazes me that they are willing to take on the devil, but if some devil in a three piece suit from the IRS or the BATF knocks on their door you will see just how brave they are."[24]

In contrast, Peters insists that Christian men neither withdraw from culture (as fundamentalists did after the 1920s Scopes trial), nor talk about a "big tent" (as Ralph Reed once did), nor counsel followers to avoid appealing to biblical authority (as Dobson's Focus on the Family does). Whereas Dobson urges followers to become politically involved because "Christians are citizens too," Peters insists that "Christians are ambassadors of Christ and ambassadors go to heads of state."[25] Exempt from the laws of the land where they reside, such ambassadors proclaim their king: "The God you worship in ignorance I now reveal to you!"

In this spirit, *Remnant Resolves* concludes by quoting 2 Chronicles 7:14. As the last words of Peters's public reading, this verse rings out from the Temple Mount over this land like the Liberty Bell. With this act, SFA uses memory as a political technology to appropriate a key text of the Christian right. Eight years earlier, when the Christian right had come to D.C. for its April 1980 Washington for Jesus rally, its leaders chose 2 Chronicles 7:14 as their theme text. According to political scientist Matthew Moen, "The importance of that Bible verse to the Christian Right transcends 'Washington for Jesus.' It has really been the movement's statement of purpose: to turn an immoral United States toward God so that He might forgive her and rebuild her glory. Recognizing the significance of that passage, Stan Hastey [of the Baptist Joint Committee on Public Affairs] labeled it 'the controlling text of the religious right.' "[26]

Remnant Resolves' appropriation of 2 Chronicles is not just any appropriation, because this divine promise is not just any promise. Second Chronicles 7 narrates the primordial moment to which both Josiah and Hezekiah staged a "return." After King Solomon dedicated the Jerusalem Temple, Yahweh appeared to him in a dream, reiterated the covenant he had made with Solomon's father, David, and declared that because he has chosen the Temple for himself, if "my people who are called by my name . . . turn from their wicked ways, then I will hear from heaven, will forgive their sin, and heal their land" (2 Chronicles 7:14). By concluding *Remnant Resolves* with this verse, SFA annexes the Christian right's articulation of the verse—simply takes it over as if the verse were a plot of land to be conquered and colonized, claimed for Christian Identity.

Concluding with 2 Chronicles 7:14 suggests that *Remnant Resolves,* like Josiah's lost-found book of the law, is performative. More pretext than text, it fantasizes the Bible as a repository of divine power that believers can tap into by mimetically reenacting covenant promises like 2 Chronicles 7:14. All the remnant need do is "add faith and stir and the true King, God and Savior becomes real to us."[27] If the nation heeds its warning and follows the blueprint outlined in *Remnant Resolves,* then the United States will get the real thing: a literal kingdom where Jesus is king and Christian men are empowered to represent that overpowering Hand. Delivering on this promise literally is Peters's goal and therefore his brand name.

The Paramilitary Romance and Nichemarketing

Real Nations Love Jesus

From this hostile competition, one might assume that Peters shuns the Christian right. Indeed, Peters at first dismissed Christian Reconstructionism as "fully saturated by Jews."[28] Yet over the years, Peters has quoted increasingly from Rousas Rushdoony and Gary DeMar, as well as Peter Marshall and David Barton (for examples, see chapter 4).[29] Peters envisions this relationship in gendered terms: before people can eat the strong meat of the Word, he says, they must be given (mother's) milk.[30] The gender metaphor expresses the central paradox of mainstreaming: Peters seeks to move Christian Identity mainstream, but he does so in hopes of moving the mainstream right.

For example, in a 1993 sermon celebrating July 4 (delivered after sharing a stage with Barton), Peters urges Barton to go one step further: "When you start investigating the Christian roots of this country, you cannot help but come face to face with the reality of the racial roots of this country. . . . Those men who are going back and discovering our Christian roots had better, if they've got the Spirit of God upon them, be honest. They were not only Christian, but they were one race of people and in the Constitution they made known that they were concerned about one group of people."[31]

Peters portrays white supremacy as the foregone conclusion of returning to the nation's religious roots: "Be honest." Yet such links are never automatic. After the Oklahoma City bombing, for example, many militia leaders professed openness to all races and creeds. Although some of these protestations were about damage control, some were genuine: the militia movement is not monolithic.[32] Yet many Constitutionalists do distinguish between "sovereign citizens," whose rights stem from the divinely inspired "organic" Constitution (defined as the original Constitution and the Bill of Rights), and "14th Amendment citizens," whose rights stem from man-made additions. In this invented tradition, women and people of color became citizens by virtue of the federal government and therefore must obey its laws. In contrast, white men became citizens by virtue of divine decree; hence when a white man destroys his driver's license, marriage certificate, and social security card, he reactivates his sovereign status and need no longer obey the federal government.

The Christian right also distinguishes rights given by God from rights created by secular humanist elites. Instead of distinguishing sovereign from amended citizens, however, the Christian right distinguishes civil from special rights. Although the details of these invented traditions differ, both set into motion the cultural silences that swirl around race and sexuality to create "others" whose unruly bodies can then be cast outside the sacred circle of citizenship. Cultural critic Alisa Solomon explains:

> Through its various attacks—on gays, immigrants, African Americans— the Right insists on "deserving" citizens who must demonstrate their worthiness of constitutional protections. The rhetorical tropes aimed at exclusion of these "aliens" and "cheats" are almost interchangeably applied to all three groups. Queers, for example, are derided in the same terms as the "welfare queen," who is, of course, always figured as black. Both are depicted as sexually incontinent, immoral beings who try to trick the state out of scarce resources. "Special rights," forged in the cauldron of antigay initiatives, became an instrumental phrase in the restructuring of "welfare as we know it." . . . What's more, the welfare reform effort relied, in turn, on the increasingly mainstream disdain for public spending of any sort—a view made popular by the Right's relentless assault on the National Endowment for the Arts. . . . [In sum,] anyone whose sexuality cannot be maritally contained—homosexuals and unwed mothers most of all—are cast out from civil protections, and in the Right's fantasy, from citizenry itself.[33]

Thus, whereas it is important to recognize the diverse attitudes among Christian Constitutionalists regarding racism, it is equally important not to get lost amid these feedback loops. After all, the Founding Fathers did not just happen to be silent on the inalienable rights of other races. Benjamin Franklin brought to the Constitutional Convention a strong resolution against the slave trade written by the Pennsylvania Abolition Society; the resolution stayed in his pocket.[34] The result of this and similar silences was a Constitution that, though founded on overt protestations of "no taxation without representation," defined political representation through coded language combining "agendas for individual freedom" with "mechanisms of devastating racial oppression."[35] Hence, W. E. B. Du Bois argued in *Black Reconstruction* that any constitutionalism that idealizes literal fidelity to the founders' original intent cannot break free of the racial violence at the nation's origin. How much less capable of breaking free is a sensibility that idealizes the Constitution as God's plan for this nation.

As did their models, the biblical kings Josiah and Hezekiah, both Dobson and Peters use "traditional religion" as an image. Its invocation of the past signifies the pleasure of protest and passion. Thus, as chapter 2 suggested, calls for religious return have less in common with the desire to return to a bygone age (à la the Amish) and more with Coca-Cola's marketing campaign, in which the company resurrected its original contour bottle (introduced in 1916 to differentiate Coke from the competition) to "unleash the power of nostalgia."[36] Long ago, there was a nation inspired by God and infused with a preordained potency, whose power was lost to unseen conspirators. The appeal of this fantasy lies not in the past but in its future promise. All one need do is recapture that stolen, forgotten self and the nation will rise again.

This is why pointing out contradictions in the Right's countermemories does not bring the Right tumbling down like a house of cards. Emptiness is key to how this image appeals. "It is precisely through such displacement," argues theorist Slavoj Žižek, "that desire is constituted." Žižek explains:

> The element that holds together a given community cannot be reduced to a point of symbolic identification: the bond linking its members always implies a shared relationship toward a Thing, toward Enjoyment incarnated. This relationship towards the Thing, structured by means of fantasies, is what is at stake when we speak of the menace to our "way of life"

presented by the Other. . . . This Nation-Thing is determined by a set of contradictory properties. It appears to us as "our Thing" (perhaps we could say *cosa nostra*), as something accessible only to us, as something "they," the others, cannot grasp, but which is nonetheless constantly menaced by "them." It appears as what gives plenitude and vivacity to our life, and yet the only way we can determine it is by resorting to different versions of an empty tautology: all we can say about it is, ultimately, that the Thing is "itself," "the real Thing," "what it is really about," and so on. . . . The structure here is the same as that of the Holy Spirit in Christianity. The Holy Spirit *is* the community of believers in which Christ lives after His death; to believe in Him is to believe in belief itself— to believe that I'm not alone, that I'm a member of the community of believers. . . . In other words, the whole meaning of the Thing consists in the fact that "it means something" to people.[37]

I suggest that this paradox of desire—the emptiness of the Nation Thing as envisioned on the screen of communication technologies—explains what Michael Barkun describes as the *irony* of recent convergences between Christian Identity and the Christian right. Whereas in the late 1980s, "the radical right was an isolated, insular subculture, detached from and shunned by the larger society," by the 1990s things had changed. In his epilogue updating *Religion and the Racist Right: The Origins of the Christian Identity Movement,* Barkun observes: "The circumstantial ties between the [Oklahoma City] bombing and the radical right should have definitively de-legitimized the radical right. But instead of reinforcing its pariah status, the bombing helped move it toward the mainstream, supplying it with the kind of media access it never previously enjoyed and attributing to it a power about which it had only fantasized. Such media access, in a time of rising anti-government sentiment, has opened new recruiting possibilities, while the attribution of power has made the fringe right an increasingly attractive prize for some mainstream politicians to covet."[38] Barkun attributes this change to three "bridging mechanisms." First, militias now provide "transition points" so that "rather than shift abruptly from 'normal' to 'abnormal' politics, one can move by stages." Second, Christian Identity repackaged its racism as antigovernment politics. Finally, its conspiratorial sensibility has proliferated into evangelical Protestantism and the New Age movement (as Barkun notes) but also, and more important (I contend), into a social sector that Barkun does not consider: mainstream pop culture.[39]

Communications technologies have created a new beast: "the mass-mediated human, whose sense of space and time, whose emotional repertoires and deepest motivations cannot be extricated from what has emanated through the airwaves."[40] Through their pioneering use of mass communications technologies, both Peters and Dobson use the biblical image of the nation/body as God's Temple to reconstruct the emotional repertoires and motivations through which people do the Nation Thing. This image rearticulates mainstream hopes and fears—hopes and fears that find their primary articulation in popular culture and, specifically, in the paramilitary romance that emerged in the 1970s and 1980s in response to challenges associated with the 1960s.

A key challenge of that era was Vietnam, which many (mostly white) Americans experienced as a crisis in the masculinity of the American soldier and, by extension, in the nation. The United States had lost, in the eyes of American racial consciousness, to an effeminate inferior race from the technologically backward Third World.[41] In response, military and political leaders narrated a cultural memory that denied defeat. By insisting that the nation had lost because of its "self-imposed restraint," these leaders set about repairing belief in national and technological supremacy by remasculinizing the nation.[42]

This official memory had a popular counterpart, which sociologist William Gibson calls the "New War" genre. Throughout the 1970s and 1980s, Hollywood produced action-adventure blockbusters (such as *Dirty Harry* and *Rambo*) by the score. Men's fiction (consider Reagan's favorite author, Tom Clancy, whose Jack Ryan series includes *The Hunt for Red October* and *Patriot Games*) also proliferated, with some twenty to forty series released each year. In 1975, former Green Beret commander Robert Brown founded *Soldier of Fortune* as a magazine for "the independent warrior who must step in to fill the dangerous void created by America's failure in Vietnam." Brown sold up to 185,000 copies per issue to readers who were college-educated, married, and spent $1,000 annually on firearms and accessories, which were hyped through a complex interplay of nostalgia (marketing a .45, for example, as an "affordable legend") and fantasy (so that buying Rambo's weapon was promoted as a way to make Rambo, or the myth of masculinity that his knife embodied, real). Alongside the popularity of military-style automatic firearms went new recreation possibilities, including combat training schools, firing ranges, and paintball.[43]

Gibson traces the popularity of this New War genre to the fact that "mobilization for war had been a constant part of American life since the beginning of WWII in 1941. . . . The long cold war against communism had for decades been presented not as a manageable conflict with a socioeconomic system that differed from Western democracy and capitalism, but rather as a holy war against the presence of the devil in the modern world."[44] Thus, apocalypticism has long provided a stage for the formation of national and masculine identity, as well as their interimbrication (using one to prop up the other to avoid acknowledging that this emperor has no clothes). Given such intimate and lengthy training in apocalypse as identity, when faced with loss at home and abroad in the aftermath of the 1960s, "white men," Gibson suggests, "began to dream, to fantasize remaking the world and returning to an imaginary golden age, a time before Vietnam, before feminism, before civil rights," before deindustrialization and downsizing of all kinds.[45]

Whereas traditional war movies and Westerns, which faded out after Vietnam, tended to engender identifications with law enforcement or the military, the New War hero is paramilitary. Birthed into warriorship by the loss of his wife and children (who die, usually because the government lacked the courage to keep its promise of protection), the New War hero fights alone or with a small band of outlaw warriors. An old war hero like James Bond found female agents in his bed only to win them over so that they want him warm and alive; paramilitary warriors find Black Widow women whose embrace leads to death—theirs or his.[46] The old war hero derived his martial prowess from his moral character and therefore needed nothing more than conventional weapons; the paramilitary warrior derives his power from customized weaponry that functions as a signature extension of his hard body/phallus.[47]

Intense and phantasmatic weaponry is necessary for an age in which the masculine style of a John Wayne seems embarrassingly naïve. Vietnam revealed the virtuous war depicted by Westerns and WWII movies to be an illusion. No longer could one simply ignore the gap between men and Real Men. Hence, the paramilitary warrior divests himself of the phallus—but only to reclaim it as most truly his own, in part through fetishized weap-

90 / Lift High the Cross

onry and in part through vivid marks of male self-torture (as in the case of John J. "what you call hell he calls home" Rambo). The fantasy that the paramilitary romance offers is that male pain purifies power, rendering it once again legitimate, moral, innocent, even wise. In this version of the romance of male protectionism, white men rise up like a phoenix from the ashes of victimization, sufficiently strong to take action and take control, restoring this nation to its original state: God's holy Temple.[48]

Perhaps the most extreme white supremacist rearticulation of the paramilitary romance, Louis Beam's strategy of "leaderless resistance," comes right out of the New War genre. In response to the increasing government crackdown stimulated by the terrorism of The Order, Beam advocated that white supremacists form independent paramilitary cells (in contrast to the top-down military model of the Klan, which enables lawyers like Morris Dees to sue organizations as corporations responsible for the illegal acts of their members). Like Rambo, Beam had fought in Vietnam; when he returned stateside, Beam "took the war back home."[49] As leader of the Texas branch of David Duke's Knights of the Ku Klux Klan, Beam formed paramilitary units that in 1981 intimidated Vietnamese shrimp fishermen in Galveston Bay.[50]

Yet, in the 1980s, white supremacists were not alone in forming their identities in terms of the paramilitary romance: rather than declaring a War on Poverty, Reagan declared a War on Drug Dealers and supported the Nicaraguan Contras. Likewise, in his analysis of the 1992 standoff at Ruby Ridge between Christian Identity believer Randy Weaver and federal authorities seeking Weaver's arrest (an event that, along with Waco, catalyzed the militia movement), sociologist James Aho attributes the escalation of this standoff, which lasted ten days and took the lives of three people, to the fact that all four major protagonists trained in paramilitarism with Special Forces. Weaver dropped out of community college in 1968 to join the army, where he was assigned to the Green Berets. Although he never went to Vietnam, he became an expert in field engineering and the M-14 rifle. William Degan, who died at Ruby Ridge, served as an armed infantryman in Vietnam. After the war, he put his skills to use in the Special Operations Group of the U.S. Marshal Service. Degan had been given the task of delivering Weaver's subpoena, along with fellow federal marshal Jack Cluff. Cluff had been an army helicopter gun crew chief in Vietnam from 1968 to 1969, providing air support for a Green Beret unit that was training Cambodian soldiers, for which he earned twenty-six medals. Bo Gritz (the Populist Party leader who negotiated Weaver down from the mountain, thanks in part to a letter of introduction from Pete Peters), served as an intelligence officer and reconnaissance chief for a Green Beret unit in Vietnam from 1968 to 1969. According to Aho, Gritz was the most decorated Green Beret in Vietnam. After the war, he commanded U.S. Special Forces in Latin America and later headed "special activities" for the U.S. Army General Staff at the Pentagon. In 1983, he led the original mission to Laos to rescue American POWs whom Gritz believed were abandoned by the federal government as part of its effort to cover up CIA involvement in cocaine trafficking as a way to fund its covert counterinsurgency efforts. Writes Aho: "It was Gritz himself who served as role model for the bluff and swagger man-of-action who in the face of government corruption and indifference seizes the day in the movie thrillers *Uncommon Valor, Missing in Action,* and *Rambo: First Blood Part II.* Bo Gritz is not merely a product of American paramilitary culture; he is its archetype."[51] Is it surprising, then, Aho asks, that the two sides played into, and played out, each other's worst fears and fantasies? Both were acting the same script.

Gibson suggests that a similar set of values informed those he interviewed at *Soldier of Fortune*'s annual conferences from 1985 to 1987. He writes:

> Being *active*—in contrast to the passivity of the general population—was a key value to the conventioneers. As active men, they considered themselves *responsible* for their own welfare and that of their families. A former U.S. Army Special Forces instructor who now ran a "Base Operational School" in Mesa, Arizona, praised his clients as "normal blue-collar and white-collar people who don't think the federal government is going to take care of them in a stressful time." A Hawaiian aircraft mechanic and member of an Army National Guard Unit spoke more personally: "We feel that it may come a time when it's up to the head of the household to take care of his family. On this planet, there are guys who are doers and guys who are watchers."[52]

Gibson's interviews reveal explicit attempts by white supremacists to recruit *Soldier of Fortune* readers. The magazine's advertising manager routinely discarded potential ads that contained the words "KKK" and "Nazi," eventually discarding ads containing the word "Christian" as well. But the manager's method was not foolproof. In 1981, William Pierce, founder of the neo-Nazi organization The National Vanguard and author of *The Turner Diaries,* bought the magazine's mailing list and sent copies of his catalogue to subscribers.[53] Gibson suggests that the magazine's readers were a "natural" constituency for white supremacists, who needed merely to link the *Soldier of Fortune*'s existing anticommunist ideology—with its well-grooved articulation between national freedom and male protectionism—with the anti-Semitic identification of communism with Judaism. Yet getting individuals to make that link is not automatic. Indeed, the advertising manager at *Soldier of Fortune* learned he had slipped up when outraged subscribers called in protest.

Increasingly, as Barkun notes, militias provide a bridge for people to transition step by step. The militia manual *Citizen Soldier* by Robert Bradley (sold by Peters) features a colonial militiaman on its cover and promises advice on "How to protect your home, family and freedom when the government can't." Convinced that federal fiscal policies concerning the national debt and social programs will result in national insolvency, Bradley warns that when the government becomes unable to fund welfare, inner cities will erupt in racial and ethnic unrest just as Los Angeles erupted after the Simi Valley verdict (aided and abetted by white liberals seeking to install socialism). Bradley counsels people to be prepared by forming a neighborhood watch from which they can recruit potential militia members.

Bradley forms his apocalyptic imaginary on a racialized national topography: white suburban homes versus dark inner cities. I explore these connections at greater depth in chapter 8, after examining Dobson's presentation of his Focus on the Family ministry as fighting to preserve suburban family values from inner-city lawlessness. There, I draw on historian Paul Boyer to show the roots of this primal scene of racial/urban unrest in post-WWII prophecy novels, which often coupled racialized images of social disintegration in inner cities with portraits of corrupt government officials luring the people into slumber.[54]

As the following case study demonstrates, because Dobson's radio audience extends well beyond the narrow confines of prophecy circles, Dobson rarely invokes biblical apocalypse overtly. Yet, when he is at his most adamant about identifying his ministry with "the defense of righteousness," he is at his most apocalyptic. For example, in a 1993 newsletter to constituents, Dobson recounts how he learned that "our mission in support of righteousness must be offensive in nature, not merely defensive," when he and his wife Shirley were touring "the Holy Land." Standing "among archaeological digs and ancient battlegrounds," James and Shirley Dobson see: "Their world, like ours, was divided between God's Kingdom and the domain of Satan." On the western shore of the Sea of Galilee lived the devout Jews to whom Jesus preached, and on the other side lived "the Canaanites whom Joshua had driven out of the [sic] Israel and who practiced the Greek form of fertility cults . . . [including] the ancient worship of Baal, the god of nature—lightning and thunder." Faced with this geography, what did Jesus do? Dobson recalls Mark 4:35–5:13, in which Jesus, when he and his disciples were in a boat on the Sea of Galilee, rowed "directly toward the forbidden world." Dobson concludes: "Jesus did not remain in the safety of the Western territory. He constantly sought out evil and confronted it head-on."

Similarly, visiting a cave at Ceasarea Phillipi (identified as a center for Baal worship) reminds Dobson of a biblical passage that is also set there: Matthew 16:13–16. In this passage, Jesus asks his disciples who they think he is and Peter responds, "You are the Messiah, the Son of the Living God." Dobson comments:

> Then Jesus said something very important to our understanding: "And I say unto thee, That Thou art Peter, and upon this rock I will build my church; and the gates of hell shall not prevail against it" (Matthew 16:18). I have always interpreted that reference to the "gates of hell" as a defensive statement. In other words, I presumed Jesus was assuring us believers that we would not be overcome by the forces of evil. But look at the wording again. When Jesus spoke of "the gates," He referred to the entrance of a walled city—a fortress. We would all agree that a fortress is not an offensive weapon—it is a defensive structure. "Gates" do not attack anyone. They are designed to protect those who are huddled within. Jesus was not telling the disciples that the church would somehow survive Satan's assault. He was assuring us the enemy would not prevail against *our* onslaught! We are to take the Good News directly into his territory and penetrate the stronghold of wickedness. This is accomplished not with the weapons of war but with the powerful force of love and persuasion.[55]

As the next case study shows, Dobson's primary identification is with sentimentality. Hence he eschews military arms to take up arms of another kind: the force of love and persuasion. Yet, identifying with sentimentality does not lead Dobson to confine his mission, stated as "preserving the Bible-based family," to defensive warfare. Instead, he maps the biblical text onto an apocalyptic geography that divides the world into the Christian West and the Baal-worshipping rest and thereby transforms talk of crucifixion—a self-sacrifice—into orders to lift high the cross and launch an offensive assault.

The Paradox of Hard-Sell Style: How to Keep the Hate You Find

This shared orientation within the apocalyptic imaginary of the paramilitary romance does not mean that Peters and Dobson, or the white supremacist and the Christian right, are identical. Both Peters and Dobson insist on the necessity of engaging with the mainstream offensively, but Peters identifies with the bravado of Clint "make-my-day" Eastwood, whereas Dobson sounds more like Arnold Schwartzenegger in *Kindergarten Cop*, learning that a real man would rather be a head of the household than a paramilitary warrior. As indicated by my earlier reading of *Remnant Resolves'* appropriation of 2 Chronicles 7:14, I interpret these competing identifications as nichemarketing.

Nichemarketing explains the paradoxical nature of Peters's mainstreaming projects. Rather than indicating his willingness to work within the system, Peters practices mainstreaming to speak the silences that lie at the heart of how America does the Nation Thing—and to speak these silences even better than *Soldier of Fortune* or Rambo; even better than Special Forces, the Reagan administration, or Christian Constitutionalism; even better than the softer version of male "headship" promoted by the Christian right. Yet, as we've seen, performing silences requires ideological work: the work of memory, the work of marketing.

Immediately following SFA's stint with *Remnant Resolves* at the Capitol, Peters and three associates attended a pastor conference held by Bill Gothard because "some in our midst are coming up with false teachings and perversions of Romans 13, advocating blind obedience to the State and I discovered they were getting this material from Bill Gothard."[56] While lunching with Baptist ministers after Gothard's first lecture, Peters

Apocalyptic Violence / 95

inquired about the assault rifle ban Congress was then debating in response to the 1989 Stockton killings (in which Patrick Purdy, a fan of the New War genre, used a military-style assault weapon to attack a schoolyard of Southeast Asian children). Asked Peters: " 'Gentlemen, if House Bill 669 passes, it could mean the confiscation of our weapons. If it does pass, are you going to tell your congregation to obey the civil authorities and turn them in?' There was no answer until finally one preacher, with a lowered head and voice said, 'I'm not turning mine in.' [Peters's associate] Brother Weiland, who was sitting next to me said, 'That's not what he asked.' Then, after a few moments of silence the preacher said, 'I would probably tell them NOT to turn them in.' "[57]

Encouraged, Peters accompanied his newsletter with a pamphlet entitled *Everything You Wanted to Know (and Preachers Were Afraid to Tell You) about Gun Control.* Denouncing "pietistic so-called Christians" for whom freedom means only freedom from sin, Peters quotes Luke 22:35– 36 ("Let him who has no sword sell his robe and buy one") and explains: "The sword of that day WAS A LETHAL WEAPON, equivalent in our time to a pistol, a rifle, a machine gun and, yes, an assault rifle."[58] Arguing that "the phony churches and preachers of our day have caused our warrior types to feel archaic, unneeded, and less than Christian," Peters does not merely accuse the religious establishment of failing to preserve the faith. As he sees it, "America's decline and weakening can be attributed to the switch from a (strong, logical, masculine) Bible-based Christianity to a (weak, emotional, illogical, feminine) non-Biblical *Judeo*-Christianity."[59] When the church is a Christian's greatest enemy, the extremity of the times mandates extreme tactics.[60] In Peters's conclusion, the Ol' Time Religion meets the "active" man of the paramilitary romance: "KNOW YOU NEED YOUR GUN TO PROTECT YOURSELF AGAINST GOVERNMENT should it ever become a de facto, out-of-control, unGodly, law perverting, oppressive system. The bigger issue is not hunter's rights or defense against criminals but the Government itself. To some brainwashed, apathetic people this statement may sound bizarre, even frightening, but the writings and teachings of our forefathers show it is not new. . . . The citizens who hold onto their guns with a vise-like grip become a caution and warning light to any oppressive government and a statement they are ready to do their duty if need be."[61]

Peters was not alone in interpreting federal gun control legislation responding to the 1989 Stockton killings as the first step in a state-run communist conspiracy. Within the various overlapping subcultures of gun enthusiasts, many gun owners read the Second Amendment as a sacred covenant. This countermemory champions the right to bear arms as enabling the colonists to beat the British and their descendants to defeat the Indians. Explains Gibson: "From this religious or mythological perspective, the semiautomatic combat rifle came to symbolize the entire American creation myth, and gun control in turn represented an abridgement of God's covenant by the forces of evil."[62] As Peters puts it, "Our people have a law written on their hearts (Hebrews 8:10) which seems to tell them to hold on to their guns. . . . Not only are our public enemies trying to disarm the people, but you can nearly anticipate another public massacre (like in Stockton, California) which would enhance their effort. Almost as a natural reaction, groups of people are arousing and making countering moves. We report on this on page 26 of this newsletter and have reprinted an anonymous mailing recently sent to us. Isaiah 52:1–2 will happen."[63] The anonymous mailing to which Peters refers came from the Patrick Henry cell of the Constitutional Militia of America. The "natural reaction" he celebrates is what we now know as the militia movement.[64]

Thus, even Peters, whose mode of leadership is primarily pastoral, speaks violence loud and proud. Even after the Oklahoma City bombing— or perhaps especially in light of the "ironical" way the bombing moved Christian Identity mainstream—Peters wears his identification with the radical right as proof of his authenticity. Echoing the popular country song that croons "I was country before country was cool," Peters proclaims, "I was Identity before Identity was cool."[65] His analogy casts the Christian right as the numerous cross-over country music artists who have appropriated country music for material gain, removing country from its roots and softening it beyond recognition.

It would be a mistake, however, to read nichemarketing at face value. After a decade interviewing white supremacists, psychologist Raphael Ezekiel describes leaders' deployment of violence as theater: a structure of feeling in which leaders perform "the almost-unspoken possibility . . . that makes the organization visible and that draws members." Ezekiel reads leaders' invocations of violence as command performances whose terms and limits are influenced by the constituents leaders seek to recruit, mobilize, and retain. Whereas most constituents have no wish either to go to jail for their beliefs or even to harm some nonwhite person, followers are attracted by the thrill implicit in the threat of violence, in being involved with "something serious." As a result, leaders must balance "giving members a sense that they are running a risk and making members fearful." Likewise, although both the proverbial loose cannon and the organized terrorist cell are disavowed by leaders, they provide "the vital infusion of *violence as possibility*" necessary for the movement's reputation and aura.[66] Hence Scott Appleby calls calculated ambiguity regarding violence "a hallmark of the discourse of religious extremists."[67]

As indicated by *Everything You Always Wanted to Know (and Preachers Were Afraid to Tell You) about Gun Control,* Peters is not averse to taking violence as his not quite unspoken subtext, akin to sex. This pamphlet champions militias. Yet in the same breath, Peters eschews offensive violence, containing militias within the mainstreaming philosophy of *Remnant Resolves* by representing armed citizens as "a caution and a warning light," a.k.a. deterrence. Likewise, in *The Bible: Handbook for Survivalists, Racists, Tax Protestors, Militants and Right-wing Extremists,* after citing biblical precedents for these practices, Peters qualifies: "It is not the purpose of this writing to promote or advocate violence, but rather to stir a Christian people to such a stance that none would dare provoke violence."[68]

At the same time that Peters eschews armed insurrection, he dreams of white Christian men who stand sufficiently tall and whose style is sufficiently militant to intimidate others, including federal authorities, into backing down for fear that physical violence will break out. This is a power fantasy: to be so threatening that one need not use force to get what one wants. It is also a fantasy about bearing the marks of a mystical destiny, made visible in race and gender, that compels others to submit. And it is above all a dream of an impossible kind of fullness. Peters projects an ideal body image whose boundaries coincide with those of the national body politic. On the one hand, this fullness is secured by a fantasy of God the Great Geneticist who writes his law on white hearts. On the other hand, this fullness is secured by a constitutionalist countermemory that reveres the gun as this Law's visible manifestation (much as Rambo's trademark knife bridges the gap between real men and Real men).

In keeping with this desire to have his cake and eat it too, Peters denounces violent confrontation with the government at the present time as

98 / Lift High the Cross

foolish—both for the long-term survival of the movement and for Peters himself, who can be held legally responsible. Decrying the Oklahoma City bombing as instigated by the government to justify persecuting the Patriot movement, Peters established a litmus test: anyone who insists on waging offensive physical warfare is either a fool, he warns, or (more likely) an agent provocateur.[69] Such protestations are sincere. They are also, and equally, about maintaining multiple layers of deniability. And they are no less about keeping hope alive through a hard sell in which violence is the image that lures.

Precisely because violence functions as fantasy and lure, violence must also be held at bay—close, but not too close. When it comes to violence, white supremacist desire, precisely because it is desire, insists on having it both ways: identifying with violence as a fantasized possibility that is perpetually deferred precisely so that members can keep on desiring.[70]

Like desire, mainstreaming is paradoxical. The Oklahoma City bombing mainstreamed Christian Identity in ways *Remnant Resolves* did not. And Peters's efforts to mainstream Christian Identity while moving the mainstream right move Peters as well. For if mainstreaming works by rearticulating cultural vectors—the racism at the heart of Christian Constitutionalism, the apocalyptic masculinity engendered by the paramilitary romance—then the cultural vectors that Peters strives to respin can also move him to places he did not intend to go.

An End to Mainstreaming:
Forget Our American Forefathers!

In 1988, when Pete and Cheri Peters returned home from the summer Bible Camp at which SFA wrote *Remnant Resolves,* the nearby university town of Fort Collins, Colorado, was embroiled in controversy. The Town Council was considering an ordinance banning discrimination against gays and lesbians in housing and employment. After holding hearings that drew about 350 people, the Council put the ordinance to popular vote in the upcoming November election.[71]

Representing himself to the press as just another "conservative minister" (in the words of the *Denver Post*), Peters denounced the ordinance in several radio sermons, which he advertised in local papers: "Will Fort Collins Become the Choice City for Sexual Perverts? Should Christians

Apocalyptic Violence / 99

Ever Obey Such an Ordinance? Should society consider sodomy, which is called a crime against nature in common law, a class one felony? Tune in this Sunday and next!"[72]

Peters even hosted Dobson associate Rev. David Noebel from Colorado Springs, whom Peters billed as having "the courage to speak out" with "shocking facts" about "the other side of the so-called alternate life style called homosexuality."[73] A John Bircher until 1987, Noebel's commitment to antigay politics stems from his work with Billy Hargis, head of the Anti-Communist Crusade. In 1965 Hargis appointed Noebel head of The Summit, a summer school in Manitou Springs, Colorado, that prepares teens to resist the communist forces (allegedly) dominating colleges and pop culture.[74] In 1974 it was discovered that Hargis had had sexual relations with students, including several men. Three years later, Noebel published *The Homosexual Revolution,* which he dedicated to Anita Bryant in praise of her antigay campaign in Florida. Adopting the stance of male protector, Noebel proclaimed it time for "Christian leadership" to speak out lest people wonder why a woman and mother was heading this battle.[75] Throughout the book Noebel constructs his authority by portraying himself as a "veteran" who has seen "the horrors of youth seduction by expert male homosexuals, who skillfully initiate their victims into a world of absolute vileness and degradation."[76] Noebel's "veteranness" was crucial in the formation of Colorado for Family Values (the group that successfully sponsored Amendment 2, the statewide ballot initiative that prohibited including sexual orientation in antidiscrimination legislation), which developed out of a meeting of Noebel, Tony Marco, and Kevin Tebedo in the basement of Pulpit Rock Church in Colorado Springs when Noebel was guest teaching a Sunday school class.[77]

Claiming that homosexuality is "fast becoming America's number 1 social issue," *The Homosexual Revolution* warns, "Overnight, homosexuality has mushroomed into a menacing abomination. Sodomites by the millions have come out of the closet—defiant, militant, organized—clamoring for 'rights' and respectability." Noebel encloses the word rights in quotes, for "in fact, homosexuals want not simply equal treatment before the law, but, rather, preferred treatment. Not only do they want to enjoy their lifestyles privately, but also they want to demonstrate those same deviant lifestyles publicly." Noebel's fear of flaunting demonstrates that the issue at stake in distinguishing "special" from civil rights is not the actual existence of gay people but our social existence: who gets to give us a name, who must feel shame.[78]

As indicated by his dedication, title, and "veteran" identification, Noebel's organizing narrative is the paramilitary romance. Consider his chapter "The Politics of Homosexuality," whose epigraph observes that "homosexuality is an affliction the KGB delights to discover." Noebel's object lesson is Great Britain, which, after WWI, experienced a "culture of rebellion" that openly accepted homosexuality. As a result (Noebel claims), when England was first confronted with Hitler, the nation adopted a posture of appeasement. Citing Carter's pledge during his presidential campaign to separate his personal religious beliefs against homosexuality from his political life, Noebel warns that the United States after Vietnam

> . . . stands before the Communist enemy much like England stood before the Nazi enemy. If we make homosexuality as respectable as England did in the twenties and thirties, we surely will be swept away with the previous nations of the world who believed they could defile the laws of God.
>
> The hour is late. We must publicly and privately stand for spiritual and moral values as revealed by God in the Bible and stand resolutely against the homosexual revolution or we, too, will die.[79]

Drawing on the antigay campaigns of the McCarthy era, Noebel represents homosexuality as "a kind of national death wish" that seeks to "change the natural order created by God Himself."[80] Thus Noebel (and, as I shall soon show, Peters as well) casts homosexuality as a rejection of God's Law on a bodily level. Noebel reads this physical rejection as the outward sign of an inner rejection of God's grace (a satanic sacrament, if you will). Such spiritual death is national in scope, for not only is the body the Temple of the Holy Spirit, but the nation, too, is God's holy Temple. Behind the open acceptance of homosexuality, then, Noebel sees a communist plot designed to take over the nation from within (or behind) by separating church from state. This theocratic countermemory uses popular prejudices regarding homosexuality to link people into a theocratic populism. Its populism, however, derives not from a commitment to democracy but from a fusion of anticommunism with a particular way of imagining the body. This fusion engenders presumptions of a God-given natural law, which Noebel converts into the political necessity of fusing God's Law with the law of the land—"or we, too, will die."[81]

The power of this threat is not literal but imaginary. In our society, homosexuality does mark destruction—not of the national body politic but of the imagined body through which one acquires intelligibility and social existence: "I will be destroyed if I love in that way."[82] A child enters into "the family" by undergoing prohibitions: one identifies with whites, not blacks; one is male, not female, and thus desires women, not men. Writes Judith Butler:

> Becoming a "man" within this logic requires repudiating femininity as a precondition of the heterosexualization of desire and its fundamental ambivalence. If a man becomes heterosexual by repudiating the feminine, where could that repudiation live except in an identification which his heterosexual career seeks to deny? Indeed, the desire for the feminine is marked by that repudiation: he wants the woman he would never be. He wouldn't be caught dead being her: therefore he wants her. She is his repudiated identification (a repudiation he sustains as at once identification and the object of his desire). One of the most anxious aims of his desire will be to elaborate the difference between him and her, and he will seek to discover and install proof of that difference. . . . That refusal to desire, that sacrifice of desire under the force of prohibition, will incorporate homosexuality as an identification with masculinity. But this masculinity will be haunted by the love it cannot grieve.[83]

Hence the paramilitary identification of the new war hero, who must prove/perform his masculinity repeatedly by repudiating those loves the culture cannot grieve. As Linda Kintz observes, "Metaphorically, an apocalyptic national crisis is often figured in terms that suggest sodomy, in which the enemy sneaks up from behind or attempts to penetrate the hero's armored safety. . . . The hero must thus always fight on two fronts, against both the enemy and the establishment. In this world, liberalism is heavily coded as a sign not only of duplicity and moral corruption but of cowardice and character defects as well."[84]

Drawing on mainstream stereotypes of gays and lesbians as narcissistic and immature, this way of imagining the body casts homosexuality as the very epitome of sin or hubris: the glorification of "I want" in defiance of God's creation order. As Peters puts it in "Sodomites Seduce City Council": "Who said they were worthy of death? God. Turn to Leviticus 20:13 if you don't believe me. . . . God is setting up laws for society [that] are perfect and just. . . . We come along [saying], 'We've found a better solution, God. We don't know why you were so hard and so unjust.' . . . We've got this false theology that says we've got a better way to deal with this: pass an ordinance that says we can't discriminate. I think Leviticus 20:13 is pretty discriminatory. So sit back Christians and do nothing. The next time they will outlaw Leviticus 20:13. . . . They will keep going until they destroy every vestige of Christian values."[85] To keep chaos at bay and shore up physical and national defenses, Real men must submit to no one—except that large hand, surrounded by light, that descends from the heavens holding a scroll: *Remnant Resolves.* Through this projected male body/ego, the assertion of "male headship" is converted into an experience of submission.

Peters follows this championing of a literal reading of Leviticus 20, his brand name, by quoting Christian Reconstructionist Rousas Rushdoony to the effect that the state, while professing neutrality to religion, has established a new religion: secular humanism. He warns, "Any revival of Christian strength will thus precipitate major conflict because it will threaten the humanist establishment." For Peters, God's law constitutes a sort of genetic tinder, encoded on the hearts of white Christians, so that all one needs is a catalyzing spark and men will be Real men once again. A side of Peters welcomes this threat:

> I pray that they [the Town Council] recognize the seriousness of the decision that lies before them. This puts the Christian who believes in protecting the Christian lifestyle called the Way in the position of being criminal. It will eventually, and I'm not advocating this, but I'm gonna tell you what happens, if men keep passing laws like this it will eventually lead to death. . . . Eventually some man is gonna follow the law that is written on his heart and there's already some of them out there. Not necessarily in the churches—the churches run 'em off—they're in the bars. But they know what the just punishment is for homosexuality. And if one of these days a homosexual is going to try to recruit one of their kids they're gonna stand up for the laws of God.[86]

Arguing in large part against the cold war, Edward Steichen's 1950s photo exhibit *The Family of Man* captioned a series of pictures depicting heterosexual couples from around the globe with the phrase "We two make a multitude." In the hands of Noebel and Peters, this hope becomes a fear. Gays and lesbians cannot reproduce so they must recruit—your children.[87] This bodily imaginary sanctions prejudice as the "natural" instinct to protect one's children.

In contrast to Peters's overt championing of the violence of Leviticus 20, Noebel explicitly disclaims any hatred of, or desire to discriminate against, gays and lesbians.[88] Yet identifying homosexuality as the epitome of sin underlies both his claim to "love the sinner but hate the sin" as well as his selection of homosexuality from a biblical list of sins as the sin most worthy of censure. Formed within the 1950s anticommunist Old Right, Noebel warns, "Not only will homosexuality characterize the end-time as it characterized the end-time of Sodom, but the anti-Christ himself could well be a homosexual. . . . Is it any wonder that some people already are writing about an international coterie of homosexual activity vying for political power?"[89]

Likewise, in its Amendment 2 campaign, Colorado for Family Values (CFV) sought to distance itself from the overt hatred of leaders like Peters. The group sponsored a "No Room for Hatred" campaign with the motto "Rather than scorn: hope for homosexuals" and ads offering referral to DoveTail, an ex-gay ministry.[90] The group also sponsored campaign ads featuring people of color claiming: "Sexual orientation is not an underprivileged class needing protection. It is a powerful special interest group" and "A 'Yes' vote on Amendment Two will maintain the integrity of true minority protections by not allowing sexual orientation protected status." These ads affirmed the racism implicit in identifying civil rights as "special help" given to those who, in the words of Tony Marco, "need an extra leg up" while simultaneously positioning the Right in the position of the protector.[91]

In the election action seminar and kit that CFV marketed to groups interested in installing similar antigay amendments in their state constitutions, CFV Communications Specialist Mark Olsen argued that the uniqueness of "The CFV Philosophical Model" consists in the way it deliberately transvalued "the D word," as when people say it is good to be a discriminating shopper. According to Olsen, "When I say to discriminate is to choose, and just because some people choose on the wrong basis doesn't mean you take away all rights to choose, heads nod. People understand that. Yes the word discrimination has some really ugly baggage [unintelligible] into it from the civil rights fights of the 1960s, but it's not permanent."[92] Olsen tells the story of Bob Smith, who "loved to tell jokes about homosexuality. He got a good gut laugh out of it. He understood there was something abnormal. But he was adamantly opposed to Amendment 2 as homophobic and wrong to discriminate. He's got something in his gut and something down here in his heart about how a person's supposed to vote, but there's no communication in between. It's a no-man's land, created by our opposition." Drawing on C. S. Lewis, Olsen argues that Bob Smith has become "a man without a chest." The special rights rhetoric of CFV, however, "built a bridge, a lifeline, over that no-man's land. I think this is where swing voters are at. They know something is wrong with homosexuality in their gut but they don't think they can vote for it [Amendment 2]." Olsen notes a similar "syndrome" regarding abortion: people whose religious beliefs oppose abortion feel they have no right to impose purely personal dogma on others. Rebuts Olsen:

> But revulsion to homosexuality is something the Holy Spirit put there and very little amount of political rhetoric [on the part of gay rights advocates] is going to change that. . . . People *want* to support us. . . . But they won't on the basis of morality and revulsion alone in today's climate with the kind of rhetoric that is being aimed at us by the opposition. It's a very important part of American and especially the Western ethic: "I don't agree with you, but I don't want society to mistreat you." That's what homosexuals have played on. People don't like homosexuality, but it's wrong to discriminate. The fallacy in there is unaddressed: the issue of discrimination. We need to tell people that opposing militant homosexuality is the height of fairness. It prevents mistreatment. . . . We didn't omit moral objections and revulsions—we gave people a way to access all of them. . . . You can take a really inflammatory and provocative fact and you won't lose those elements but you'll gain a lot more if you put it in context and document that fact. . . . There are some facts that we presented that do make people want to hate. They make people want to pick up a gun. The fact is, we said: Facts don't hate, they just are. . . . Our campaign did go into the emotional, the visceral, people's gut level feelings about homosexuality. But by placing them in a common sense, rational context, we told the voters it was OK to consider them in their voting discussions.

Added Will Perkins: "This approach gave people hard-nose, real life objective reasons for voting how they felt."[93]

Olsen dramatizes these "real-life reasons" in his "docu-novel" *Refuge*, which narrates the paramilitary romance in an antigay key. *Refuge* tells the story of Vern Yates, a software specialist with a "hip Christian aesthetic," who opposed Amendment 2 as discriminatory only to lose his family to a liberal government gone out of control. Vern finds himself in an America at the beck and call of militant gay activists whose calls for "tolerance" and "equal rights" mask an aggressive plan to smash "the strangle-hold of Judeo-Christian dogma" by convincing social services to take conservative children from their parents (saving them from homophobic indoctrination) and forcing its true believers into hiding in the Colorado mountains, where they are tracked by an HIV-positive butch dyke named Sonya. Olsen concludes his antigay apocalypse with this warning: "To those of us following these trends, the picture of America shown by *Refuge* seems entirely possible—if her citizens don't stand up and contend for their rights. . . . So, please get involved. Let's keep this book a work of fiction. Let's keep it from becoming an awful prophecy of life to come in America."[94]

Seen in terms of a bodily imaginary in which gays and lesbians reject God's most basic law of procreation, antigay politics can function as a bridge between the theocratic Right (be it Christian Identity or Christian Reconstructionism) and sections of the Right that eschew the antidemocratic sentiments implicit in theocracy (although, as we shall soon see, this bridge is neither logically necessary nor sociologically automatic.) What makes this bridge possible is the Christian Constitutionalist identification of Christianity as the sole source of this nation's health, strength, and success. The Right engenders credibility for the Christian Constitutionalist identification of Christianity as the source of the nation's strength and success by articulating its ideological claims of supremacy "in those places where things are felt before they are thought or believed," in people's most intimate memories of familiarity and familiality—fused as these memories often are with biblical memories and images, whose cadences and possibilities articulate with unspeakable hopes and fears.[95] From a fantasy about sexuality and the body, to the Christian Constitutionalist identification of Christianity as the sole source of the nation's health and strength, to theocracy: from the body, to the national body politic, to the Church as "the community of believers in which Christ lives after death"—thus does apocalypse fuse fears for children/the future into the paramilitary romance of men protecting their own by cleansing the national body.

Peters himself acknowledges using this issue to reinvigorate his ministry—both internally ("recharging his batteries" when he was feeling dry for sermon material) and externally (drawing public attention).[96] My sense is that Peters saw opposing the ordinance as a no-brainer, a mainstreaming opportunity for which he expected little opposition. In the short term, this was true: when the issue was put to popular vote, 56.8 percent of the votes cast opposed expanding antidiscrimination protections to include sexual orientation.[97]

During the campaign, Peters's church never filed as a political action committee, mostly (I believe) because Peters does not see himself as part of "the system." In response, the Colorado Attorney General sued the church for failure to file a contributions and expenditures report as required by the Colorado Campaign Reform Act.

When notified by the Larimer County Clerk of his election code violation, Peters asked: "As an ambassador of Jesus Christ, a Christian pastor and evangelist with Holy instructions to, among other things, proclaim the word of God, how and when did I and my labors as a Christian pastor fall under your jurisdiction?"[98] Working within the framework outlined in *Remnant Resolves*, he proclaimed: "When the LaPorte Church of Christ publicly opposed the sin of homosexuality and the promotion of that sin by the Fort Collins City Council, it was doing so out of the worship of Christ." Hence he refused to hire a lawyer, claiming Jesus Christ was the church's lawyer: "When the Pastor of the LaPorte Church of Christ appears in court he has done so in the presence of two or three Christian witnesses[;] thus Jesus Christ, the church's counselor is present and Christ through His spirit has and will give counsel."[99] In a move that proved controversial in the Christian Patriot movement, Peters decided to "just stand on the word of God" in his legal briefs.[100] Working within the fundamentalist hermeneutic of constitutionalism, Peters invoked Public Law 97–280, in which Congress declared 1983 "The Year of the Bible," claiming that this declaration put the government on record acknowledging the Bible as law.[101]

Thus, in his court briefs, Peters represented himself as simply quoting the government back to itself. Drawing on the common (although false)

Apocalyptic Violence / 107

interpretation of the Founding Fathers as suspicious of strong government, Peters argued that insofar as the court was originally established "to serve as a check and balance" on state power, the court must "instruct the state to let the church be."[102] Instead, the court sided with the state, and in May 1993, after the fine had exceeded $10,000, the state seized the church and auctioned its contents.[103]

Peters's response can be read as a classic case of the authoritarian personality, but his stubborn insistence can also be read as image creation: Peters's version of Coke's contour bottle "recognizable the world over without trace of brand identification."[104] Indeed, representing his court battle as an issue of religious liberty enabled him to cross over into media networks of the Christian right. James Kennedy's *The Coral Ridge Hour* featured Peters on a show entitled "Taking Liberties: The Betrayal of Our Heritage," which concluded its account of Peters's court battle with these words: "What has happened to the LaPorte Church of Christ is not an isolated incident. Indeed, there is a concerted effort to strip away our religious liberties in this country. . . . Today in America liberty for Christians is at risk." The program's only reference to Peters's white supremacist beliefs was indecipherable: "Although many Christians would disagree with some aspects of Pastor Peters's theology [which remained unspecified], most would agree with his resolve to stand for his faith."[105]

A similar silence surrounded Peters's appearance on *Keystone On the Line,* a cable TV talk show on the evangelical Keystone Inspirational Network. The program's host introduced Peters as "this fantastic man who stood up in this day and age," noting later that, "If there was ever someone who was speaking out in these last days, Pete, it is certainly you. And I believe we need more John Bunyans just like you."[106] This guest appearance launched Peters's own cable TV show on the evangelical network, called *Truth for the Times.*

Moreover, image creation is not just for others. Faced with defeat, rather than abandoning his ultimate concern and acknowledging that God's genetic law never gets sparked as it should, Peters turns "aggression toward the ideal and its unfulfillability . . . inward, and this self-aggression becomes the primary structure of conscience. . . . Oddly, the psyche's moralism appears to be an index of its own thwarted grief and illegible rage."[107]

Thus, when the court denied his appeal on April 6, 1992, Peters upped his ante, writing a pamphlet whose cover proclaimed *Death Penalty for Homosexuals Is Prescribed in the Bible.* He told reporters that the fine had inspired him to counterattack the gay and lesbian community.[108] His pamphlet also attacked Amendment 2, which was up for statewide vote the following fall. The pamphlet denounces "lukewarm, cowardly, goody goody, praise the Lord, Judeo-Christians" for campaigning against special rights for gays and lesbians while supporting civil rights: "Now the historical record shows, forty years ago, the family values in America would never allow homosexuals to have free speech, free assembly, safety, etc., and thus, the homosexual was afraid to come out of the closet. Now lukewarm Judeo-Christians consider it family values to allow them to do so. Such values are not Bible values, for the Bible allows those who continue in the sin of homosexuality, no such rights."[109] In contrast, Peters insists, "LAW BY ITS VERY NATURE IS INTOLERANT AND DISCRIMINATORY" insofar as lawbreakers suffer the consequences of their actions: "This is particularly true concerning the subject of homosexuality where young people are led to believe they can make up their own law, that is, choose their own sexual preference. They are not being told that there is the existing Law of their Creator, God, that is not to be disobeyed without grave consequences" (*Death Penalty,* 3; emphasis in original).

Like Noebel, Peters means "grave" literally. Citing research from Paul Cameron's (discredited) Family Research Institute, Peters notes that homosexuality brings disease, serial murders, and "the death of the family name or lineage" (*Death Penalty,* 8).[110] "Yet, homosexuals do not mind promoting their lifestyle, which is, in reality, to promote the death penalty" (7). Framed through the paramilitary romance, homosexuality means their death or yours: "After all, the Bible says not only is the homosexual worthy of the death penalty, but also those who give approval to it [homosexuality]" (8). Lest God's people also be judged worthy of death, the nation must be cleansed: "When the people of the land repent, they demand that just that be done [that the nation be cleansed], revival takes place, and consequently a healing of the land" (9).

As in *Remnant Resolves,* quoting 2 Chronicles 7:14 is a way to trump the Christian right. Peters proposes a counteramendment—no lukewarm Amendment 2 but "the real thing." Noting that twenty-five states already have sodomy laws, Peters urges Christians to campaign "state by state (as the homosexuals have done)" for a law that would make the death penalty

Apocalyptic Violence / 109

mandatory for gays and lesbians (*Death Penalty*, 7). He frames his proposal as a prophetic ultimatum: "History shows, however, that it is just a matter of time before courageous men rise up and do what unrighteous government refuses to do. . . . There will be far less death and suffering if society simply enforces Sodomy Criminal laws in every state in the union according to His righteous, existing Law. The facts of this writing show it can and should be done. Pray Christians take the initiative and do so lest a worst judgement of death befalls us as a nation" (25).

Although the plot of this fantasy is familiar (thus did Peters conclude *Remnant Resolves* and respond to the assault rifle ban), something crucial has changed. Before his court battle, Peters tempered representations of violence with the belief that Christian men can performatively invoke the kingdom by catalyzing the law written genetically on the hearts of the white race and recorded in its Constitution. Thus, although Peters had recommended this same counteramendment in 1988 while opposing the Fort Collins ordinance, at that time he tempered talk of the death penalty with qualifiers: "I don't believe in vigilantism."[111] Likewise, when Christian Identity adherents in Shelby, North Carolina, were accused of killing five gay men in 1987 to "avenge Yahweh on homosexuals," Peters testified in court that the adherents' Christian Identity beliefs, far from indicating motivation for the crime, actually proved their innocence. He reasoned that Christian Identity teaches that the execution of gays and lesbians must come not from vigilantes, but from the government. When God's law is enforced by vigilantes it is delegitimated.[112] Obviously, one cannot take such statements at face value. But neither am I willing to dismiss them as hypocrisy or expediency. Peters believed that if he sparked the divine law genetically encoded on white hearts and established in the Constitution, God's kingdom would come.

In Peters's 1992 death penalty pamphlet, disclaimers and rejections of vigilante action disappear. Disillusioned regarding the possibility of speaking to the state's "true nature," he shifts from advocating civic intolerance (the use of legal force or legitimate violence against "outsiders") to permitting violent intolerance (the use of illegal force against the "outsider").[113] Peters still hedges his talk of executing gays and lesbians with prayer that Christians take legal initiatives. Committed to long-term white supremacist organizing, he is not about to become Order founder Robert

Mathews. Instead, he reimagines the connection between the human and the divine: the Constitution no longer does the trick.

As indicated by its dedication, the primary target of Peters's *Death Penalty* pamphlet is former Green Beret and Rambo model Bo Gritz, who in 1992 was running for president on the Populist Party ticket.[114] When speaking to Christian Identity ministers during his campaign, Gritz refused to endorse capital punishment for gays and lesbians.[115] In *Death Penalty,* Peters accuses Gritz of blasphemy for claiming to stand on God's Law as the source of the nation's strength while affirming the "live and let live" individualism that is such a common point of Western regional identification.[116] Peters's denunciation of Gritz was divisive, something he did not do lightly. His usual mode of operation, although something at which he has had little success, is to try to bring the fragmentary and fractious Right together.[117] Not this time. Arguing against Gritz, however, also pushed Peters to rethink his own commitment to Christian Constitutionalism:

> Earlier I spoke of an individual who was running for high office. That individual took the position that although he did not agree with homosexuality, he felt that if two people were consenting adults, then this is America, and they have a right of choice. Does that sound familiar? He is not alone. That is the type of thinking that is prevalent today. . . . In this country, we do not call it Baalism, we call it Constitutionalism. . . . We have forsaken the commandments of the Lord, and we have followed the Baals, but we do not see ourselves as Baal worshippers. We see ourselves as tolerant, Constitutionalists, Christians and conservatives. Those Constitutionalists who take this position consider themselves Christians who are upholding Christian values. What have they *really* done? They have simply repeated the actions of their forefathers in the wilderness.[118]

The wilderness in question is not the North American West, but the wilderness of the Dead Sea into which the biblical Hebrews escaped from slavery to worship their god. Here Peters rereads that moment on which "The Greatest Love Story Never Told" turned: at the foot of Mount Sinai, just when Moses is pledging the nation's troth to keep God's covenant, the people ask Aaron to make a golden calf (which symbolized the Canaanite god Baal). Comments Peters: "They were not worshipping the calf any-

Apocalyptic Violence / 111

more than we worship the donkey or the elephant that represents our political parties" (*Baal,* 53). Likewise, when the white race came to America, they fought to be free, thanked God—and then held a Convention that replaced God's law with the rule of the people and erected another golden calf: the Constitution.

Peters includes himself in his indictment: "Since the time of the Constitutional Convention, we have had preacher after preacher, and I am one of them, who has said that the framers of this Constitution were men of God, Christian men" (*Baal,* 69). Now, however, he denounces the invented traditions of Christian Constitutionalism as just that: invented. The Constitution, he charges, does not mention Christ or God's Word; it allows for homosexuality, abortion, usury, and people of other races to rule over whites. Hinting at distinctions between First- and Fourteenth-Amendment citizens, Peters asks: "*Have you ever known a sacred or divinely inspired document that needed to be amended?* . . . If we return to some of the moorings that our American forefathers gave us, we have gained nothing. I say, let us take the initiative now. Let us go forward and surpass those men. They were good men, but there is nothing in the Scriptures that says we cannot be better men. Forget our American forefathers" (73, 69; emphasis added).

Whereas Peters went to D.C. with *Remnant Resolves* delighting in the power of his performance as a man giving warning, now he denounces this mainstreaming strategy as idolatry. Catherine Wessinger analyzes Christian Constitutionalists as practicing a kind of magic that seeks to "appropriate the enemy's power by imitating their actions and their use of words possessing power."[119] Whereas Peters once trusted the courts, as guardians of the divinely ordained Constitution, to protect him, when his court briefs fail to produce the desired result, he concludes—not that God's law is not written genetically on the hearts of the white race—but that the state is a myth whose power is created by people in their imaginations, when really "it is like the Wizard of Oz, they are just pudgy little men, and who should be afraid of whom?" (*Baal,* 3).

Peters's battle with the state of Colorado illustrates the self-fulfilling prophecy that haunts apocalyptic movements. This includes millennial movements that eschew violent confrontation, for even disengagement can lead to conflict. Indeed, given "the complex network of laws and regulations that governs a modern society, whether in regulation of firearms, tax payments, or the treatment of children [much less election laws]," Barkun contends that such conflicts are inevitable.[120] Peters's reflections seem to agree with Barkun's assessment, although he draws different conclusions. Said theoretically, Peters concludes that his fight is with the specifically modern form of power that accompanied the rise of the nation-state: biopower. As Peters puts it: "Baal is regarded as 'owner.' Have you ever thought about the idea that someone owns you? Does the company store or the corporation you work for own you? . . . As for me, I belong to God and it bothers me that some state god has decided that I am one of his resources. . . . *We did not recognize at the time that was a religious battle we were fighting. Our battle against the creeping takeover of socialism, and their use of subsidies, grants, tax exemptions, Social Security, public (government) schools, welfare, all loosely termed the New Deal and now the New World Order, is a religious battle*" (*Baal*, 22–23; emphasis added). Having long derided the Christian right for mistaking "the powers, principalities and world-forces of this present darkness" as *spiritual* Satans, Peters emerges from his battle with the state deriding Christian Constitutionalists and militias for waging a *political* battle. Thus does Peters claim the other side of his brand name.

Certainly, Peters has always insisted that those who fight only for the Constitution fight in vain. For example, in the SFA newsletter promoting the then-emergent phenomenon of militias, Peters prefaced his reprint of a flier from the Constitutional Militia with the following reminder: "Note: It has no appeals to Jesus Christ, the source of all liberty, truth and freedom."[121] Yet, whereas before, Peters appended notes, after his court battle, which he credits with "helping me focus on the issue of submission," he avows, "I have been guilty of thinking that before we tear something down, we should find a replacement. It is like telling God we will go through the Red Sea, but not until He tells us where to find food on the other side. . . . Someone will say, 'Well, if we do not have the Constitution, what can we do?' Let us go forward and find out. Maybe God has it all under control after all, and if we just begin doing our part, that kingdom will emerge" (*Baal*, 18, 63, 79).

Whereas Dan Gayman responded to the federal crackdown on the supremacist constellation in the early 1980s by urging followers to submit to authority, Peters cites the vision of the biblical book Daniel, in which a stone crushes a statue that represents state power. "What happens when you make that choice for God?" Peters asks. "The Kingdom begins to come into existence, and it begins to crush the Baals. The Kingdom is that stone that is cut out of the mountain without hands. That stone is being cut by those who refuse to be ruled over by tyrants and those who call out for their King. Let us choose Him as our King, as our Lawgiver and as our Judge, and He will save us" (*Baal*, 117). As Peters puts it, just as people told the Wright brothers "Man can't fly," so people say "You can't see the Kingdom now." Oh, yes, we can, Peters avows. If Israel had a Kingdom before, Israel can have a Kingdom again—if she dares to renew and cleanse herself. Even if you don't completely believe, Peters promises, if you begin to comprehend that the Kingdom is now, "then in one or two generations our children will see the streets of gold in that great City." For when I deny "His presence and His reigning right here and now . . . I have denied the Kingdom to my children" (158–59).

Peters gives up on mainstreaming as performatively invoking the Kingdom. Much of that strategy seems to have been about enjoyment: projecting a body image, standing tall, stepping into the impossible fullness of a body image that is projected outward into a world. Mainstreaming for Peters was about putting your body on the line and acquiring the fullness of self that you know you really are.

Peters loses that. But he doesn't give up on his belief. Nor does he grieve. Instead, he redoubles his belief in God's Law by internalizing it, thereby keeping his desire alive through fabricating an interior world. Having lost the Constitution as the link between humans and the divine, Peters still dreams of being the spark that re-fuses—only now, the stage on which he seeks to performatively invoke God's kingdom is first and foremost spiritual: an even more radical version of human belief, shorn of this-worldly supports. In place of the fullness of performing one's masculine body as identical with the national body, Peters offers a future body: the children. This new understanding of spiritual warfare heightens the tension between fantasy and reality, rather than lessening it.

When this chapter began I noted that one thing religion does is help people negotiate the gap between ideals, the way the world ought to be, and reality, the accidental, happenstance, and uncontrollable way the world is. Although religion can be hyped in ways that facilitate an active refusal to acknowledge the existence of its own phantoms, it can also be used to confront precisely those problems that are so structurally deep and collectively embedded that they defy any attempt at a quick fix. Much depends on how power is imagined.

Peters's career as a Christian Identity leader illustrates the ambivalence of the desire for the sacred. Religion can facilitate catharsis by articulating losses and failures into a structure of disavowal that resolutely forgets its failures and disowns the violence at its origin. Yet religion can also empower people to confront these losses and failures in the hope of transvaluing conditions of absolute impossibility into conditions for possible action. The key to such a transvaluation is developing the willingness to remember and actively avow the loss and violence that runs through memories and histories. The following case study investigates this ambivalence from a different angle, by exploring the softer style of today's Christian right, exemplified by James Dobson's Focus on the Family ministry.

The Christian Right,

Focus on the Family, and James Dobson

6 The Power of Soft-Sell Style

Building a Multimillion-Dollar Ministry
by Subverting Feminism

Its Vast Scope:
82 Ministries in over 98 Countries

When I visited Focus on the Family in Colorado Springs during the summer of 1994, I was amazed at the vast amount of people and money flowing through its doors. Focus on the Family was receiving an average of 3,000 to 4,000 phone calls and 8,600 letters each day.[1] With an annual operating budget in 1993 of just over $88 million,[2] the organization employed over 1,300 people. One year later, its estimated income topped $101 million.[3] When I visited, the forty-seven-acre campus housed two buildings: a distribution center, out of which employees were shipping six thousand parcels of books, cassette tapes, and videos daily, and an administration center, out of which over fifty different ministries were then operating.[4] Three years later, the number of ministries jumped to its current figure of 82, which now operate in over 98 countries.[5] Weeks after my visit, a welcome center opened, complete with interactive displays, built from a $4 million donation by corporate conservative Ed Prince. Describing the welcome center, Dobson quipped, "It isn't Disney World, but it's as close as we're likely to get."[6] Dobson's words, alongside the scope of his multimedia ministry, indicate how conservative Bible-believing religiosity has shifted during the last quarter of the previous century; no longer wearing strict separation from the secular world as their badge of authenticity, Bible believers appropriate and reinflect middle-class institutions. For this project, Dobson has generated considerable support. Although Focus on the Family receives contributions from corporate conservatives like the Prince family and Richard DeVos (Amway), by its own account the organization has traditionally received the bulk of its monies from individual contributions ranging from ten to forty dollars.[7]

Although the building-block donations might be small, the scale is vast. Focus on the Family produces nine radio programs, heard on almost five thousand stations worldwide. The original program featuring James Dobson is heard 15,325 times each week around the world.[8] The ministry's flagship publication, *Focus on the Family Magazine,* is received in 2.3 million homes each month.[9] Dobson's name is "practically synonymous" with Christian video; his *Focus on the Family* series, estimated to have been seen by over 40 million people, defined and dominated the market.[10] In addition to producing radio and video series for children, Focus on the Family publishes ten monthly magazines that are sent to more than 2.3 million people and targeted demographically (seniors, single parents, physicians, teachers) and fifteen to twenty new book titles each year as well as two to three editions in its five children's book series.[11] The organization selects two books a month as premiums for subscribers; selected books double their retail sales.[12] In addition to the over one hundred full-time employees who provide a mail and telephone counseling service, outreach programs include a Crisis Pregnancy Center that supports three thousand local antiabortion centers; a Physicians Resource Council; a lending library that is currently operating in over 375 corporations across the nation; and a pastoral support ministry that funds a weekly briefing (faxed to over three thousand ministers), twice-a-month gatherings of pastors in major cities, and evangelistic basketball camps for inner-city kids.[13] A Public Policy Division educates Christians about political issues; its weekly fax, *Family Issues Alert,* reaches thirty-six hundred subscribers, and its *Citizen* magazine reaches seventy-five thousand subscribers.[14] The organization also works to create and support Family Policy Councils in each state which disseminate materials, monitor state legislatures, and coordinate local conservative groups.[15]

Organizational History

Building a Million-Dollar Ministry by Rearticulating Feminism

Dobson was touted as the Christian right's "new rising star" by Jerry Falwell when he dissolved the Moral Majority in 1989. Yet Dobson's ministry can seem like a contradiction, for Dobson is not a minister. He received a doctorate in psychology from the University of Southern California in 1967, as Watts was still smoldering, UCLA students were staging sit-ins, and Martin Luther King spoke against the Vietnam War.

Outraged by what he perceived as the flagrant defiance of the youth movement, Dobson responded by writing a child-rearing manual in which he counsels the nation's parents not to fear asserting their authority. Published in 1970, *Dare to Discipline* has been a best-seller for nearly twenty years, with sales topping three million copies.[16] Dobson's official biographer describes the historical import of *Dare to Discipline* as follows: "Though it is out of date and bears the flavor of the Vietnam War and that troubled era, the book still appeals to those who know that the values we abandoned as a nation during that historic period are still valid and must be readopted if we are to survive as a people. . . . James Dobson's arrival on the scene coincided exactly with a revolutionary social movement that shook America to its foundations. He was God's man for that hour, and he was ready for the assignment."[17]

Dare to Discipline exemplifies the soft-sell style that Dobson would later come to perfect. Although he stresses "the vital function of authority," he does not communicate this message in an authoritarian tone (although it would not be hard to cite biblical texts supporting his contention that parents must "lay down the law" for their children). Instead, he adopts a motivational style, offering practical and workable solutions to everyday problems (setting limits, using rewards). He illustrates this advice with anecdotes from his own family life, cultivating a sense of authenticity through this intimacy. Yet the intimacy of his motivational style is political. Dobson frames his encouraging words—*dare* to discipline!—with asides and prefaces that trace young people's political protest to the "permissive democracy" adopted in America's families during the cold war era.[18] He frames student involvement in the protest movements within the biblical trope of God calling a misguided younger generation to put aside their stiff-necked rebellion and respectfully return to the ways of their fathers.

Dare to Discipline brought Dobson numerous opportunities to speak across the country. With the advent of 1970s feminism, he sought to counter feminist criticisms of the family by offering seminars to churches urging that America not forsake its focus on the family. When these seminars drew two thousand to three thousand people a weekend (at $12 a

Soft-Sell Style / 121

head), Dobson left his joint positions as professor of pediatrics at the University of California School of Medicine and director of behavioral research at the Children's Hospital of Los Angeles. On June 7, 1977, he incorporated Focus on the Family in Arcadia, California. Housed in a two-room suite with one half-time secretary, Focus on the Family then consisted of a film series made by taping Dobson's seminars and his twenty-five-minute weekly radio talk show.

By his own account, Dobson's political conscience seems to have been pricked by Phyllis Schlafly's campaign against the Equal Rights Amendment. As Dobson tells it, the Right was politicized principally by white middle-class feminist claims to "speak for all women."[19] For Dobson (as for many conservatives), such claims were epitomized by the national conference for the International Women's Year held in Houston in 1977. Looking back on that eventful year, Dobson envisions millions of women sitting at home watching the events at Houston on TV and asking themselves, "How did all that federal money get funneled into the hands of such radical people? Why isn't *my* point of view represented?"[20]

Yet feminism also helped a good portion of Dobson's constituency develop the ears to hear his message. Interviewing conservatives in the Silicon Valley, Judith Stacey found that some women converted to evangelical religion in the 1980s as a way to cope with the economic uncertainty of the electronics industry and to fulfill ideals they had learned from feminism. She argues that the belief that the man heads the household in practice can afford women a considerable amount of *personal* power: by conceding the husband's authority as a last resort, women can exercise power during the other moments.[21]

Certainly, women are the average Dobson listener, although not necessarily the stay-at-home moms whom Dobson privileges. Surveys of *Focus* magazine readers reveal that nearly half the households have a mother who works full-time outside the home, with many probably working part time; half the men and a quarter of the women have undergraduate or graduate degrees; most are thirty-something (in contrast to viewers of televangelism, who tend to be elderly); and more than 90 percent voted in the 1988 presidential elections.[22]

Whereas Dobson's account of his own politicization envisions women wondering "Why isn't *my* point of view represented?", Focus on the Family revolves around the authority of DR. Dobson. Just as turn-of-the-century fundamentalism sought to reassert male control over religion (which had become a predominantly female space), so today's Christian right seeks to reclaim home and church as domains of male leadership.[23] Thus, Dobson answers Freud's question "What do women want?" by claiming to provide a "better solution" to the cultural devaluation of women and women's work than feminist politics.

For example, in his 1975 release *What Wives Wish Their Husbands Knew about Women,* Dobson chastises men for "our lifetime ego trip" and urges them to make emotional commitments a priority. When he discusses the biblical command that women submit to their husbands (Ephesians 5:22–24), he articulates this command as an injunction that *men* must nurture their wives.[24] Insisting that the responsibility for a marriage relationship does not lie at the door of women alone, Dobson elaborates specifics for what men can do, many of which sound like standard feminist advice. Urging women to explain their needs to their husbands, he explicitly rejects the self-abasing codependence that derives a woman's value solely from her connection to a man and offers practical advice for communication that bolsters women's self-esteem.

Dobson here is voicing what anthropologist Susan Harding calls a "widespread finesse" of the biblical injunction regarding female submission/male headship that became common as the fundamentalist regime of separate gender spheres ended around 1980 (with women increasingly working outside the home and men increasingly including being a husband and a father in their identity). In her study of Falwell's Moral Majority, Harding notes that this metamorphosis reveals "how much [the Bible's] plain meaning, [its] absolutes, that moral order, can change during the course of a decade or two."[25] Dobson, however, puts his reinterpretation of Ephesians in the service of calling women to recognize not the role of human interpretation in making the Bible speak to people today, but the unchanging nature of God's Law as written in genetic code.

For Dobson acknowledges that *What Wives Wish* will be read mostly by women, not men. He is primarily telling women what they want. Rather than connecting women's personal discontent with politics by analyzing gender as a relation of power, Dobson puts his calls for respecting women and women's work in the service of getting women to accept and respect their biological differences as "God-designed." Indeed, "males and females are in fact different from one another in every cell in their bodies, because they have a different chromosomal pattern."[26] Dobson represents the alleged naturalness of gender difference, its seeming "givenness," as rooting our social order in the creation order. He calls this "the biblical concept of masculinity and femininity," which, he warns:

> We must not abandon . . . at this delicate stage of our national history. Not that every woman must become a mother, mind you, or even a homemaker. But those who do must be honored and supported. There should be a clear delineation between maleness and femaleness, exemplified by clothing, customs and function. . . . Boys and girls should be taught that the sexes are equal in worth but very different from one another. Girls should know that they are girls, and boys should know that they are boys. And for the rest of us, self-awareness begins with an understanding of our sexual identity. . . . Everything we do is influenced by our gender assignment. The first element of our self-identity as toddlers comes from our identification as boys and girls. Any confusion at that point . . . or in the relationship between the sexes . . . must be seen as threatening to the stability of sex itself.[27]

Just as "men's and women's bodies were crafted to 'fit' together sexually," he contends, "in the same way the emotional apparatus of males and females is designed to interlock . . . like hand in glove."[28] From bodies to emotions to social roles, Dobson constructs a chain of ontological articulations grounded in genetic biological differences: "The husband is called to provide leadership and love, while the wife is called to follow the leadership of the husband, nourishing and loving the family."[29] Eithne Johnson notes that this discourse does give women a certain power. Whereas Dobson explains depression, loneliness, and anger as rooted in female biology, if women accept the gender facts of life, they can exercise "sexual persuasion over men and disciplinary authority over children"—turning the raw (be it male sexual desire or aggressive childish wills) into the cooked.[30]

This ontological chain linking sex, gender, and desire is the Christian right's version of the genetic code that white supremacists such as Peters imagine to be written in the hearts of the white race. Both Peters and Dobson reinscribe the Law of the Father through mystical access to a transcendent identity that is rooted in the body. For Peters, the transcendent identity is race; for Dobson, it is gender that is invested with the aura of the sacred.[31] This is not to say there are no overlaps between race and gender; I explore those in chapters 7 and 8. But gender is where Dobson stakes his claim.

By envisioning gender as sacred, Dobson does not need to cut off completely women's mobility by citing biblical passages that command women to be silent in church (as does Peters in his reading of Hosea: "That's once"). Instead, by taking up feminist sites of investment (children, sexuality, relationships, community, emotions) and changing their evaluative accent, Dobson rearticulates feminist insights and investments into a conservative sensibility. In the process, he separates women's personal empowerment from feminist politics. Such a soft-sell style is especially appealing to white middle-class women, for it enables them to secure their own empowerment without confronting larger systems and structures.[32]

Sowing the Wind and Reaping the Whirlwind

Dobson has increasingly sought to transfer the influence of his electronic forum into political clout. Just a few years after the Houston Conference, President Carter announced a White House Conference on the Family. After writing letters to the White House and getting no reply, Dobson announced that he wanted to sit on the committee, and eighty thousand followers contacted the White House, successfully securing his position.[33] During the Reagan and Bush administrations, Dobson claims to have served in various roles, including the National Advisory Committee to the Office of Juvenile Justice and Delinquency Prevention, Citizen's Advisory Panel for Tax Reform, Attorney General Edwin Meese's Commission on Pornography, and the Panel on Teen Pregnancy Prevention. In 1996 Dobson was appointed to the National Gambling Impact Study Commission.[34]

Dobson's involvement with Carter's 1980 Conference on the Family connected him to other Christian conservative activists and businessmen. One result was the Family Research Council (FRC), formed to "ensure representation for the Christian perspective" in Washington.[35] In December 1988, during a time of financial crisis, the FRC became part of Focus on the Family's public policy outreach. Although the FRC became independent in October 1992, organizational ties remain close.[36]

Dobson has increasingly sought to heighten his Washington profile. During the 1996 presidential primaries, most of the Republican candidates made the trek to speak with Dobson at Focus on the Family. In 1998 he denounced the GOP for using the Christian right as foot soldiers to get Republicans elected and then refusing to enact its moral agenda. After Dobson threatened to leave the GOP and "take as many people with me as possible," the party responded by convening a "values summit" focusing on his concerns.[37] Meanwhile, Dobson began endorsing a series of candidates running for open seats in the U.S. House of Representatives, including Operation Rescue founder Randall Terry in New York, who was granted a thirty-second radio spot.[38]

Given that Dobson has always framed his imperative that the nation focus on the family in political terms, there is a tension between on one hand the ultimate issues at stake in Focus on the Family's ministry, leading Dobson to engage in Washington power politicking, and on the other hand its soft-sell style, which features Dr. Dobson dispensing motivational advice on how to cope with the everyday stresses of modern life.

The Ambiguities of Soft-Sell Style

Mission Statements

This tension runs through the ministry. In the video with which the tour of Focus on the Family headquarters begins, Dobson acknowledges a gap between the organization's mission statement and its clientele's perception:

> There is a lot of confusion regarding why the organization exists. If you stop one thousand people on the street who know something about Focus on the Family and ask them the primary purpose for [the organization's] existing, most will miss it. Most will say: to hold a family together. We care a lot about that and we put a lot of our investment and time in that, but that's not the primary thing. The number one goal is the same as a church. Our number one objective is to cooperate with the Holy Spirit in spreading the Good News, the Gospel of Jesus Christ, to as many people as we possibly can around the globe. That's our primary purpose and that's the Great Commission. We do that through families, and trying to hold the family together. What better way is there to evangelize the whole next generation of children than to help mothers and fathers love each other and understand their theology and communicate it to their children. . . . What good does it do really to teach mothers and fathers to run a family if

they don't know Jesus Christ? That *has* to be the foundation, the ground-floor, and that's the essence really of who Focus on the Family is.[39]

A more recent brochure explains the advantages of this gap: the family is a coded evangelism strategy:

> *A Reason to Be:* In a godless society where human hearts have become hardened to traditional Christian evangelism, Focus on the Family is developing new approaches to reaching a world that does not know the Savior. We've discovered that people who might never attend church or allow someone to witness to them will listen to what the Bible says about a meaningful home life. Thus, the connection between meeting the family's relational needs and addressing its spiritual emptiness is the key to helping us present the Gospel of Jesus Christ in homes across the country. . . . Focus on the Family's primary goal is to win souls for Christ. . . . We believe that our unwillingness to compromise on this primary objective is one of the reasons God has chosen to bless Focus on the Family.[40]

Dobson's soft-sell style exploits connections between the boom in pop spirituality and the boom in pop psychology/self-help, both of which are related in complex ways to the stress of living in postmodernity. Reading Dobson, I am continually struck by his ability to articulate how contradictory postmodern life feels to those sufficiently privileged to live in its spaces: the sense of being overwhelmed by limitless choices coupled with a pervasive feeling of powerlessness and emptiness; the high affective stimulation combined with apathy, indifference, and boredom; the surplus of information but relative scarcity of meaning. How calculated Dobson's strategy can be is indicated by an April 1996 newsletter in which he notes: "In scheduling our radio broadcasts, for example, we select highly practical topics that will interest people with no particular Christian commitment. Tucked within these discussions are elements of what we believe, although the presentation is subtle and inoffensive. Then, about every three weeks, we typically schedule what is called a 'harvest program,' which focuses on a testimony or dramatic story of personal conversion. Repeatedly, we hear from people who became interested in the broadcast almost accidentally while spinning the radio dial, and then were introduced to Jesus Christ during one of these harvest programs."[41]

Yet followers can rely on Dobson's advice on parenting and marriage

Soft-Sell Style / 127

without having to invest in (or even tune in to) the conservative Christianity he promotes. For example, one woman I interviewed had turned to Dobson for help when she went through a divorce that left her with three kids to raise while still young herself. She had heard Dobson on the radio and was also active in a Southern Baptist church in Texas where his materials were used in Sunday school. When I asked her why she read and listened to Dobson, she told me, "My concern was having the strength in my own life [to raise my kids] and trying to develop some sort of system whereby I felt secure. . . . Dobson said things to me that made sense. That children need routine. And [that children need] a sense of security developed from equal parts responsibility and discipline. He showed me that discipline could relate to love. . . . I needed to have a strong sense of control. I needed to be in control even though I wasn't deep-down. He showed me how to do that."[42] She talked about other books written by child experts that left her feeling inadequate and even less in control of her situation: "They told you to be a supermom . . . or were constantly warning 'If a mother does this she will ruin her children.'" In Dobson's motivational style she found relief from this societal pressure that blames mothers: "From him I learned I could only do what I could do!"

She went on to note her disagreement with religious proselytizing, taking a few jabs at Jerry Falwell as she said with scorn, "THAT is religion! It's exactly why I left the church!" Yet even though she left the Southern Baptists, she still relies on Dobson's Bible-based philosophy to raise her stepson. When I noted that some people would classify Dobson with the intolerant proselytizers and the bigoted Falwell, her denial was an immediate and spirited "Oh, I never got that!"

Because Focus on the Family offers so many ministries, people come to the organization by different paths. If your primary access is through children's videos or through Dobson's newspaper column dispensing advice for parents, you might develop a different sense of who Focus on the Family is than if you first encounter the organization through its public policy initiatives. This is true of detractors as well. When I spoke with Colorado Springs residents who opposed Focus on the Family's public policy work, several residents explicitly exempted Dobson's parenting advice from criticism because they deemed such advice to be of a different order than promotion of Amendment 2.

Although the current tax code also deems parenting advice and public policy work to be of a different order, I would not want to limit understanding of the Christian right to the legal limits of the tax code. To my mind, the most powerful work performed by an organization like Focus on the Family is how it links personal, cultural, and biblical memories of the family to a particular understanding of power, bodies, economics, and children—and makes these links seem, if not inevitable and necessary, at least the best available.

The Fifth Pillar

To carry out the Great Commission "through a practical outreach for homes," Focus on the Family has adopted five pillars proclaimed as "recommendations of the Creator himself." The first four pillars affirm the preeminence of evangelism; the life-long nature of the marriage between a man and a woman; the value of children as a heritage and blessing for which parents are accountable to God; and the sanctity of human life from conception to grave. When I was visiting in 1994, a fifth pillar had just been adopted: "We believe that God has ordained three basic institutions—the church, the family, and the government—for the benefit of all humankind. The family exists to propagate the race and to provide a safe and secure haven in which to nurture, teach and love the younger generation. The church exists to minister to individuals and families by sharing the love of God and the message of repentance and salvation through the blood of Christ. The government exists to maintain cultural equilibrium and to provide a framework for social order."[43] With this pillar, Focus on the Family affirms a plurality of social spheres, or secularization. Secularization refers to three related but distinct processes. The first moment of secularization refers to the historical processes that functionally differentiated the state, the economy, and science from the religious sphere. The second moment refers to the privatization of religion (involving the shift from organized religion to individualized spirituality). The third moment refers to the decline of religion. Whereas the first moment of functional differentiation forms the structure of modern Western society, the existence of plural social spheres does not necessitate that religion will become privatized or that religion will wither away. Instead, the different moments can be negotiated differently.[44]

Focus on the Family's fifth pillar affirms secularization and pluralism in the historical sense. By adopting this pillar, the organization explicitly rejected envisioning the Christian nature of the United States in terms of a theocracy in which the church officially controls the government, science, the economy, or even private morality as taught within the home. Yet, the fifth pillar also claims these different social spheres are ordained by God. In so doing, the fifth pillar picks up and reworks the ambiguous legacy of the Social Gospel. Social Gospellers sought to Christianize culture—not by fighting for church control over science, economics, or government, but by infusing white middle-class Protestant values into everyday life by identifying Protestant norms with civilization. As a result, certain institutions, practices, discourses, and cultural spaces became invested with religious resonance even when no explicit religious references are made. This turn-of-the-century project to "Christianize culture" helped slip religion and religious authority out of the realm of knowledge-power (where it was fast being replaced by science) and into the realm of ignorance-power. This rearticulation helped white middle-class Protestant values to continue to speak powerfully in contemporary American culture because they had been infused silently.[45]

Rather than calling for church control over the different social spheres, Focus on the Family seeks to determine how people move through the spaces that link (or separate) these different social spheres. Unlike sociologists who argue that a plurality of social spheres spells out the inevitable demise of the Right, I contend that the Christian right is contesting secularization by playing its different moments against each other.[46] Foregrounding the family as our central mattering map positions the family, and memory, as a disciplinary apparatus. If "focus on the family" is the national imperative, then "dare to discipline" is the corollary. In a fast-paced world where people struggle to sustain relationships, sentimental invocations of the family use memory to shape and discipline how we move through a plurality of possibilities. Rather than overtly prohibiting the range of possible options, focusing on the family subtly determines which possibilities are available for people to invest in and which possibilities become immaterial. So that, despite our different starting points, we end up "coming home."

7 Remembering the Sixties as Pop Cultural Conspiracy

"Everyone's Best Interest Group"

Back to the Future

After interviewing fundamentalists for two years, historian and psycho-analyst Charles Strozier concluded, "In various ways death and its equiv-alents, along with constant efforts to hold off fragmentation, play a central role in the self experiences of fundamentalists."[1]

In his essay "Mourning and Melancholia," Freud imagines grieving as a process of internalizing that which we have lost.[2] When we grieve, we psychically inscribe loss on, in, and as our bodies. Grieving hollows out spaces, structures loss into ourselves so deeply that loving those we lost be-comes part of our everyday process of going on. Rather than holding off death and fragmentation, we take impermanence in—and through that gesture develop and deepen our capacity to love. In this case, loss is some-thing we do.

In contrast, fundamentalist narratives form identity in the teeth of loss, as a gesture of disbelief in death's finality. In this way of hoping in things unseen (for there are others), a theology that incorporates loss is a contra-diction in terms: God cannot lose by definition of absolute power. This form of Christianity values Christ's crucifixion and resurrection less for salvific healing through frailty and fragmentation and more for vanquish-ing death; consider European cathedrals whose stained glass windows depict Christ as king emerging from the grave like a general victorious in battle, having given his blood so that his followers need nevermore.[3] For Billy Graham, "The conquest of death is the ultimate goal of Chris-tianity."[4] It is this hope that joins religion and the family so deeply for James Dobson, who tells parents that the Great Commission begins at home: family values start with converting your children so that the family remains intact even in death.

"You Can't Go Home Again": The Function of Nostalgia

Thinking about Dobson's countermemory as centrally concerned with loss helps explain one of its most puzzling features. Dobson designs his June 1994 newsletter to resemble a photo album commemorating his fortieth high school reunion, complete with pictures of his school as it looked in 1954; the cheerleaders ("This is how I remember the girls in my class" reads the facsimile handwritten caption); his wife Shirley as homecoming queen; his college tennis team; Dobson driving a 1949 Mercury; as well as a shot of his classmates in 1994. Dobson dishes up this nostalgia to argue against historians like Stephanie Coontz, whose research reveals the 1950s family as "the way we never were."[5] Take it from the "eyewitness account of a teenager who was there in 1954," Dobson says, "it was a very good year."

Yet, the first version of *Dare to Discipline* (copyrighted 1970) identifies the demon decade in which everything came tumbling down with those very good years: the 1950s. Here Dobson blames student involvement in the antiwar and civil rights movements on "modern" child-rearing practices (advocated most famously by Dr. Spock) that took hold during the 1950s and fostered "permissive democracy."[6] Indeed, the Focus on the Family logo features not June and Ward Cleaver but a Victorian couple with child.

Dobson's shifting Golden Ages suggest that the point of nostalgia is neither the psychoanalytic aim of forming identity through loss nor the traditionalist aim of returning to a bygone era (à la the Amish). Dobson himself concludes his newsletter celebrating 1954 by conceding: "Can we return to the 'Happy Days' of the Fifties? No. It is still impossible to back up on a freeway. As the late novelist Thomas Wolfe wrote, 'You can't go home again.'"[7]

But one can invoke the past, and the home, as a gesture that enables people to protest the present—and to experience their protest not as theocratic domination (à la Christian Identity) but in more intimate and domestic terms: as keeping faith with one's cultural heritage, preserving the family intact even in death. In this chapter, I explore how evoking sentimental memories of loss enables Dobson to represent his conservative politics of family values not as an assertion of majority power but as an act of religious compassion.

Remembering 1968: Authority, Pop Culture, and the "Five Bad Ideas"

In his May 1993 newsletter Dobson marks the twenty-fifth anniversary of the year 1968 by staging an elaborate memory-work. Sounding like Freud, Dobson urges his listeners to "repeat, recollect and work through" the 1960s. Although this "flashback journey" involves painful memories, he promises that "only by examining the turmoil of our past can we understand ourselves and the world in which we live. . . . Whether we realize it or not, we have been influenced enormously by those hairy, unwashed kids in psychedelic vans that we used to be. . . . If we are to bring stability to our shattered world, with its broken children, its unstable families, its devastated minorities, its addictive victims, and its search for meaning, we must go back to the fork in the road where we went astray. We took a wrong turn back there in our youth, departing from the biblical standard and substituting our own puny ideas for the wisdom of the ages. And heaven knows, we've paid a dear price for that miscalculation."[8] Dobson accompanied this newsletter with a series of radio broadcasts that featured former-hippies-turned-Focus-on-the-Family-employees, who reenacted a 1960s-style sit-in and testified to how they were "saved from the sixties."[9]

Dobson frames this memory-work cum testimonial within the contemporary context of Bill Clinton's presidency. Many journalists pointed to Clinton, the first baby boom president, as signifying a shift in generational power. Dobson reads Clinton as a sign that the 1960s youth counterculture that spawned our most serious social problems is now "in authority at the highest levels! . . . It is really important to see the linkage between this irresponsible behavior that is going on—and which now *our government* seems to be perpetuating—and the source of it. We need to go back to that fork in the road and re-examine the decision that took us in that direction."[10]

Dobson is not passively remembering: this is active memory management. For Dobson, this is important not least because many of his current followers are baby boomers. By framing his attack on the 1960s as memory-work, he avoids condemning the "naive young people . . . [who] were caught in the riptide." Just as Dobson (mis)identifies himself with the baby boom generation (in 1968 he was no hairy, unwashed kid in a psychedelic van but an over-thirty research professor with a suit and briefcase), so he refrains from refuting their trenchant social criticisms.

Remembering the Sixties / 133

For example, on the tape, Linda says: "I was a cause person. And I saw that the church was not responding to what my contemporaries were calling the social justice issues of the day. . . . Part of it for me goes back even further. As a third grader, in order to attend school in Texas I had to get dog tags and blood typed; and wear those dog tags; and we had air-raid drills. I think that part of our breaking loose was that whole fear in the 1950s—nuclear war and constraints. When we grew up we said, 'There are more noble things than the cold war,' and began to push those limits." Rather than debating the nobility of the cold war, Dobson frames the discussion in ways that move being "a cause person" out of the realm of social revolution and into the realm of focusing on the family. He cannot make his panel forget their memories of 1968. He can, however, construct a countermemory that does not so much banish their social critiques as it reshapes them, linking them with certain affective sites (such as the family) while delinking them from other sites (such as collective politics).

Yet there looms quite a gap between Watts and Vietnam on the one hand and disciplining the baby boom generation on the other. Dobson covers over this gap by narrating 1960s civil rights movements through the biblical trope of God's corrective love calling a stiff-necked generation to turn away from rebellion and remember the ways of their fathers: "Down through the ages, people have dreamed and longed for a day when their major troubles would be resolved: 'If we just didn't have this terrible war to fight; if we could eliminate this famine, or this depression, or this plague.' At last in post-war America, 1950–1970, a generation was born on which all the coveted goodness was heaped. But instead of bringing exuberance and gratitude, there has come antagonism and contempt for the generation that worked to provide it."[11]

Thus, although Dobson rarely cites chapter and verse, biblicizing contemporary issues is no less central to his political project than it is to Peters's. Rather than thumping the relevant biblical passages, Dobson uses biblical masterplots to determine how popular memories get articulated. Specifically, he traces the nation's most serious contemporary problems— "broken children, unstable families, devastated minorities, addictive victims, and meaninglessness"—back to "five bad ideas" that gained popular acceptance during the 1960s: drugs and rock music, the sexual revolution, feminism, "God is dead" theology, and divorce.[12]

Of these big bad ideas, Dobson zeroes in on number 4 as the source of

134 / *Lift High the Cross*

the nation's "wrong turn." As he tells it, the crisis that white middle-class Protestantism underwent during the 1960s created a void that Satan filled with popular culture, in whose spaces young people found/created alternative identities and imagined communities that extended beyond their families and environments of origin. Dobson calls the 1960s the era when "authority went out of style,"[13] replaced by figures like "John Lennon, an outspoken atheist, [who] stunned the religious community in 1966 by saying, 'Christianity will go. It will vanish and shrink. . . . We're more popular than Jesus now.' "[14] In Lennon's quip, Dobson hears the decade's rallying cry: God is dead—long live pop culture!

Dobson's focus on pop culture derives from David Noebel. I introduced Noebel in chapter 5, when Peters drew on Noebel's expertise in his antigay campaign. Before writing *The Homosexual Revolution,* Noebel was authoring books titled *The Marxist Minstrels: A Handbook on Communist Subversion of Music* and *Communism, Hypnotism and the Beatles.* In these books, Noebel identifies sexual licentiousness and "primitive" music with people of color and subversion.[15] According to Noebel, young people have a built-in inhibitory reflex implanted by "their parents, churches and society. It entails such things as decent behavior, prohibiting the coed from taking off her dress in public, tearing up the auditorium, creating havoc and battling with authorities." But rock music's beat puts young people in a highly excited, hypnotic state in which they can be told to do anything, from sex to political revolution, with race providing the switchpoint. Noebel warns: "The Beatles, Rolling Stones, or any rock group, for example, need only mass hypnotize thousands of American youth, condition their emotions through the beat of their 'music' and then have someone give the word for riot and revolt. The consequences are imponderable. Watts, Detroit, Newark and its 'burn, baby, burn' would fade into significance."[16]

In *Children at Risk,* Dobson updates Noebel's argument. Dobson analyzes the wild external stimulation of the unrestrained rhythms, eerie lights, wild behavior, and large crowd of a rock concert as social engineering that brainwashes teenagers by destroying their individuality and creating a passion for social conformity.[17] "His peer group becomes lord and master, until finally, the wonderful freedom of youth is traded for slavery and domination" (*Children,* 7). In this view, young people have a wonderful freedom: to follow their social conditioning.

Although it is tempting to dismiss such views of popular culture as outdated survivals that the information highway will leave in the dust, Dobson is not seeking to return to a world before communications technologies; his own ministry depends on them. Instead, what Dobson rightly perceives is that popular culture has become *the* site for the construction of authority in people's everyday lives. Lawrence Grossberg calls this "the most obvious and perhaps the most frightening thing about contemporary popular culture . . . [namely,] that it matters so much to so many different people. . . . There is no necessary reason why the affective relationship is located primarily on the terrain of commercial popular culture. But it is certainly the case that, for the vast majority of people in advanced capitalist societies, this is the primary space where affective relationships are articulated. It is here that people seek actively to construct their own identities, partly because there seems no other space available."[18] Grossberg gives the example of singing a pop song; we literally take someone else's words into our mouths, authorizing them to speak for us. And we do it with all our hearts: think about seeing the person in the car next to you belting out a song. We actively construct individual identities by locating ourselves within circuits of power.[19]

Dobson's elaborate memory-work suggests that the culture wars are not so much about competing systems of moral authority (liberal vs. conservative) as about controlling this feedback loop whereby we create personal empowerment for ourselves by giving someone else authority in our lives.[20] Constructing a conservative countermemory is less about winning on a particular issue (the nobility of the cold war), and more about determining "the very possibility and nature of authority, of who or what has the right to speak for others, to stand in their place, to construct their mattering maps."[21] The goal of Dobson's memory-work is to ventriloquate authority in the vernacular of "the popular."

This strategy both resembles and differs from that of the British Right. In *Hard Road to Renewal,* Stuart Hall demonstrates how Thatcherism resurrected nostalgic images of the British Empire less to re-create an empire on which the sun never sets than to articulate an authoritarian populism "in which each step towards a more authoritarian posture is accompanied by a powerful groundswell of popular legitimacy. . . . The state comes to provide just that 'sense of direction' which the public feels society has lost."[22] In contrast, political scientist Alan Wolfe observes that what other countries see as the "meat and potatoes" of politics is met in the United States with "boredom, resentment and sporadic attention." This apathy contrasts sharply with culture, which "grabs everyone's attention all of the time. . . . [Americans] practice politics in cultural terms. . . . Unable to abolish war, they have abolished politics; the state has not withered away, but the amount of attention paid to its affairs has withered badly."[23] Grossberg sharpens Wolfe's observations by suggesting that such depoliticization is not natural to being an American, but must be actively produced.

Hence the importance of remembering, repeating, and working through 1968. Dobson seeks to rework modern sensibilities regarding political struggle, resistance, and power by narrating that decade in terms of apocalyptic conspiracy:

> Nothing short of a great Civil War of Values rages today throughout North America. . . . Instead of fighting for territory and military conquest, however, the struggle now is for the hearts and minds of the people. . . . On one side of this Continental Divide are the traditionalists whose values begin with the basic assumption that "God *is*" . . . Until approximately thirty years ago, these biblically-based concepts were the dominant values and beliefs in Western society. Not everyone agreed, of course, but most did. . . . Then, slowly at first, another way of looking at the world began to emerge. It evolved from the basic assumption that "God isn't" . . . It has been said that never in human history has a culture discarded its belief system more quickly than America did in the sixties . . . children are the prize to the winners of the second great Civil War. . . . The predominant value system of an entire culture can be overhauled in one generation, or certainly in two, by those with unlimited access to children. (*Children*, 19–21, 35)

Dobson calls his followers to fight this "well-thought out and coordinated conspiracy" lest the nation see the day when an entire generation of children have no memory of the Christian concepts that "made this country great" (39, 60).[24]

Dobson's appeals to the Civil War are not unique. In his presidential speeches, Ronald Reagan frequently conjured the specter of the Civil War (and the apocalyptic discourse that surrounded it) to convey the nation's destiny and the redemptive quality of the struggle against communism.[25]

Such cultural memories constitute the current link in a signifying chain that has long formed national and masculine identity through apocalyptic narratives that perceive difference as the devil and loss as betrayal (see chapter 5).

In remembering the 1960s as a Civil War of Values, Dobson draws on the way apocalyptic conspiracy theories enable people to acknowledge the reality of change while rejecting grief by imagining loss as theft. In chapter 4, I explored how Peters conjures a cabal of Jewish leaders masterminding a secular humanist conspiracy that has taken control of the government and uses pop culture to promote deviant sexuality to erase the genetic memory of the white race and thus steal their birthright. Likewise, Dobson imagines a secular humanist conspiracy arising out of 1960s youth counterculture, with its fascination for Black Power, feminism, gay rights, and Eastern spiritualities, while America's parents "were preoccupied at home" (*Children*, 35). Unseen by this silent majority and therefore unstopped, this "alien" force captured the power centers of society and is now using pop culture to annihilate all memory of Christian concepts by reprogramming sexual and gender mores to steal the hearts and minds of your children—and with them, your power to determine the nation's future (viii).

Historian David Blight has argued that when the shooting stopped in 1865, the struggle continued as a contest over how the nation would remember the Civil War and thereby re-member its torn social body. Lost Cause champions joined northern industrialists in reunifying the nation by depoliticizing the war, celebrating the experience of individual soldiers while ignoring issues such as "slavery, secession, emancipation, black equality, even disloyalty and treason." Instead, the war was seen as "essentially a conflict between white men; both sides fought well, Americans against Americans, and there was glory enough to go around."[26] In contrast to this reidentification of the nation with white citizens, Frederick Douglass narrated a countermemory that focused on black emancipation as a source for national regeneration.

Likewise, when the turbulence of the 1960s subsided, the struggle continued as a contest over how we remember that decade and thereby re-member the nation. Much like champions of the Lost Cause, the point of Dobson's Civil War of Values is to reidentify "the majority" with the nation. Dobson himself concedes that before the 1960s "not everyone agreed" with biblically based concepts, "of course, but most did." And in that Golden Age (be it the 1950s, the 1920s, or the Victorian era) it was this majority that mattered, determining everything from public policy to public schools. Indeed, Dobson's countermemory identifies Protestantism with religion absolutely and without qualification ("God is . . .")— despite, for instance, John Lennon's involvement with Maharishi Mahesh Yogi. Dobson's Civil War of Values cannot see such pluralism, which is both religious and ethnic, facilitated as it was by Lyndon Johnson's lifting quotas on Asian immigration.

Instead, Dobson's Civil War identifies the not-everyone-agreed-but-most-did majority with the common people, who carry the memory of the nation's founders written in their hearts: "Our godly forefathers [the Puritans] acted as though they had swallowed 'gyroscopes' that helped them distinguish between right and wrong. . . . Those internal gyroscopes still operate deep within the spirits of the American people. The majority of us carry a memory of our Christian heritage even though every effort has been made to extinguish and ridicule it. . . . This characteristic has prevailed within us for nearly three hundred years, going back to the influence of the Puritans and the framers of the U.S. Constitution" (*Children*, 42). Whereas Peters imagines God's Law to be genetically encoded on white hearts, Dobson waxes sentimental about "the heritage of faith" or "the beliefs and values that were handed down by their ancestors" (43–44). In both cases, however, national origins—the Constitution, the Puritans—are invoked to represent an exclusionary authoritarianism as populism.

Dobson's Civil War pits the common people who preserve ancient memories against the elite special interest groups that emerged out of 1960s social movements and captured the public sphere. Consider his remarks on sex education:

> Why do bureaucrats, researchers, Planned-Parenthood types fight so hard to preserve adolescent promiscuity? . . . Kids jumping into bed with each other are supporting entire industries of grateful adults. The abortion business alone brings in an estimated $600 million annually. . . . How about the condom manufacturers or the producers of spermicide, "the pill," IUDs, or diaphragms? Would they want their businesses decimated by a sweeping wave of morality among the young? I doubt it. . . .
>
> At the top of the list of those who profit from adolescent irrespon-

sibility, however, are those who purportedly fight it! Planned Parenthood and similar organizations would simply fade away if they were ever successful in eliminating teen pregnancies. They currently receive an estimated $106 million in federal subsidies to carry out their mission, plus approximately $200 million in contributions from private sources. Do you *really* believe that they want to kill the goose that lays those golden eggs? . . . It's a matter of self-preservation. (*Children,* 13–14)

In addition to Planned Parenthood, Dobson castigates welfare workers and recipients, teachers' unions, multiculturalists, environmentalists, feminists, and affirmative action proponents—carpetbaggers all, who deliberately create the problems they profess to solve in order to obtain benefits for themselves in the form of government grants. Dobson eschews the overt racial theocracy of Christian Identity and even the more coded racism of Christian Patriots who use the First and Fourteenth Amendments to distinguish first- from second-class citizens; nevertheless, his countermemory pits the tax-paying family on one side of the common good against tax-receiving special interests on the other: "minorities" against We the People.

Domesticating Difference: The Family as a Divide-and-Conquer Strategy

While Dobson calls Christians to protest in the name of the family, his conservative politics of family values relies on, and furthers, alienation from government and civil society, insisting that the family would be fine if government-funded special interests would just stay out. Paradoxically, then, his countermemory heightens personal empowerment to (re)produce political apathy, positioning parents against collective political action, which he demonizes as a militant secular humanist conspiracy to reprogram society's mores.

Recall how Dobson built Focus on the Family by appropriating feminism: "The feminists . . . had some good ideas in the beginning, including equal pay for equal work and the rights of women to be respected and taken seriously in the workplace. Congressmen and state legislators were quick to grasp this opportunity to impress 50 percent of the voters, and they rapidly translated many feminist ideas into law. Heady with success and encouraged by an enthusiastic press, the *real* agenda of radical feminists came into focus. They wanted the whole pie!"[27] By differentiating reasonable protest from "the real agenda of radical feminists," Dobson reinscribes difference within a new frontier: not along the line of feminists versus traditional women, but along the line of assimilable feminists versus militant feminists. This frontier transvalues in four directions: (1) it deflects feminist criticism of misogyny as a systemic problem (legislators were quick to impress 50 percent of the voters) as (2) it invokes stereotypical fears about women (whose desire cannot be satisfied); in the process, (3) it demonizes politics (radical feminists with a militant agenda) by (4) depoliticizing difference (a few good ideas rapidly embraced as law). The result is paradoxical: women have freedom—to resist women's liberation.

Dobson makes a similar move when dealing with the gay, lesbian, bisexual, and transgender liberation movement. Claiming to "hate the sin but love the sinner," Dobson would have nothing to do with Peters's calls to institute Levitical prescriptions of the death penalty for gays and lesbians. Instead, he constructs a division not along the line of gay-affirmative versus gay-hating, but along a new frontier that differentiates "good" homosexuals, who discipline homoerotic desires (either by not acting on those desires or by feeling shame when you do), from militant homosexual activists, who want the whole pie (social legitimacy for homosexuality).[28] Again, the result is paradoxical: queer people deserve respect as children of God—and therefore should reject their homosexuality.

Likewise, Dobson identifies the family values movement as the "next stage of the civil rights revolution," arguing that what blocks African Americans today is their lack of family values.[29] He traces this lack to "the grant initiatives designed to assist children and families. Chaos reigns supreme in the inner cities where most of the effort was directed" (*Children*, 31). As proof of the family's ability to conjure African Americans into the middle class, Focus on the Family features a handful of black conservatives such as Kay James and Tony Evans in leadership positions. This retelling of the civil rights era insists that the nation rejected race discrimination in the 1960s—and therefore must eschew affirmative action today.

In constructing a pedigree for Christian right activism, these invocations of the civil rights movement work to substitute Christians for African Americans. For example, in *Children at Risk*, Dobson coauthor Gary Bauer declares that, without education vouchers and institutionalized prayer in public schools, millions of Christian Americans will be "politically disenfranchised," forced "to go to the back of the bus" (281). Likewise, Dobson identifies Randall Terry and Operation Rescue with Christians like Corrie Ten Boom, who broke the law to protect Jews from Nazi extermination, or Dietrich Bonhoeffer, who called the Christian church to "jam the wheels" of totalitarian dictatorships. *Children at Risk* explains why secular humanists target children by citing the Nazi Youth Corps (106). Invoking the Holocaust enables Dobson to project himself as inclusive (he is, after all, no Holocaust denier) while reversing the sense of these memories by using them to portray Christians as the new minority targeted for extinction in the 1990s by an atheistic modern state in whose invisible war most Americans have become complicit without knowing—just like the German church under Hitler.

Throughout these rearticulations, Dobson deploys the rhetoric of remembrance to efface difference while professing compassionate inclusion. On one side of the Bible-based family, Dobson positions "accidental" differences that society can assimilate and ignore. On the other side, he positions "subversive" differences that threaten the social order. Nostalgic invocations of "the family" offer an impossible dream: the acceptable other who self-disciplines so successfully that he or she can be added to the social order without disruption, without needing to be granted "special" rights to succeed. Underneath this impossible American dream lies a fantasy of a fictional time when white middle-class male Protestant hegemony was not protested as a relation of power.

Thus Dobson's photo album/newsletter celebrates 1954, the same year that the Supreme Court declared "separate but equal" schools unconstitutional. Although Dobson acknowledges that segregation was wrong, this acknowledgment does not affect his evaluation of those high school years as a time when "America was great because America was good." He acknowledges racial difference to politically neutralize difference so that it has no public impact.[30] The result is, once again, paradoxical: people have power—to submit to authority.

Nichemarketing and National Memory:
The Community Impact Seminar

Although Dobson and Focus on the Family have rejected overt calls for a Christian political party or for Christian theocracy, they do so to reidentify Protestant hegemony with public power, acknowledging and blurring distinctions among church, state, and religiosity.

Dobson acknowledges these differences, for instance, when he insists that public schools "of course" cannot teach students that they must have a personal relationship with Jesus Christ: this is *church* doctrine. He blurs these distinctions, however, when he insists that public schools can and must teach students the absolute value of the heterosexual, monogamous, lifelong marriage as the only acceptable arrangement of gender, sexuality, and affection: this is the nation's *cultural heritage of religious values* (*Children*, 18).

This is not an easy line to walk. By studying two different versions of the ministry's Community Impact Seminar, you can watch Focus on the Family craft it. The early version of the seminar (used through 1991) espoused an overtly theocratic countermemory indebted to a Christian Reconstructionist thinker who has shared a stage with none other than Pete Peters: David Barton (see chapter 5). In contrast, the seminar's later version warns participants against proclaiming the United States a Christian nation.

The Community Impact Seminars identify the uniqueness of our time by the fact that "never have so many people believed in so little."[31] What Dobson and his organization get right about the age is the depth of popular apathy: people feel unable to believe in anything enough to commit themselves to it, thereby giving it authority in their lives. This loss, a far deeper issue than competing systems of authority, lies at the heart of the postmodern crisis, and Dobson articulates this sense of loss to himself. The "impact" that these seminars hope to produce, then, is to rearticulate this contemporary crisis of authority and belief so that Bible-based family values seem to be, if not The Answer, at least the best option available.

Each seminar concludes by urging participants to start community action committees within their local church. These committees are intended to involve the church as a corporate entity in the public sphere while "discipling" church members into becoming politically active. The committees also integrate people into an interlocking infrastructure that blankets the nation on multiple levels: national, state, local nonprofit, as well as the local church.[32]

This alternative infrastructure seeks to counter "the secular humanist takeover" in which society's "gatekeepers" force their ideas on the people, whose Christian values these gatekeepers neither reflect nor respect. The seminars (especially the later version) single out education as the culprit for creating a gap between the elites who head social institutions and the people they are supposed to represent. Seminar leaders propound institutional reform as the ultimate goal: "Helping men and women to leave the homosexual lifestyle is immeasurably more difficult than keeping them out of it in the first place. The ravages of divorce are well-documented; preventing the breakup of a marriage (including making it difficult to get a divorce) makes more sense than trying to pick up the pieces" (CIS, 1993, 51).

Yet, much as the Left once pointed to Stalin as evidence that changing institutional power can fail to bring revolutionary change, the Community Impact Seminar points to Carter and Reagan as evidence that electing Christians can fail to ensure victory: "Two years ago, the City of San Francisco passed a gay rights ordinance. The conservative Christian community rallied and overturned it. Can you guess what happened the following year? The liberals rallied and overturned the conservatives. This is the future for Christian activism; we're going to win ground and lose it again until we capture cultural consensus. We must address the crisis of authority in culture" (CIS, 1993, 50).

Arguing that trying to mobilize a moral majority was the biggest mistake conservative Christians made in the 1980s, seminar leaders contend that secular elites have excluded Christianity not just from public institutions, but from the private hearts and minds of the people. Before conservative Christians try to mobilize the majority of Americans who identify as Christian, they must first make that majority think in Christian rather than secular terms.

What is meant by thinking in Christian terms? The seminar quotes a 1989 poll that found that, whereas 61 percent of the population agree that abortion is morally wrong, 74 percent agree that abortion ought to remain legal. How, seminar leaders ask, can Christians morally oppose abortion yet feel they ought not expect others to agree? How can Christians feel the pressure of a Kantian "ought" not just regarding their own values but equally regarding the contradictory values of their neighbors? The Community Impact Seminar targets precisely this space where identifications conflict in order to dismiss the multiple commitments that enable assertions like "abortion is morally wrong but ought to be legal" as sheer hypocrisy (or, in the language of Colorado for Family Values, as emasculation: being "a man without a chest"; see chapter 5). The seminar is designed to empower conservative Christians to feel compelled to impact their moral beliefs not just on their own families but also on their communities—and to represent this duty in such a way that using laws to restrict abortion, homosexuality, and divorce, for instance, will feel less like Augustine "coercing others to come in" to the church and more like empowering their neighbors to do what they really want but do not dare.

To facilitate this reversal, seminar leaders shift from lecture format to drama, piping in over the P.A. the "voices of the ancestors" that thunder from on high. The voices dramatize the signing of the Mayflower Compact, "hardly what one would call a foundation for secular government." Daniel Webster praises Plymouth Rock as the spot where "Christianity, and civilization and letters made their first lodgment in a country covered with wilderness and peopled by barbarians." Patrick Henry insists that "this great nation was founded, not by religionists, but by Christians, not on religions, but on the Gospel of Jesus Christ!" And first Chief Justice John Jay reminds "you and me to elect only Christians as our leaders." These ancestral voices are offered as testimony to "the widely and deeply held understanding of these people that religion, the Christian religion of the Bible, is the only legitimate basis for government and the only legitimate hope for freedom." According to seminar leaders, the United States was "designed to work only on a Christian foundation" and "much of the damage we see around us" derives from separating church from state (*CIS*, 1991, 17–23).

According to this countermemory, strict church-state separation is a recent revision dating to the 1947 case *Everson v. Board of Education.* Seminar leaders teach that the First Amendment was intended to establish a *one-way wall* that prohibits the government from declaring one Protestant church supreme over other churches. However, the First Amendment was never intended to disestablish Christianity from its status as supreme moral arbiter whose pronunciations provide the foundation of civility and therefore of civil law.

When Dobson's public policy division revised its Community Impact Seminar (after 1991), it retained both the dramatized "voices of the founders" and the dismissal of church-state separation as a recent revision. Yes, religion has been excluded from the public square. Yes, Christians have been disenfranchised. "Do you feel this way?" the speaker asks, and the crowd roars back an affirmative five hundred strong. Yet the newer version prefaces its dramatization of the countermemory with a caveat warning participants against identifying Christianity with the nation, as if "We built it, we founded it, and we are going to get it back!" When the audience laughs, the speaker acknowledges, "It's funny, but if you were an American Muslim, Hindu or atheist, how would you respond?" The audience's discomfort increases as seminar leaders reiterate their warning against declaring the United States a Christian nation: "Well-meaning yet unwise use of the phrase by Christians has helped hard-core separatists confuse average Americans, leading them to believe that Christians wanting to play their part in the values debate are really extremists" (*CIS*, 1993, 20).

Having learned that overt assertions of power play into popular perceptions of the Christian right as extremist, seminar leaders acknowledge that, yes, other beliefs did influence the Constitution. Yet these others are no sooner overtly invoked than they are immediately denied significance. Citing historian Sidney Ahlstrom, seminar leaders imagine the hegemony exercised by white middle-class Protestants at the time of the nation's founding not as an expression of a will to power, but as a populist consensus: "Christians are not just another special interest group; we are an 'everyone's best interest group.' The power politics of sheer majoritarianism, even if they help to win a battle, would surely serve to lose the war. Compassion is to be the hallmark and primary motive of our work in society" (*CIS*, 1993, 51).

Eschewing the iron fist of legal and physical force, Focus on the Family urges Christians to wield the velvet glove of cultural power. Seminar leaders cite Benjamin Franklin, who, though no orthodox Christian, lived in a world dominated by the Christian worldview and therefore thought in biblical symbolism, especially when he wanted to appeal to the conscience of his fellows. Although seminar leaders train participants to

146 / Lift High the Cross

frame their political work without directly appealing to biblical authority, their ultimate goal is to establish a fundamentalist version of the Bible as the nation's public language—while denying that making others speak your language enacts a relation of power. To the contrary, in *Children at Risk,* Gary Bauer quotes E. D. Hirsch asserting that the loss of biblical hegemony harms minority children:

> [Hirsch] says that the Bible is the source of literacy among English-speaking peoples. He even notes that in India, where over 450 languages and dialects are spoken, English is the national language of commerce and government. In order to understand their national language, Hirsch says, Indians must study the Bible. Even though their religion is predominantly Hindu or Muslim, Indians recognize their need for cultural literacy. . . . We now know that liberalism's "Thirty Years' War" against Bible-reading in our public schools has also had devastating *educational* consequences. And the primary victims of this misguided drive have been inner-city minority children from single-parent families. . . . What we need to be a successful nation is an appreciation of our motto: *E Pluribus Unum.* Vice President Al Gore got this one wrong recently. He thought it meant: "From one, many." But it really means: "From many, one." That has been our national goal for over two centuries. It's still a worthy goal. But it can never be accomplished if multicultural education is adopted which attacks Whites, males, and our Judeo-Christian heritage. (203)

At the seminar I attended in 1994, although no one protested the claim that Christians must renounce citing the Bible, they vociferously resisted the caveat against proclaiming America a Christian nation. During the question-and-answer period, one man objected, "You seem to say we were once a Christian nation, but we are no longer and we will never be again." The audience cheered this man; they were with him. Seminar leaders responded by insisting repeatedly that pluralism "is a sociological fact" that conservative Christians can ill afford to ignore.[33]

These tensions reveal what sociologist Matthew Moen has called an attempted "education campaign" regarding rhetorical style on the part of Christian right leaders. Moen cites an interview he conducted in 1989 with Bauer, in which Bauer remarked, "The heightened sensitivity to language is particularly present at the leadership level. In the 'rank and file,' the task has not been sufficiently completed." Moen suggests that the softening rhetoric is less about softening political aims and more about nichemarketing.[34] Seminar leaders coached participants in how to avoid couching their claims in appeals to biblical authority, but they did nothing to help participants develop the skills necessary to inhabit a public square where pluralism is a sociological fact of life.

To the contrary, although seminar leaders explicitly reject the historical revisionism of Christian Reconstructionism and acknowledge that the United States was never *legally* a Christian nation, they insist that "we can say with historical integrity that America, at its founding, was a *culturally* Christian nation." Differentiating this cultural strategy from the more explicitly electoral aims of theocracy and Christian Reconstructionism enables Focus on the Family to disassociate "preserving the Bible-based family" from extremism—and thereby to disavow the power relations that undergird its promotion of biblical family values as "everyone's best interest group." We are fighting for everyone, the rhetoric goes, because everyone has a family. Yet Focus on the Family's acknowledgment of pluralism as a *sociological* fact does not extend to acknowledging as a *natural* fact that people arrange the sexual and affective dimensions of their private lives differently, that not everyone contains sexuality within marriage and not everyone identifies those they love within the concept of a "family."

Instead, Focus on the Family acknowledges pluralism as a sociological fact to differentiate it from natural. Drawing on the fundamentalist evaluation of the Bible as "God's owner's manual to life," Dobson transvalues the Bible into a book of natural law, asserting that the natural world and human nature are Christian in essence.[35] So, for example, when Dobson is asked if AIDS is God's punishment on gays and lesbians, he likens AIDS not to the punishing hand of God, but to gravity. If you defy natural laws and jump out the window, of course you will hit the ground. And if you defy natural laws and have sex with the same sex, of course you will become diseased! Dobson also suggests that if black people do not keep their families intact, it is just common sense that they will be poor.

Likewise, Dobson's public policy division produces reports that argue against homosexuality, single-parent families, and the Kinsey report not by citing the Bible, but by amassing sociological data. Much like the campaign to spin Amendment 2 as nondiscriminatory, these public policy reports are stamped with a seal proclaiming them "A Matter of Facts."

Rather than advocating the literal application of biblical law, Focus on the Family argues that public policy must be based on Christian values, for it is Christian values—Dobson's gyroscopes—that enabled men in the state of nature to form a social contract and enter into civil society by agreeing to sublimate their nasty, brutish, and short-lived desires for "the common good." Seminar leaders represent Christians as "everyone's best interest group" because Christianity constitutes the nation's sole cultural capital:

> We are like a man who has ceased to make deposits into his bank account and now lives upon his savings. Each new withdrawal brings him closer to bankruptcy, but so long as the bank clears his checks he doesn't pay attention to his balance. Our culture is living on the moral bank account of our forefathers. There is a vestige of Christian morality which still lingers in the culture. Current expressions of human dignity, morality and social order are possible only because of our Christian heritage. But the account is running low, and we haven't made a deposit in quite a while. . . . The cultural richness of Europe and America could never have been produced by such a [relativist] mindset; what we have left is simply the whittled down remnant of the past. (*CIS*, 1993, 31–33)

Much as people often perceive their families through a screen onto which they project the family they wish they were, so a politics of family values mediates our vision of that imagined community we call America by projecting a fantasy of social consensus. Yet this fantasy hinges on disavowal. The classic formulation of disavowal is Freud's analysis of castration anxiety: It is not that men are vulnerable; it is that women lack a penis. In the case of the Christian right, this disavowal is formulated as: It is not that white middle-class Protestant hegemony is vulnerable, shattered, incomplete, immoral in its absolution of power; it is that secular society cannot make moral choices because it lacks the capacity to believe in absolutes.

What makes disavowal strategies complicated is that they have a certain, albeit misplaced, truth. In the case of castration anxiety, whether or not women have a penis is not the point. The point is that no one has a penis that measures up to The Phallus and the absolute power and knowledge that this symbol idealizes. In the case of the culture wars, what Dobson gets right is that people feel powerless. Yet he turns this recognition into a misrecognition: It is not that we need to find new ways of negotiating difference, envisioning community and imagining power. It is that our society has abandoned its founding consensus and listens not just to the voices of the ancestors but to all voices equally, thereby falling down the slippery slope of an anything-goes relativism.[36]

Whereas for Focus on the Family, listening to all voices equally entails forfeiting the capacity to take a stand on the things that matter, I understand pluralism differently. Pluralism calls us to communicate in ways that are less about asserting where I am right and defending against where you are wrong and more about relationship. And relationship always calls us to something bigger: to step into a larger and less certain space where things are not determined in advance, where we can hold conflicting and contradictory truths. The goal of engaging with others who define right and wrong differently is not necessarily to agree (not everything is infinitely negotiable), but rather to open to being changed through dialogue, which in my experience most often means changing how I hold my beliefs. This might sound pretty, but it can feel gruesome, for one cannot control or foresee how one might be changed. It's the way that being powerful in the world often means you let yourself be powerless much of the time.

Sex, Children, and Conspiracy Theory

Dobson is able to access this space in which people feel powerless and turn it toward the Right—thereby holding at bay a more inclusive understanding of truth, difference, and power—less by the persuasive power of his historical reconstructions or his conservative politics, I contend, and more by using sentimental and scandalous images of children as an affective magnet for multiple moral panics, all of which wander across the public/private divide.[37]

Dobson uses the rhetoric of "saving the children" to reverse the sixty-year-old evangelical tradition of seeing the world as a "wrecked vessel" from which Christians should save only souls.[38] In the current cultural climate, Dobson argues, Christian parents cannot save their children's souls without first saving their children from the culture war.

Dobson's appeals to people's hopes and fears for their children also work more broadly (hence his ministry's description of the family as an evangelizing tool that speaks to people "who might never attend church or allow someone to witness to them").[39] Children function as a condensed cipher for deep fears regarding changing relations of power. Dobson accesses these fears and rearticulates them within cold war discourse, portraying Christian concepts of sexuality as the only thing that can keep Americans from being made into "perfectly mobile and infinitely manipulable creatures" vulnerable to brainwashing by the totalitarian state: "Society as it has been—with its Judeo-Christian origins—must be redesigned and reconstructed. There is only one way to accomplish a feat of that magnitude, and that is to isolate kids from their parents and reprogram their values. Sex, therefore, is the hydrogen bomb that permits the destruction of things as they are and a simultaneous reconstruction of the new order" (*Children*, 48–49).[40]

As stunning as this image of sex as an H-bomb is, these fears are not all hype. Sociologist Martin Reisebrodt has argued that although fundamentalists mobilize for many reasons, the key is "the dramatic reduction in the chances of the fundamentalist milieu to reproduce itself culturally."[41] This jeopardy is both real and perceived. It is real in that government is playing an increasing role in children's lives, often via mediating institutions such as schools and public libraries. Yet this jeopardy is perceived because children have never simply reproduced parental worldviews, not even in traditionalist societies. Although we think of tradition as static and unchanging, traditions are also open-ended by definition. A tradition that is not open to being made to speak in new ways to new situations would not be passed on for long.

Dobson invokes sentimental and scandalous images of children to hold this fluidity (and the loss it implies) at bay. He appeals to the private intimacies of heart and hearth: however complicated the world might become, parents have an unquestioned right and duty to take a stand and take control. Children are the site whereby authority can be made to seem possible again, believable, even natural, or at the very least necessary.

Dobson's appeals to heart and hearth rest on biological intimacies, the natural supremacy that parents exert over children who "belong" to them by blood. It is this biological imaginary that enables Dobson to gloss over the reality that children live in much broader and more public social worlds than the private family. He works this ambiguity in the reverse direction: as surely as parents exercise authority over their own children, so surely do parents have the right to exercise ownership over the culture in which their children are being raised. This ownership extends to resisting public policies (regarding taxes, nonprofit status for churches, and multicultural curricula) that threaten "their own." Dobson invokes children as a site of unquestioned control. Or, at least, as a site where we think we "should" be in control.

And there's the rub: "the family" demarcates a space of no small anxiety. Focus on the Family has argued against expanding the definition of the family beyond "a group of individuals related to one another by marriage, blood, or adoption." Yet marriage, blood, and adoption do not "naturally" make people a family. Shirley Dobson has written a book entitled *Let's Make a Memory* filled with arts and crafts projects for mothers to do with their children at each of the year's seasons: women make the family by making memories. In his preface, Dobson acknowledges the anxiety that underlies this "making": "The great value of traditions comes through as a family gains a sense of identity, a belongingness. All of us desperately need to feel we're not just a cluster of people living together in a house, but a family that's conscious of its uniqueness, its personality, character and heritage, and that our special relationships of love and companionship make us a unit."[42] The whole existence of Focus on the Family testifies to the way that families are not born but made.

Likewise, whereas Dobson represents parental supremacy as "natural," the point of Dr. Dobson's advice-giving role is to argue that authority does not just happen: parents must make it happen through disciplinary rituals enacting submission and control. He asserts: "It is the ultimate paradox of childhood that a youngster wants to be controlled, but insists that his parents earn the right to control him. . . . Nothing brings a parent and child closer together than for the mother and father to win decisively after being defiantly challenged. . . . The parent's demonstration of his authority builds respect like no other process, and the child will often reveal his affection when the emotion has passed."[43] For Dobson, rituals of submission, such as spanking, create the human capacity to bond. He posits this fusion of pain, power, and love as the condition for human connection. Whereas in my reading of Freud I suggested that it is through "doing" loss that we become social beings, Dobson holds loss at bay by arguing that we become social beings through "doing" power and submission:

It is imperative that a child learns to respect his parents—not to satisfy their egos, but because his relationship with them provides the basis for his later attitude toward all other people. His early view of parental authority becomes the cornerstone of his future outlook on school authority, law enforcement officers, employers, and others with whom he will eventually live and work. . . . This factor is also of vital importance to Christian parents who wish to transmit their love for Jesus Christ to their sons and daughters. Why? Because young children typically identify their parents . . . and especially their fathers—with God. Therefore, if Mom and Dad are not worthy of respect, then neither are their morals, their country, their values and beliefs, or even their religious faith.[44]

Dobson shares a story about his shock at seeing "this close identification between God and me in the mind of our son before he was two years old." One day, when Dobson was traveling on business, Shirley asked their son to say grace before meals. The child prayed: "I love you, Daddy. Amen." Dobson acknowledges that the story unsettled him, but rather than leading him to question this identification, he reads his discomfort as proving the purity of his motives: "It was too big a job and I didn't want the responsibility. But I had no choice, nor do you. God has given us the assignment of representing Him during the formative years of parenting. . . . Scary, huh?"[45]

What is seductive in Dobson's philosophy of child discipline is the way he articulates a child's need for discipline, structure, and limits as a struggle for power—and concomitantly, how he narrates parental respect as won through war. Dobson is often criticized by fundamentalists for his focus on building children's self-esteem, yet he stands within a strand of Protestantism that sees the human will as the source of sin and therefore sees parents as charged with breaking a child's will as part of a spiritual warfare waged against Satan—who is, after all, not just the ultimate enemy, but an intimate enemy as well.[46]

Dobson represents parenting as a soft-style version of Rambo: Arnold Schwartzenegger in *Kindergarten Cop* learning that he would rather lead in the family than be an isolated paramilitary warrior. Yet both the hard and soft versions of the paramilitary romance wage similar battles: an apocalyptic struggle for the salvation of the nation in which the legitimacy of male power is rewon by imagining men as victims of an effeminizing and alien government (see chapter 5). In these scenarios, men do not exercise power because they want to. They didn't ask to be men and their desires are not the issue. They must simply submit to what Dobson terms their "gender assignment" and *dare* to discipline!

Here, masculinity, precisely as an ideal, rests on and reinforces internalized aggression. In such a setup, exercising power can indeed be an experience of submission and lack of agency. Yet the truth of such insights depends on how one holds them. Although Dobson sees that masculinity is a performance—an ideal no one just naturally is—rather than opening up space for disidentification, he reidentifies with the masculine warrior ideal all the more tightly by identifying the father on earth with the Father in heaven, mistaking the penis for the Phallus.

In parenting, there are moments when this confusion falls apart and the gap shines forth stark, emergent, and raw. These moments confront us with the fact that no subject is the absolute subject supposed to know, that no father is the Father. Such moments present choices. Dobson chooses to acknowledge the gap between men and Real men (scary, huh?) only to close the space more tightly through an erotics of domination (I had no choice, nor do you). Yet we can negotiate this gap differently. We can open this space further and forge connections out of this unknowing. We can teach children to recognize limits as well as the consequences of their actions without "showing them who is boss." Limits, consequences, discipline—all call us to develop skills in negotiating and opening to the mysterious ways in which people are interdependent, not separate from one another, although we are different.

Dobson holds this space of loss at bay by imagining parental authority within an erotics of domination. Parents must play the role of "boss-man," however unwanted, because they must submit to their divine assignment and because children secretly desire to submit. Much as Peters uses romance to overcome resistance to the idea of a racist God (see chapter 4), Dobson traces the biological intimacies of parental supremacy to the possessiveness that (for him) defines sexual intercourse as that moment when a man and a woman "become one flesh" (Genesis 2:23–24; *Children*, 58). Whereas Peters reads the opening chapters of Genesis as narrating the creation of the white race, Dobson reads these chapters as narrating the creation of binary male and female genders and therefore as inscribing heterosexuality within the order of creation. For Dobson, this sexual fantasy interlocks immediately with the romantic fantasy of gender in which opposites find their other half and live happily ever after. Implicit in this family romance is a myth of self-sufficiency, according to which contemporary families would be fine if people would just stay out and leave the happy couple alone.

Contrary to popular misperceptions of fundamentalists, then, Dobson does not see sex as a necessary evil.[47] For Dobson, sexuality is our most primary energy. Whereas in *Dare to Discipline,* he castigates the "scientific experts" whose theories of child rearing led the nation to lose confidence in its heritage of biblical wisdom (which had been "handed down generation to generation from the time of Christ"), Dobson idealizes and fights to preserve the modern family created by those scientific experts he loves to hate.[48] But the point of his nostalgia was never historical accuracy. The point was discipline.

In large measure (and here I am looking toward the topic of the next chapter), this discipline is about maintaining middle-class status.[49] Historian George Mosse has argued that the emergence of nationalism in the nineteenth century was intimately connected with white middle-class norms regarding respectable sexuality. Dobson cites Joseph Daniel Unwin (the Victorian thinker with whom Peters became entranced while reading Rushdoony's *The Institutes of Biblical Law,* a classic Christian Reconstructionist text; see chapter 5), who frames the issues as a quasi-mathematical law: a civilization's level of cultural attainment is inversely proportional to the openness of its sexual regulations regarding extramarital and premarital sex.[50]

Drawing on Unwin, Dobson identifies sexuality as our deepest truth. It is the heart of personality: "Self-awareness begins with an understanding of our sexual identity. . . . Everything we do is influenced by our gender assignment."[51] It is the heart of religion: "Premarital chastity and marital monogamy are centerpieces of nearly all major religions. To destroy these ancient concepts in the minds of today's children is to weaken or totally negate their faith" (*Children,* 48). And it is the heart of the nation, analogous to the hydrogen bomb with its power to annihilate the soul of Western civilization while leaving its external buildings and structures intact for totalitarian takeover (46–47).

No small part of the appeal behind Dobson's use of children as an affective magnet derives from the way he links these very modern images

Remembering the Sixties / 155

and identifications to the Bible. This biblicization is deeply contradictory. One has to look hard to find the family that Dobson idealizes in the Bible. Would it be the bigamous family of Jacob/Israel, who gave the nation its name? Or perhaps the unmarried teen mother who gave us Jesus? Yet, as I explored in chapter 4, the Bible persistently associates sex with national threat. Pentateuchal texts narrate the creation of Israel as a nation through stories representing women and other peoples as sexually deviant, morally promiscuous, and idolatrous.[52] Both the Deuteronomic history and the prophets (especially Hosea, Isaiah, and Ezekiel) recount the rise and fall of Israel as a nation through sexuality: stories of Bathsheba run through the biblical account of David's reign, stories of domestic abuse run through the biblical account of Israel's conquest of the Promised Land in Judges, and Hosea's marriage metaphor fuses adulterous women with national security risk and religious apostasy.[53] Perhaps, then, Dobson's nostalgia for the Bible-based family (much like Peters's nostalgia for the Ten Lost Tribes) is less about the Bible and more about national power—symbolized in children's bodies.

Whereas Freud presented the discipline that civilization exacts as a source of discontent, Dobson presents this discipline as true contentment. For the mechanism by which society effects sexual discipline (according to Dobson) is private property: having a mate, a family, and a home of one's own. By these means, he seeks to produce desire for discipline.

In *Discipline and Punish,* Foucault develops the notion that in modern societies, power acts not only through oppression and repression but primarily through producing knowledge and desire. Writing in the context of analyzing how modern societies moved from public rituals of torture and execution to the modern penal system, Foucault reflects:

> It would be wrong to say that the soul is an illusion, or an ideological effect. On the contrary, it exists, it has a reality, it is produced permanently around, on, within the body by the functioning of a power that is exercised on those punished—and in a more general way, on those one supervises, trains and corrects, over madmen, children at home and at school, the colonized, over those who are stuck at a machine and supervised the rest of their lives. This is the historical reality of this soul, which, unlike the soul represented by Christian theology, is not born in sin and punishment, but is born rather out of methods of punishment, supervi-

sion and constraint. . . . But let there be no misunderstanding. . . . The man described for us, whom we are invited to free, is already in himself the effect of a subjection much more profound than himself. A "soul" inhabits him and brings him into existence, which is itself a factor in the mastery that power exercises over the body. The soul is the effect and instrument of a political anatomy; the soul is the prison of the body.[54]

Dobson's elaborate memory-work suggests that the Bible-based family is the prison of the body, the effect and instrument of a political anatomy. Perhaps this is why we need so much encouragement to focus on it; perhaps this fundamental ambivalence toward the family necessitates the elaborate nostalgia of its invocation. The following chapter takes up this idea in detail by exploring how Dobson deploys the family as a disciplinary technology to engender desires (expressed in the intimate language of gender and sexuality) that splice people into politicoeconomic structures, institutions, and ideologies, all while erasing the lines that connect the private family to the public structures that enable it—an erasure whose political anatomy is not innocent of race and class.

8 Nichemarketing the Family Homestead

*Rearticulating Mainstream Silences in the
Romance of Privatism*

Studying Focus on the Family's memory-work reveals how the Christian right uses the Bible-based family as a disciplined mobility. This family works less by issuing prohibitions than by producing possible paths of investment and desire. Explains Lawrence Grossberg: "The affective plane is organized according to maps which direct people's investments in and into the world. These maps . . . tell people where, how and with what intensities they can be absorbed into the world and into their lives. . . . They 'tell' people how to use and how to generate energy, how to navigate their way into and through various moods and passions, and how to live within emotional and ideological histories."[1] Consider how highways enable us to move faster by structuring the flow of traffic through determining where cars enter and exit. Similarly, focusing on the family enables people to move through an overstimulating environment whose relentless solicitations engender an active indifference lest one's boundaries be perpetually breached.

Whereas sentimental invocations of the family enable people to invest in their worlds (no mean feat), relentlessly focusing popular investments within the private family makes it exceedingly difficult for people to invest in more public forms of social connection. This exclusion happens because collective social movements are explicitly demonized ("secular humanist engineering"), but also because people's investments are so relentlessly privatized that it becomes difficult to see, much less invest in, the public. The result is a national body politic that denies its broader interconnectedness. This ignorance is structural, less a matter of individual prejudices than of structuring people's care for themselves and their loved ones so that collectivity simply fails to appear as a possibility in which it makes sense to invest.

Such ignorance does not simply happen: it must be actively produced and sustained. In this chapter, I read Focus on the Family's institutional memories of its 1991 move from the Los Angeles vicinity to suburban Colorado Springs, whose Chamber of Commerce recruited Dobson's ministry as part of an economic development scheme to diversify the city's economy. Shot through with ellipses and substitutions, these institutional memories demonstrate how the family can reproduce ignorance. Focusing on the family means telling history and making memories in ways that privilege the private family while eclipsing the public that nurtures this family form. As a result, promoting a cultural focus on the family can splice people into an economic agenda focused on private business—an agenda they might not agree with, intend, or even be aware of. Such splicing is an act of power. Writes Grossberg: "The real source of both contemporary forms of depoliticization and of the increasingly conservative tone of life in the United States depend on the production of a new regime of everyday life. . . . Everyday life becomes the site for and the mode of a new apparatus of power, aimed at depoliticizing significant segments of the population by erasing the lines that connect everyday life to the political and economic realities that are its conditions of possibility."[2]

This erasure is effected through dual senses of the term "private." Private can refer to the realm of heart, hearth, and individual pursuit of happiness, exemplified in such adages as "A man's home is his castle." But private can also refer to the realm of private business and the private market, idealized in the figure of the independent, self-starting entrepreneur.[3] These two senses of the term come together in the belief underlying the American dream "that there exists some private, safe, secure place— our neighborhoods, our churches, above all, the family—that would give us everything we needed if only the government would stay out."[4]

By working these two senses of the term private (sometimes with each other and sometimes against each other), privatism allies We The People with multinational corporations, situating them in the same structural position: opposed to big government. Invoking the family to speak economic fears while eliding the structural nature of economic inequality, the new right represents market discipline as morality-inducing, thereby enabling the nation to write off whole segments of the population in the name of human connection.

Religion plays a key role in the new right's ability to hold this contradictory alliance together and render its paradoxes productive. By investing "the family" with the aura of the sacred, the Christian right idealizes the family as a moral frontier that rides the juncture between national heritage and domestic memories. Mapped onto the national landscape as a moral topography, the Bible-based family underscores the hope of privatism with fears of urban apocalypse, thereby entangling economics with race, gender, sexuality, and children in a poetics of control.

Confronted with this tangle, what I want to do more than anything else is untangle it: separate religion from family from gender from sex from economics. Yet the power is in the tangle, in the larger cultural framework of privatism whose individual threads coproduce each other. The question posed by such a politics of family values is: Do we open and rethink this tangle? Or do we allow this tangle to rethink us?[5]

For rethink us it will. I conclude this chapter by demonstrating how Pete Peters invokes the variegated strands of this tangle to mainstream Christian Identity by constructing convergences with more mainstream sections of the right-wing continuum. Calling the Christian right on its bluff, Peters derives power for white supremacy by respinning the structural ignorance at work in privatism's mythic geography of urban apocalypse to promote militias as simply the logical extension of a politics that mobilizes people to protect the Bible-based family.

Better Homes and Gardens:
Capitalism and the Construction of Intimate Identity

It used to be you turned to a neighbor for help and support. But there are none. If there were, there'd be no Focus on the Family. Take my case. My wife and I live in a place where there's no one around during the day, no one at all to talk to. That's why people come to Dr. Dobson for his advice.—Tom Hess, editor of Focus on the Family's *Citizen* magazine[6]

"The welcome mat is always out," promise the advertisements in *Focus on the Family* magazine. The year I visited Focus on the Family's campus in Colorado Springs, about one hundred thousand people tramped across the mat and took the tour,[7] which featured a visit to the studio where Dobson records his radio program. "Dr. Dobson sits at the head of the table, facing the gallery. Mike Trout, his cohost, sits at Dobson's right," the tour guide informed, adding, "When you're hearing the broadcast, remember yourself sitting here." Intimate invitations like these help listeners identify with Focus on the Family by imagining themselves part of a community despite a lack of face-to-face connection. By making institutional memories, Focus on the Family smooths over the gap between the image of intimate connection through which it promotes its services and the reality of being a mass media enterprise. Consider the following: "*Coming home.* We all know how good it feels to come home. A tired youngster dragging his sled back into the house, where hot chocolate and a warm fire await . . . the end of a homemaker's day-long battle with traffic, supermarket crowds and a cranky toddler . . . Dad's headlights shining on the garage door after a tough shift at the plant. *Coming home* means spending time with those you love most—your family."[8]

Thus begins founder and president James Dobson's letter introducing Focus on the Family's 1993 annual report. A corporation's annual report does more than record its financial standing; the genre is one of the nation's premiere fantasy texts. In its annual report, an organization accounts for financial in- and out-flows by narrating history, memory, identity, vision. Entitled *Coming Home,* Focus on the Family's 1993 annual report (which visitors were given at the end of the tour) frames its finances by commemorating the September 25, 1993 dedication ceremony for the buildings through which the tour walks: "This past year,[9] *coming home* took on a similar meaning for Focus on the Family," continues Dobson. "We finally realized our long-cherished goal of establishing a campus of our own."

In keeping with this imagery, the ministry's main administration building preserves architectural features of a home. In contrast, its previous headquarters in Pomona, a satellite suburb of Los Angeles, were located in a modern office building with walls of sheer glass. Despite this architectural nostalgia, however, the administrative center does not appear on the cover of the annual report commemorating its construction. For the report's fantasy, even the suburbs are not suburban enough. Instead, the cover features the nation's most cherished idyll: a single-family home pioneering the empty plain all by itself with no other inhabitants in sight, just the sun setting behind a three-storey farmhouse whose downstairs lights are warmly lit within—a contemporary Little House on the Prairie.

Yet Laura Ingalls Wilder and her family did not just come home to a

The Romance of Privatism / 161

little house on the prairie. Frontier families depended on local communities, including various communities of color, as well as on national policies that used public monies to fund exploration and dispossession of the land, repression of the indigenous peoples who were already "coming home" there, as well as systems of transportation and communication.[10] Indeed, rough drafts of Wilder's memoirs were extensively revised by her daughter during the 1930s as an ideological attack on the New Deal welfare state.[11]

Just as the Wilder family did not come home to their Little House on the Prairie without historical revision, neither does Dad just come home to the suburbs after a tough shift at the plant, nor Mom after a long day battling traffic and supermarket crowds. According to Stephanie Coontz, the 1950s suburban family and the frontier family "probably tie for the honor of being the most heavily subsidized in American history, as well as for the privilege of having had more of their advantages paid for by minorities and the lower classes."[12] From the artificially low down payments and interest rates that enabled almost half of 1950s suburban homeowners to purchase homes; to the sewers, utilities, highways, and other public improvements that made suburban communities livable; right down to the technical innovations (aluminum clapboards, prefab walls and ceilings, plywood paneling) that brought single-family homes within the financial reach of the white working class—all were made possible by public funds diverted from urban areas that were increasingly red-lined, relegated to people of color.[13] Writes Coontz: "By the end of the 1950s, Los Angeles epitomized the kind of city such policies produced. Once served by an efficient and widely used mass-transit system, the city was carved up into multilane freeways, overpasses and viaducts. By the end of the decade, two thirds of central Los Angeles had been paved over to make room for cars."[14] The family car, the suburban home—this is how "the family" disciplines: by structuring the types of movements and connections that are publicly available, "the family" enables us not to see those who inhabit the urban spaces over which our cars speed home unimpeded on the freeway.

A similar suburban/urban geography of exodus plays out nationally. Californians seeking cheaper living conditions, safer homes, and quieter neighborhoods have relocated. In Colorado, the three hundred-some families that Focus on the Family transferred to Colorado Springs were not the only people to flee California for the Rocky Mountain State. According to the U.S. Census, between July 1, 1992, and July 1, 1993, Colorado's population jumped by 101,282 to reach 3,565,957, with roughly one-third moving from California.[15] Californians moved to places like Colorado Springs, which a local political scientist describes as a "suburb in search of a city," with its suburban-style government, lack of an industrial base, and over three-quarters Anglo population.[16]

Whereas many analysts have situated the rise of the new right in reference to its religious and political context, I am arguing that we also need to consider the geography that underlies the emergence of the suburban family home as the central site of national identity. In *City of Quartz: Excavating the Future in Los Angeles,* Mike Davis notes that turn-of-the-century Los Angeles was the first municipality in the nation to zone districts exclusively for upscale, single-family homes. Along with exclusionary zoning came "restrictive covenants," which stipulated minimum required costs for home construction and excluded non-Caucasians and sometimes non-Christians (except as servants). The first homeowners associations appeared in Los Angeles in the 1920s when white homeowners banded together to prevent people of color from buying homes outside the ghetto. Homeowners associations were helped sometimes by the Chamber of Commerce and sometimes by the Ku Klux Klan.[17]

When the U.S. Supreme Court ruled against restrictive covenants in 1948, Californians hatched a new strategy to construct a single-family barrier: private incorporation. Incorporated communities control zoning and land use while contracting out vital services (such as fire and police) to county and state governments (often at cut-rate prices), thereby passing the tab on to taxpayers.[18] In his study of the twenty-six such cities formed in Los Angeles County between 1954 and 1960, Gary Miller documents how pro-incorporation literature consistently portrayed homes as threatened by exorbitant taxes that were levied to pay for redistributional services (like welfare) and bureaucratic salaries, thereby linking the protection of property values with "gut issues" such as race, class, and antigovernmentalism.[19]

Similar links fueled the California tax revolts of the late 1970s, many of which were organized out of homeowners associations.[20] Dubbing this movement the "Watts riot of the middle classes," Davis observes that land inflation in Southern California from 1975 to 1979 meant that the state

The Romance of Privatism / 163

raised tax assessments just as the court ordered school busing: "In rousing their neighbors, tax protestors frequently resorted to the inflammatory image of the family homestead taxed to extinction in order to finance the integration of public education and other social programs obnoxious to white suburbanites."[21]

The political activism nurtured in homeowners associations fed into a new generation of young professionals, middle managers, and entrepreneurs—so-called "Middle American Radicals"[22]—who entered state and local politics just when 1960s social movements were disintegrating. Drawing on links forged by homeowners associations, these "new conservatives" advanced a broad front of issues—antibusing, back-to-basics education, pro–school prayer, antiwelfare, anti-immigrant campaigns—which were held together through a populist middle-class sensibility that Davis aptly dubs "homestead exclusivism."[23]

It is this emerging and amorphous sensibility—which links property values to family values by means of "gut issues" like race, class, and antigovernment sentiment—that Focus on the Family seeks to foster, shape, and capitalize on (through, for instance, its national network of Family Policy Councils). During the same years that Focus on the Family was coming home to the Briargate suburbs of Colorado Springs, the suburban voting bloc was becoming the majority vote in U.S. elections.[24] Political scientists on both the Left and the Right have suggested that this change could be as significant as population migrations at the end of the nineteenth century from country to city.[25] What its precise significance will be, however, is not predetermined, and this is where organizations like Focus on the Family enter the scene.

Focus on the Family seeks to spin this shift in conservative directions by mapping the suburban/urban terrain as a moral frontier. This mythic geography pits the middle-class cult of domesticity against "the city," which is cast as the embodiment of everything the suburban family is alleged not to be: centered around adults rather than children; a place of experience rather than innocence; alien because dark; uncivilized because unproductive and unproductive because out of control.[26]

This moral topography is not unique to the Christian right. Think, for instance, of the role that L.A. plays in popular culture, from films such as *Bullworth, Grand Canyon,* and *Boyz in the Hood* to the popularity of gangsta rap (as well as how popular it has become for public figures to condemn rap music as if it were the source of misogyny and violence). Much as pop culture of the 1980s was fascinated by Vietnam as "the primary site of the national nightmare," so contemporary pop culture fixates on "the black inner city as the symbolic space of suburban anxiety."[27] Los Angeles represents the nation's contemporary heart of darkness, right down to its soundtrack: low-flying helicopters conflate Los Angeles with Vietnam, communicating the message that the nation is still at war, only now the jungle—and the apocalypse—are urban.[28]

Although this mythic geography is tightly linked to race, as political scientist Alan Wolfe argues, one cannot read people's zip code as evidence of their moral choice to disown the cities. The children of those parents who moved to the suburbs in the 1950s have by now bought homes and raised their children in the suburbs.[29] Although their family history might involve urban flight, their present experience is suburban stasis. Moreover, many people of color—African Americans, Asians, and Hispanics—have moved to the suburbs, with the result that suburbs tend to be settled along racial lines. Wolfe concludes: "None of the qualifications I have introduced to the story of suburbia as a retreat from the ideal of a more racially and economically integrated society should lead to the conclusion that such a story is a false one; nearly all the available evidence, from this study as well as others, suggests that issues of poverty and issues of suburbanization will always be intertwined. But my findings also indicate that it is not always clear how they are tied together."[30]

Determining how disparate issues "tie together" is the point of counter-memory: to spin gut issues into affective support for a political orientation regardless of whether people cognitively agree with its particular philosophy or political position. Claiming that feminists have chosen to ignore the gender "facts of life," Dobson contends that the consequences of such willful ignore-ance can be seen in inner cities, where "chaos reigns supreme."[31] Hence the wildly oscillating depictions of the inner city as a place defined by controlling black matriarchs and out-of-control black youth. Against urban confusion, Dobson pits the civility and stability of suburban family values where sex-gender disciplines people into clear and distinct roles. Or consider the analysis of Gary Bauer in *Children at Risk*:

> Nowhere is the flight from fatherhood more apparent than in the inner cities of our nation. There the full effect of the antifamily, "liberation"

The Romance of Privatism / 165

philosophy is painfully apparent. . . . Men enticed by drugs, easy sex and the other temptations of urban life have abandoned the responsibility of parenting and husbanding. . . . Our current welfare system, for example, encourages the formation of "the mother-state-child family." Uncle Sam has become a marriage partner and "father" of last resort. . . . The influence of feminism on the cultural elite is so strong that many in government and the media are unwilling to say clearly that, on the average, female-headed households are in great danger—particularly in the inner city with its many social problems.[32]

Drugs, easy sex, and temptations are neither limited to, nor more readily available in, cities than in suburbs. This geography is less about actual differences and more about the differences people imagine in their minds, drawing on stereotypes regarding people of color and poor people as out of control, overexpressive, fixated on immediate gratification, hypersexual, emasculated, and matriarchal. The line that divides people onto one side or the other is daring to discipline. And the source of this courage is the Bible-based family.

Dobson's primary theoretician for this claim is economist George Gilder, whose *Wealth and Poverty* was touted as the Bible of Reaganomics. As Gilder sees it, what poor men really need to do is "work harder than the classes above them."[33] He acknowledges that the only impetus they have to do that, given a market system that does not grant them the immediate rewards it grants the upper classes, is their hope that their children will live the good life even if they cannot:

> The short-sighted outlook of poverty stems largely from the breakdown of family responsibilities among fathers. The lives of the poor, all too often, are governed by the rhythms of tension and release that characterize the sexual experience of young men. . . . Civilized society is dependent on the submission of the short-term sexuality of young men to the extended maternal horizons of women. This is what happens in monogamous marriage. . . . If work effort is the first principle of overcoming poverty, marriage is the prime source of upwardly mobile work. . . .
>
> The key to the intractable poverty of the hardcore American poor is the dominance of single and separated men in poor communities. Black "unrelated individuals" are not much more likely to be in poverty than white

ones. The problem is neither race nor matriarchy in any meaningful sense. It is familial anarchy among the concentrated poor of the inner city, in which flamboyant and impulsive youths rather than responsible men provide the themes of aspiration.[34]

In this masculine romance, the private family functions as public compensation for men on the bottom rungs of the class ladder—"the family wage" being here reduced to the wages of masculinity, as it were—while smoothing over the painful reality of class. Used to obscure the violence that founds this social contract, the family functions as a screen memory onto which people project their hopes as they disavow the pain of a dream so perpetually deferred. Although Gilder notes that his critique also applies to whites, to my mind, this "inclusion" does not make this mythic geography any less violent.

Gilder disavows this violence by representing it as the very root of civilization, arguing that in "primitive" societies "men could not find time to make capital, could not bring themselves to work, save and forgo rewards in the name of the unseen and unknowable future. It was firm links between work, wealth, sex and children that eventually created a future-oriented psychology in the mass of Western European American men."[35] For Gilder, the Protestant work ethic was literally birthed in the bodies of children. Family ties bind men into capitalist relations through generating, by means of their access to the bodies of women and children, a future-oriented state of mind strong enough to discipline male bodies to work hard while receiving few rewards. Although Dobson explicitly distances himself from the harshness of Gilder's worldview, his more sentimental version is no less supremacist:

> Suddenly we see the beauty of the divine plan. When a man falls in love with a woman, dedicating himself to care for her and protect her and support her, he suddenly becomes the mainstay of social order. Instead of using his energies to pursue his own lusts and desires, he sweats to build a home and save for the future and seek the best job available. . . . He discovers a sense of pride—yes, masculine pride—because he is needed by his wife and children. Everyone benefits from the relationship.
>
> When a society is composed of millions of individual families that are established on this plan, then the nation is strong and stable. It is the great

contribution marriage makes to a civilization. But in its absence, ruination is inevitable. When men have no reason to harness their energies in support of the home, then drug abuse, alcoholism, sexual intrigue, job instability and aggressive behavior can be expected to run unchecked throughout the culture. That is precisely what has happened to many black inner-city families. The government pays the bills. Who needs the man? He procreates and disappears.[36]

In this mythic geography, the family functions as what film critic Kaja Silverman calls a "dominant fiction." Silverman argues that most people do not directly inhabit abstract structures like capitalism. Instead, people get spliced into macrostructures like capitalism indirectly through their imagination: through the stock images, scenes, and sequences in which people are encouraged to "find" themselves.[37]

In the mythic geography outlined above, Dobson and Gilder splice people into capitalism by idealizing the Bible-based family in ways that position people to identify market discipline as morality-inducing. Yet this morality and this Bible, not to mention this family, are all racially coded. Invoking the family as a dividing line between Western civilization and "primitives" encourages people, regardless of the color of their skin, to "find" themselves within the identity of whiteness.

Focus on the Family's 1993 annual report overlays this version of the mythic geography, with its focus on the alleged (a.k.a. mythical) origins of Western civilization out of "primitive" society, with a later moment in time: the 1950s suburban frontier. This suburban version too, however, uses the family to splice people into capitalism, in this case, consumer capitalism, by encouraging them to find themselves in the cold war apocalypse that identifies the free market with democratic freedom. Writes historian Elaine Tyler May:

> In 1959, when the baby boom and the cold war were both at their peak, Vice President Richard M. Nixon traveled to the Soviet Union to engage in what would become one of the most noted verbal sparring matches of the century. In a lengthy and often heated debate with Soviet Premier Nikita Khrushchev at the opening of the American National Exhibition in Moscow, Nixon extolled the virtues of the American way of life, while his opponent promoted the Communist system. What was remarkable about this exchange was its focus. The two leaders did not discuss missiles,

bombs, or even modes of government. Rather, they argued over the relative merits of American and Soviet washing machines, televisions and electric ranges.

In her book, May includes a photograph depicting Khrushchev and Nixon in suits and ties with government officials and reporters looking on as the two world powers survey a replica of an American ranch home complete with labor-saving appliances. "What we want is to make easier the life of our housewives," proclaimed Nixon. Claiming that "diversity" is what matters most to Americans, Nixon pointed to the evidence: "We have many different manufacturers and many different kinds of washing machines so that housewives can have a choice." May concludes: "Many observers credit this trip with establishing Nixon's political future. Clearly, Americans did not find the kitchen debate trivial. The appliance-laden ranch-home epitomized the expansive, secure lifestyle that postwar Americans wanted. . . . Suburbia would serve as a bulwark against communism and class conflict, for according to the widely shared belief articulated by Nixon, it offered a piece of the American dream for everyone."[38]

For many white women, the image of the appliance-laden ranch home was the soft-sell inducement to leave the workforce in favor of home economics. For white men, the promise of owning your own homestead offered inducement to renounce earlier visions of masculinity that had focused on a man's entrepreneurial and fiercely self-reliant spirit in favor of becoming an "organization man" who subordinates his personal ambitions to the corporation's good while providing happiness and security for his own.[39]

If the suburban ranch constituted the velvet glove of power for some, unprecedented government purges of "homosexuals and other moral perverts" constituted its iron fist for others.[40] By orienting its members within a global geopolitical order, the suburban family obscured from view those fellow Americans for whom the suburban homestead was not a viable aspiration—and who were by no means silent at the time. Just four years before Nixon celebrated diversity, Rosa Parks sparked the Montgomery bus boycott, a consumer campaign for civil rights fought in the arena of public accommodations as a wedge by which to win deeper dreams. The year after Nixon extolled freedom of choice, four black students walked into a Greensboro Woolworth, bought toothpaste and other items, then sat down at the lunch counter and demanded equal service, initiating the student phase of the civil rights movement.[41]

It is this 1950s moment, with all its velvet promise and iron restriction, that Dobson invokes so sentimentally in his 1993 annual report. This dream is what America promises: an Eden of consumer commodities discovered by Columbus, who was, after all, seeking a short route by which to obtain trade goods. In this private market version of freedom, equal opportunity means that commodities are equally available to all those who can pay.

This populist vision of consumerism as democracy works because commodities do make a certain sort of freedom possible.[42] For example, the emergence at the turn of the century of a leisure culture (exemplified by such spaces as amusement parks) made it possible for young working-class men and women to develop distinctive rituals, identities, and communities. Likewise, blues music provided a site where African American women could "autonomously work out—as audiences and performers—a working-class model of womanhood."[43] The rise of industrial capitalism in the nineteenth century meant that the home ceased to be the primary unit of economic production, so that men and (to a lesser extent) women no longer needed to live in a procreative family to survive, enabling gay and lesbian identities/communities.[44] The same changes that helped enable the emergence of homosexual identity also helped enable the emergence of heterosexual identity. No longer focused on producing hands to help in the fields (and to support parents in old age), the heterosexual family became idealized as a sacred haven in a heartless world: *the* place where human needs for intimacy, happiness, and pleasure are met—and more often than not, by consuming commodities.[45] Likewise, commodities continue to provide one of the primary ways that queer folk signal an identity as culturally unseeable as gayness to others and to ourselves.

Yet there is a blindness built into commodities, and therefore into the intimate identities created by their means. This is the blindness of privatism: focusing on the private sphere erases the public lines that connect us to one another. As a result, commodities tend to become what Marx called fetishes, by which he meant the eerie way that commodities tend to end up ruling their producers instead of being ruled by them. Writes David Harvey: "We can take our daily breakfast without a thought for the myriad people who are engaged in its production. All traces of exploitation are obliterated in the object (there are no finger marks of exploitation in the daily bread). We cannot tell from contemplation of any object in the supermarket what conditions of labor lay behind its production. The concept of fetishism explains how it is that under conditions of capitalist modernization we can be so objectively dependent on 'others' whose lives and aspirations remain so totally opaque to us."[46] This opacity results less from individual attitudes and prejudices and more from the public maps that determine how we connect (and fail to connect) the various spaces in which we live our lives: production and consumption, work and home, private business and private family.

Home Finance:
Focusing on the Family Eclipses the Public That Nurtures It

God himself has raised Colorado Springs to be a strategic center for our nation. . . . Colorado Springs is America's spiritual NORAD.
—Jim Tomberlin, pastor of the Woodmen Valley Chapel, which welcomes 2000 plus worshippers each weekend[47]

Just as focusing on the family ignores the public that enabled the Ingalls family to inhabit a little house on the prairie, so the suburban family that graces Focus on the Family's annual report covers over the public policies that brought this multimillion-dollar enterprise to a suburban campus nestled beneath Pike's Peak, fabled gateway to the West. Focus on the Family was recruited to the Springs as part of an extensive development campaign run by the Greater Colorado Springs Economic Development Council. This development campaign marketed the Springs' conservative heritage as a way to attract environmentally clean businesses that could diversify the local economy. Religion as economic development? Conservative religion as diversity? The antienvironmentalist Christian right as earth-friendly business?

Understanding how a recruiting campaign rife with such contradictions could nevertheless be quite productive requires seeing how privatism extends beyond merely economic institutions and doctrines. According to Sam Bass Warner, "Psychologically, privatism meant that the individual should seek happiness in personal independence and the search for wealth; socially, privatism meant that the individual should see his first loyalty as his immediate family, and that a community should be a union of such money-making, accumulating families; politically, privatism meant that the community should keep the peace among individual money-makers and, if possible, help to create an open and thriving setting where each citizen should have some substantial opportunity to prosper."[48] In this broader sense, privatism constitutes a cultural sensibility (or public mattering map) that works on the level of affect, guiding how people invest in, and move through, their worlds.

As such, privatism runs deep in national memories, defining the emergence of Western cities like Colorado Springs, which began as entrepreneurial enterprises (in which private investment was often stimulated by public funds).[49] According to town chronicler Marshall Sprague, the Springs was conceived by former Union general William Jackson Palmer as a promotional scheme. Palmer's dream was to make his fortune by building a railroad through land he obtained at a steal, thanks to two large estates given as grants to Europeans by Governor Manuel Armijo before the Mexican War. Yet, in a twist that Dobson would love, Palmer's vision for the Springs was crucially altered by falling in love with a lady named Queen Mellon. Rhapsodizes Sprague: "Before Queen came into Palmer's life, he had visualized the usual rough railroad towns which he would found along his 'north and south' line at intervals to be determined by prospects for agriculture and mining. But Queen split him into two people—the tough empire builder determined to conquer the wilderness and the Arthurian cavalier shielding his gentle lady from the facts of life." The result was Colorado Springs, a town that Palmer promoted both to British financiers and to his bride-to-be (who feared the roughness of the West and the wildness of its Indian inhabitants) as "an attractive place for well-to-do people on the order of Newport and Saratoga." Palmer's PR man named the town Colorado Springs because of its "nice rich eastern spa sound," even though the only springs were five miles away. Originally nicknamed "Little London," the town's architecture was British, its police officers were called bobbies, and it took tea in the British style.[50]

Colorado Springs grew through being marketed, first as a place for sheep and cattle ranching (although its land was not suitable) and then as a place to take the cure for tuberculosis (becoming unnecessary for that purpose with the discovery of modern antibiotics). The town was promoted in a different way when gold was discovered in Cripple Creek in

172 / Lift High the Cross

1891. But by the 1930s boom turned to bust as gold production dwindled and tourism declined because of the Depression.[51]

The solution? Another marketing campaign. In the 1940s entrepreneurs convinced the military that the Pike's Peak environment would be as beneficial to military personnel as it had been to health tourists in the 1870s, bringing home Camp Carson.[52] In 1948, the Springs lured Peterson Air Force Base, which today houses the North American Aerospace Defense Command (NORAD) as well as the Pacer Frontier Project for a worldwide space logistics center. In 1954 Colorado Springs became home to the U.S. Air Force Academy. The result? Population soared: from 30,000 to 75,000 in 1950, reaching 150,000 by the end of the 1950s.[53] Dependence on federal funding was furthered in 1985 with the arrival of Falcon Air Force Base, which houses the Consolidated Space Operations Center, which controls all military satellite systems through ground-to-space communication, as well as research for the Strategic Defense Initiative, whose defunding propelled Colorado Springs into its next round of boom and bust.[54] Responding to defense funding cuts in 1970, the Colorado Springs Chamber of Commerce created an Economic Development Council (EDC) to recruit private businesses to the area.[55]

These councils were a common response to economic crises in the 1970s, as cities experienced unemployment as well as a net outmigration of economic activity and population.[56] Added to this was impatience with the social programs spawned by Johnson's War on Poverty as it gradually became clear that there was no quick way to fix "the other America." Capitalizing on this disillusionment, Nixon's New Federalism defunded social programs, arguing that reliance on federal aid prevented cities from making full use of local leadership in the private sector.

The EDCs viewed the problems that deindustrialization posed to the urban landscape through the lens of privatism. The result was an urban sweepstakes in which success was defined by the ability to bring home high-tech firms and the middle-class population needed to staff them. Economists have compared this postindustrial urban sweepstakes with the eighteenth-century competition for railroad connections, in which the cities that lost became ghost towns.[57]

This postindustrial privatism was first codified by Carter's Commission for a National Agenda for the Eighties. Arguing that the national economy no longer depended on the industrial cities of the Rust Belt, the Commission suggested that leaving certain cities behind was the price of national progress, much as white suburban flight had abandoned cities two decades earlier. Urging the nation to abandon the War on Poverty in favor of funding urban development, the Commission argued that the best use of public funds is to fund private investors who will revitalize the economic base, bringing jobs and thus providing "a painless way to help the poor."[58]

This shift away from social programs toward urban development changed notions of governance. Whereas economic development had formerly been the terrain of business associations and Chambers of Commerce, now mayors and other public officials increasingly functioned as entrepreneurs. Similarly, EDCs are quasi-public organizations. They receive and administer public funds, as well as offer public incentives such as tax exemptions. Yet, as nonprofit organizations, their decisions are not directly influenced by the public.[59] Barnekov, Boyle, and Rich argue that such civic entrepreneurship turns both government and free enterprise on their head. Local government begins to act "the role of competitor and business as welfare recipient. It is a process in which the public takes enormous financial risks, while business surveys the willing suitors and moves freely to where public risk-taking is greatest."[60]

The marriage metaphor invokes gender to "naturalize" a crucial assumption: what is good for private business is good for the public. The unasked and unseen question—the question that is made not to matter— is: What is business good for? Barnekov, Boyle, and Rich argue strongly that when this question is not asked, public governance becomes subsumed under the concerns of private business.

This double bind is well illustrated in Colorado Springs. In terms of the 1970s urban sweepstakes, the Springs won: it recruited electronics and high-tech manufacturing, as well as the middle-class population these firms require.[61] Colorado Springs helped pioneer the information age. But in 1985–1986, as the personal computer market lagged and funding for Star Wars fell through, Colorado Springs went from being touted as the "Silicon Mountain" and "Space Capital of the World" to the "Foreclosure Capital of the Nation."[62]

The solution? Another marketing campaign. In 1987 the EDC consulted with the Fantus Corporation, which gave a new mandate: Diversify!—by recruiting national nonprofits and using the city's conservative heritage as a marketing pitch. Add to these recommendations the fact that EDC member Alice Worrell is a conservative evangelical and daughter of Christian college teachers. "There were a lot of names I knew from living on evangelical college campuses all my life," Alice Worrell told the *San Diego Tribune*. The result was over seventy religious ministries that by 1995 were "coming home" to Colorado Springs.[63]

The jewel in the crown of this diversification campaign was the relocation of the multimillion-dollar mass ministry of Focus on the Family, the largest religious nonprofit recruited to the Springs. Dobson has said that he relocated Focus on the Family to save $5 million a year, including at least $1 million in lower wages, another $1 million in lower insurance costs, and another $800,000 in taxes.[64] The pot was sweetened by a $4 million incentive grant from the El Pomar Foundation, whose chair, Bill Hybl, is a member of Focus on the Family.[65] Focus on the Family used the El Pomar grant to purchase forty-seven acres of land in the northern section of Colorado Springs, where its new home now sits next door to the Air Force Academy.

There has been considerable debate in Colorado Springs about whether the money used to lure these ministries has strengthened the local economy.[66] According to Worrell, these ministries employ 5,600 (out of a total workforce of 200,000).[67] Supporters also cite the increased visibility that these ministries bring to Colorado Springs: "The people who come in from outside the county on business with nonprofit organizations get the opportunity to experience the area, an opportunity that might not exist if the nonprofit organization were not there."[68]

Detractors argue that religious nonprofits pay lower-than-average salaries and are exempt from taxes on income and property. (The Colorado Constitution grants a property tax exemption for religious "worship." In 1989, just as California was tightening its tax restrictions on religious organizations, Colorado's tax code was loosened to further accommodate religious organizations by extending its definition of worship to include any activity "in furtherance of religious purposes" *as determined by the religious organization*.)[69]

This economic development strategy changed the everyday environment of Colorado Springs without open, public discussion. For many, this change in the environment was symbolized by the arrival of Focus on the

Family. This was not because Focus on the Family works primarily on local issues. Noting that "any organization that dropped $100 million into the economy would have attracted some measure of attention," a local activist described his perception of the change: "While the Springs has always been economically conservative (it's a military town), the Springs was typical of most of the West in having a live and let live attitude. This changed. . . . I don't think they anticipated what happened as a critical mass was reached and the dominant voice became a white Christian voice . . . no one organization was leading it or making stuff happen or politicizing issues. It was more a matter of people working in jobs that merge vocations with avocations becoming more political under a 'the Kingdom is now' philosophy."[70]

The Greater Colorado Springs Economic Development Council has gradually backed away from its strategy of nichemarketing the city's conservative heritage to fundamentalist nonprofits. In 1997, the EDC issued a study that reported that outsiders perceive Colorado Springs as controlled by "religious zealots." The study attributed this perception to the maelstrom of negative publicity that arose after Amendment 2 regarding the presence of the Christian right, with such headlines as "Onward Muscular Christians" (*Newsweek*), "Rise in Christian Right Divides a City" (*New York Times*), and "A House Divided? Influx of Religious Groups Rattles Springs" (*Denver Post*).[71] The EDC found this perception to be a "significant detriment to recruiting talented people [who] fear the imposition on the general public of extreme beliefs through schools and through government."[72]

On the other hand, many right–leaning inhabitants celebrated the change in the public environment as an "alternative to secularism which dominates the culture." One man I interviewed in 1994 told me with pleasure that Colorado Springs was the first "place he had lived since 1950s Catholic upstate New York where the neighborhood and the village were religious." He spoke of a friend in real estate who sends articles with big headlines proclaiming Colorado Springs "the center of intolerance" to potential clients in Southern California, hoping to recruit them to move to the Springs. His wife saw the growth as a blessing from God and a sign that God is at work in the Springs. "I hear that Focus on the Family came here because of economics, but I wonder if there is a spiritual pull," she told me. She attributed her family's decision to move to the Springs just before the boom began as an act of Providence.[73]

Our Own Private Eden:
Prosperity Theology and the Eclipse of the Public

Throughout the centuries God has chosen different cities for different tasks. Colorado Springs has been chosen to refresh and globalize Christianity.
—Rev. Ted Haggard, pastor of New Life Church[74]

Focusing on the family, I have been arguing, means telling history and making memories in ways that privilege the private family while eclipsing the public that nurtures this family form. Thus, in contrast to my account highlighting how Dobson built his ministry by subverting feminism, Focus on the Family remembers its birth as a mass media ministry in terms of Jim Dobson's personal solution to a typically male problem: traveling too much to focus on his own family, Dobson became caught between a man's need to satisfy his career ambitions and a man's need to love and lead his family. The solution? Radio ministry, which allowed Dobson to reach millions while still "coming home" each night.

The ministry's memory of its own history mirrors its representation of "the family" more generally. Postindustrial economies demand a flexible workforce, constant retooling, and high geographic mobility, as well as longer work hours coupled with an increasingly porous boundary between work and leisure. In response, Dobson speaks powerfully of the need to refuse becoming so consumed by work that you have no time for emotional or spiritual relationships. And he speaks clearly about the dangers of overcompensation, warning that you can be enslaved by the things you buy.[75] In explicit contrast to market imperatives that urge "Achieve at all costs!" and "Thou shalt consume!", Dobson offers the family as an alternative identity from which to resist such market solicitations.

Idealizing the family as a site of resistance to market imperatives is not new to today's Right. According to Stephanie Coontz, "Antebellum romanticization of the family reflected a real appreciation of the economic and psychic costs of capitalism, both for the small businessman who was thrown into increasing conflict with his employees [whereas

The Romance of Privatism / 177

before, boss and employees had worked together in a more communal fashion] and for the artisan who faced a loss of control over his work and demotion to the status of hired hand." Coontz analyzes the cult of the home as a strategy forged largely by white middle-class women who sought to help their husbands and sons negotiate a middle way between two dangerous extremes: "Work and market forces were kept from producing dangerous ambition or speculation by the doctrine that the highest good lay in the home; home was kept from becoming an alternative to work by imbuing domestic morality with the values of thrift and accumulation. . . . The worker's mother, and later, his wife provided a counterbalance to influences at work that might lead him to either reject competition altogether or set his sights too high." Eschewing market relations among family members, however, was tied to accepting market competition and insecurity as determinative of all other relations. Thus, Coontz describes the sacralization of white middle-class domesticity as a devil's wager.[76]

Coontz's analysis suggests that the sacrality of the home is produced in large part through being articulated in opposition to the market. Perhaps, then, the sacrality of gender is produced through its relation to economic class (where class, I contend, stands in tight articulation with national identity: the whole notion of the American dream). Consider the fear that informs Dobson's imaginary geography, which positions the private suburban family as the moral dividing line between those who deserve to make it and those who do not. Unlike Peters (to whom I'll turn in the next section), Dobson's preferred way of narrating such class fears is through their flip side: religious hope.

Much like the woman quoted above who reinterpreted Focus on the Family's move to suburban Colorado Springs within a religious narrative that trumps the economic, Focus on the Family narrates its mission to preserve the Bible-based family through a prosperity theology that identifies market discipline with the hand of God, and thereby splices people ever more tightly into the demands of the private market.

Consider the video *Coming Home: A Family Album,* companion to the 1993 annual report commemorating Dobson's new multimillion-dollar campus. The video opens by quoting Psalm 127: "Unless the Lord builds the house, the builders labor in vain." In the Bible (but not on the screen), this verse is paralleled with the following: "Unless the Lord watches over the city, the guard watches in vain" (Psalm 127:2). House and city are conflated: the private home and the national city on a hill.

As this biblical verse fades away, the camera pans Pike's Peak from above, like the Spirit moving over the waters or pioneers moving westward over those amber waves of grain, coming upon Focus on the Family's new home. The administration building rises before our eyes in a speeded-up time reminiscent of the way Hebrew narrative strings short subject-verb sentences quickly one after another to build a sense of rapidity. In a matter of seconds, Focus on the Family's new home rises as if inevitable: destiny manifest.

In the Bible (but again, not on the video screen), the next verse of Psalm 127 warns: "In vain you rise up early and go late to rest, toiling for the bread you eat; he supplies the needs of those he loves." After all, how does one know that the Lord is building one's house or watching over the exodus of family values followers to Colorado Springs? Whereas Psalm 127 positions the Lord's presence in a conditional clause ("Unless . . ."), the narrative voice-over, speaking as an omniscient voice coming down from on high, dispels doubt before it can arise: "The beautiful forty-seven-acre campus and home of Focus on the Family is not the result of any great scheme of man but is truly from the hand of God." Not the result of an economic development scheme, not the result of a long and enduring tradition of privatism that structures how the nation imagines community, but the result of a divine hand.

Just a year after my visit, Dobson wrote and published *When God Doesn't Make Sense,* in which he explicitly criticized prosperity theology, warning of the dangers implicit in interpreting material good fortune as a sign of divine favor.[77] Prosperity theology has a double edge. Ask Job, who said, "The Lord giveth and the Lord taketh away" after he lost his home and family because God made a bet. Yet Dobson's caution is absent when narrating how Focus on the Family came home to the Springs: "I didn't in 1977 say, 'Man, how can we build something big?' We have never sat around the table with the board and said: 'How can we get big? How can we expand this thing?' . . . It was motivated before we even realized what was happening. It came out of my father's prayer life—his relation with the Lord and his intense desire to serve him. And the Lord has just transferred that one generation down, as He did for Solomon and allowed him to build the Temple instead of David."[78]

In his last sentence, Dobson refers to 2 Samuel 7. In this text, Yahweh promises David, Israel's first king, to make David's house an everlasting dynasty, to appoint a place for the nation from which it will never be disturbed, and to allow David's son Solomon to build the Lord a house, the Jerusalem Temple. We've seen this text (and its house metaphor) before: Peters read it as proof that the white Puritans who settled New England are the literal descendants of the Ten Tribes of ancient Israel and that the land they founded is destined to be the Promised Land, where God's covenant will finally come true in the form of a racial theocracy. Although Dobson rejects such explicit theocracy, he produces his ministry in relation to this same lost promise, a promise that conflates house and nation as Temples of the Lord. Like Peters, Dobson styles his ministry as a tool in the hand of God, waging an offensive culture war to restore the Law of the Father and thus spark the divine promise recorded in 2 Chronicles 7:14: "If my people who are called by my name humble themselves and pray and seek my face and turn from their wicked ways, then I will hear from heaven, will forgive their sin, and heal their land."

Whereas Peters remembers this promise through a racial prophecy (God's Law written genetically on white hearts), Dobson narrates this biblical promise through a family prophecy in which he "finds" himself playing Solomon to his father's David. A Nazarene minister, Dobson Sr. was praying at the deathbed of his brother-in-law, petitioning the Lord to grant them just three more years to preach the gospel together. On the third day of his prayers, Dobson Sr. received a promise: "I have seen your compassion and am going to answer your petitions in a way you could never have imagined. You are going to reach literally millions of people for me, from coast to coast and around the world. But it will not be through your efforts or through the work of James McGraw [his dying brother-in-law]. It will be through your *son!*"[79] That night, his brother-in-law died; the next day, Dobson Sr. suffered a heart attack from which he never recovered. These events took place in 1977, the year James Dobson Jr. founded Focus on the Family.

By his own account, Dobson did not learn about this prophecy until 1985, when his ministry was at its nadir and he was beset by doubts about his own mission. He credits this prophecy with revolutionizing his understanding of Focus on the Family. As grainy black-and-white clips of the child Dobson toddling with his parents flash across the screen, the narrator intones: "The inspiration for the ministry of Focus on the Family can be traced directly to Dr. Dobson's relationship with his father and to the influence that godly man had on his life." Dobson portrays himself as simply doing the work of his F/father. He concludes the video's opening sequence by professing: "Nearly everything I write, nearly everything I speak about, the values I represent, what I really care about, originated with him."[80] Not me, but the F/father in me.

After this opening identifies Dobson's ministry with the Law of the F/father, the video goes on to narrate the institutional beginnings and growth of Dobson's ministry, including its involvement in politics. The video concludes with scenes of Dobson speaking to a vast amphitheater filled with thousands of people, their faces up-turned to catch his every word. The camera pans over the crowd, then pans over the Garden of the Gods to show Pike's Peak, over which is written the biblical text: "And all the people were amazed at what God had accomplished so quickly" (2 Chronicles 7:29). This quote forms a bookend with the opening biblical quotation, representing Focus on the Family's involvement with politics as a natural progression: from the house to the city, just as in Psalm 127.

A theme text for the ministry since its earliest days, 2 Chronicles 7:29 is also emblazoned in giant letters across one of the walls of Focus on the Family's new home. The quote frames the phenomenal growth of Dobson's ministry as evidence that the ministry "belongs not to Dr. Dobson nor to any group of people but to the Lord," and therefore as the embodiment of the F/father's hand, proof positive of his work in the world. This text also reveals a certain understanding of the work that the Lord is believed to be doing through the ministry, its reason for existence. This reason is one we've seen before. Chapter 5 recounted how Peters styles his ministry on the model of reforms initiated by the biblical king Josiah. Just as Josiah sought to produce national identity through religious cleansing, so Peters hopes Scriptures for America will catalyze God's kingdom by sparking a similar cleansing today. Second Chronicles 7:29 is the companion text to Peters's prototype, recounting the story of reforms initiated by King Hezekiah, Josiah's predecessor. Hezekiah assumed the throne in the Southern Kingdom after the Northern Kingdom had been conquered by Assyria (715 B.C.E.). Portraying Assyria's victory over the North as divine punishment for forsaking the worship of Israel's own god, Hezekiah removed Assyrian and local Canaanite deities from the Jerusalem Temple, declaring them outside the boundaries of Israelite monotheism. He destroyed the rival folk religion with its altars in the country, centralizing worship on the Jerusalem Temple. And he held a Passover in Jerusalem that sought to include the remnants of the northern tribes who had been conquered by Assyria.

In chapter 5 I suggested that these overlapping textual models are one way to understand how the Christian right and white supremacy converge: both Peters and Dobson style their ministries as cleansing the house/nation/Temple. In this biblical model, monotheism is performed as a political act: one God, one king, one people. This oneness is produced through a "cleansing" that creates and makes visible national boundaries, in the form of external threat and in the form of domestic discipline. Functioning as a "dominant fiction," the biblical house metaphor enables people to "find" themselves at home in the nation by internalizing the boundaries of the national body politic through producing desire for discipline in the affective form of fidelity to the F/father and thus inscribing national boundaries on individual bodies in the form of gender.

Focus on the Family represents this fidelity as a guarantee of security, a kind of heavenly insurance that reads size and prosperity through a logic of triumphalism, much as the video reversed Psalm 127's conditional "unless" into a guarantee. If the body is the Temple of the Holy Spirit, then it must be "cleansed"—and a national body politic composed of such disciplined bodies transforms the conditional "I will be your God if you will be my people" into a nation authorized by God, the direct result of his providential hand.[81]

When Peters takes *Remnant Resolves* to Washington, D.C., he practices a body politics that identifies the bodily boundaries of his own ego as Christ's ambassador with the boundaries of the national body politic in the hope that enacting this identification will catalyze the kingdom. Dobson, too, practices a body politics: narrating Focus on the Family's growth within prosperity theology identifies the ego boundaries of the male head of the household with the law of the Father, and fuses the body of Christ with the national body politic. This is the point of the video's closing scene, in which Dobson speaks to the multitudes, whose upturned faces are moved by his testimony. In her analysis of Christian video, media critic Eithne Johnson reads such scenes as constituting a "body genre" whose formal properties reproduce the experience of being born again:

In the hierarchical structure of the conservative evangelical church, the pastor is the focus of congregational attention; similarly, in these Christian tapes, the videovangelist is situated in front of a studio or seminar audience, whose members are routinely shown in close-up responding dramatically to the expert's words. . . . The cross-cutting between shots of the videovangelist and of the audience signifies the marking of their bodies in terms of the spiritual-therapeutic narrative structure of Christian salvation. The "megacommunicator" signifies the patriarchal body whose lineage is traced from God to pastor to expert. This is coupled with the studio audience, whose bodies signify the living church, the Body of believers formed by the congregants. . . . Successful videovangelism effects an emotional alignment between the audience inside the frame and the viewer outside, thereby bringing them together in the Body.[82]

In chapter 6 I argued that focusing on the family is bait-and-switch: "the family" evangelizes those who would not otherwise be open to hearing the "born-again" message. In chapter 7 I suggested that this evangelization has a political edge: Dobson's ministry rejects theocracy in favor of using the family as a cultural strategy to Christianize the nation, portraying the Christian right neither as one interpretation of Christianity nor as a political special interest group, but rather as "everyone's best interest group." Drawing on the long legacy of privatism in American cultural memories within which the sacrality of the home is produced through its opposition to the private market, and the sacrality of gender is produced through its eclipse of economic class, the video effects this identification of America as a Christian nation on the level of bodies: the camera sweeps over the enormous amphitheater that holds the vast crowd of Dobson's audience, then segues to sweep over the majesty of God's law at work in the natural world only to culminate in a biblical text in which monotheism constitutes a political act, God's law at work in the national body politic: "And all the people were amazed . . ."

Ruby Ridge and the Attack on America's Families

Focus on the Family's invocation of prosperity theology speaks to a middle-class, suburban-identified constituency. In contrast, Peters speaks precisely to those rural-identified homeowners whose property taxes rose

The Romance of Privatism / *183*

as Californians (such as Dobson and Focus on the Family) fled the suburban sprawl surrounding Los Angeles. Despite their competing regional positions, however, Peters and Dobson converge via the mythic geography of urban apocalypse that links private family and private business. Through amplifying the supremacist undertones at work in Dobson's sentimental idealization of the suburban family, Peters seeks to mainstream Christian Identity by promoting militias as simply the rural counterpart to, and Real man's version of, the politics of family values advanced by the Christian right.

Although claiming militias as embodying family values might seem quite a stretch, recall how the paramilitary romance fuses masculine and national identity through apocalyptic narratives that align antigovernment sentiment with protecting the family. Moreover, although the immediate catalyst of the paramilitary romance was national defeat in Vietnam, the work of historian Paul Boyer suggests that the post-1960s New War genre draws on the articulation of antigovernment and antiurban sentiment in post-WWII popularizations of apocalyptic prophecy writing. This genre imagined the impending apocalypse in terms of urban disintegration; it coupled racialized images of a fragmenting social fabric ("all the ooze of primitive man emerging," as one text put it) with a deep suspicion of government officials, who were represented as lulling the people into slumber.[83] Dobson's call for a national culture war to defend the family draws on this mythic geography of urban apocalypse: Middle American Radicals must take this country back from an effeminizing government that attacks the family because it lacks the courage to discipline the urban/dark masses. As I argued in chapter 5, a similar poetics of control undergirds the militia narrative: portraying militias as a natural extension of your neighborhood block watch, militia leaders prepare for the day the federal debt becomes so large that the government can no longer fund welfare and inner cities erupt, just as Los Angeles erupted after the Simi Valley verdict.[84]

Both Peters and Dobson biblicize this mythic geography, framing contemporary concerns within the biblical masterplot that imagines body, home, and nation as temples in need of cleansing. Much like the antebellum cult of domesticity, both Peters and Dobson sacralize the family to speak class fears while denying the structural nature of economic inequality. By romanticizing the private realm as a brake on capitalism's cold-

184 / *Lift High the Cross*

hearted search for profit, the Right's postmodern cult of domesticity enables people to authorize market discipline as morality-inducing. Key to this popular authorization of the market is the mediating discourse of religion, which speaks both private values and public heritage. By identifying supremacist religion with the nation, the Right's postmodern sacralization of the family promises that waging a culture war against the secular humanist elites who control the government and popular culture will bring morning again to America.

The catalytic event through which Peters has sought to spin the Christian right's politics of homestead exclusivism into an overtly white supremacist politics is the death of Vicki and Samuel Weaver at the hands of government officials in Ruby Ridge, Idaho. This event, along with Waco, galvanized militias into a grassroots movement that was capable of bridging the white supremacist and the Christian right. To conclude this chapter, I explore the underlying cultural conditions from which Ruby Ridge derived its ability to galvanize by investigating how Peters articulated Ruby Ridge within privatism's mythic geography of urban apocalypse.

In October 1992, Peters convened a weekend-long meeting in Estes Park, Colorado, to strategize response to Ruby Ridge and thereby to bring together the diverse sections of the right-wing continuum: from neo-Nazis, Christian Identity believers, and tax protestors to Second Amendment advocates and antiabortion activists.[85] Peters opened his keynote speech by proclaiming: "I'll not ask you how you are. I'll ask you how your families are: your wives, sons and daughters. I'm pleased to report to you that my family is fine, and by the grace of God Almighty I'm gonna see to it that they stay fine the best I can. . . . There is a man tonight whose family is not fine. His wife is dead. She had her head blown off with a large-caliber missile from a high-caliber rifle while she was standing at the door of her home holding her baby in her arms. Her son was killed before that. . . . We can't agree on His name. We don't agree on a Bible translation, on the day of rest, but by the God of Abraham we agree that you don't murder our wives and our children! And that's why we're here."[86] By invoking the family, Peters also excluded the possibility of responding to the FBI and BATF through withdrawal from mainstream society. Instead, he reads Ruby Ridge through the lens of the paramilitary romance: male honor requires you to defend your own against all comers—including the government.

As always, Peters biblicizes contemporary events, styling his keynote as a

The Romance of Privatism / 185

Bible study of Judges 19–21. These closing chapters in Judges are the last of a series of stories that narrate the chaos alleged to have characterized those bygone days "when there was no king in Israel" (19:1). Judges offers a retrospective justification for why the twelve tribes united under one king. Although the book's overt concern is the public politics of nation formation, the stories hinge on sexual and gender norms, for it is through such private sexual politics that the nation becomes God's Temple. In this imaginary, bodies take central stage: male bodies, female bodies, the contaminating bodies of others, the body of the king—all make visual the imaginary (because collective) body called the nation.[87]

This particular narrative begins as a man from one of the northern priestly tribes, the Levites, journeys south to collect his woman,[88] who had returned to her father's house. While journeying homeward, the two are given shelter in Gibeah by an aged kinsman. "As they were making their hearts merry," local men knock at the door and demand, "Bring out the man who came into your house, that we may know him" (19:22). Refusing, their host offers his virgin daughter; when the men remain unappeased, the Levite pushes his woman out the door. The next morning, when the Levite opens the front door to journey homeward, "Behold: there was his concubine lying at the door of the house, with her hands on the threshold" (19:27). Upon returning home, the Levite dismembers the woman's body into twelve parts, sending them "the length and breadth of Israel" (19:29). Confronted with her dismembered body parts, the twelve dispersed tribes "arise as one man" and form a militia.

Unlike his reading of Hosea's marriage metaphor, Peters does not narrate this story to sanction its violence. A gap opens here as Peters pushes away a biblical text that is too violent for him. It's as if the text reveals the limit of what society can see about itself: the disorder at the heart of this patriarchal order, the violence at the heart of culture. If the nation is a temple that must be kept clean by such sacrifices, perhaps the cost is too high.

Peters contains this potential crisis by denouncing the Levite: "Far as I'm concerned he wasn't much of a man. It's because of him that she's dead to begin with. He's no hero to me."[89] In Peters's reading, the cure for the violence against women through which men bond to form the patriarchal nation lies in being *more* of a man, not less—close, but not too close:

186 / *Lift High the Cross*

remember what the men wanted. Sounding like Dobson in *Children at Risk,* Peters warns that an invisible war is being waged against Christians without their knowledge:

> There seems to be a war out there. A lot of people aren't concerned about this little boy who lay lifeless in the dirt and a wife who drops her baby to the floor because they were nothing more than white supremacists. Well, my wife is white and my son is white and they are not just some cheap, lousy white supremacists! And I love them. And I know that man loved his wife and his sons. They have got some great white hunters turned loose. They shoot two [obscure] and they shoot does and they'll keep shooting until we say enough is enough. When Herod went marching into town to kill all those babies, I've often wondered, how could you do that? . . . It had grown to the point that they could do whatever they want. And if we let this get by, it'll grow to that point and they can do whatever they want.[90]

Note how Peters seeks to produce bonds among feuding factions of the right-wing continuum by reiterating the focalization of the biblical text. Behold: standing just before the door of her home, she falls—only here the mute cry of the silent hands takes voice in the cry of the baby who tumbles out of Vicki Weaver's arms. Much as Dobson represents Christians as the new minority targeted for annihilation by the secular humanist state, the official report issued by the Estes Park meeting charged the government with targeting the Weaver family for "trespass, military aggression, oppression and genocide" because of their Christian Identity beliefs.[91] Elsewhere, Peters indicts the "reversed perspective" that talks incessantly about family values but criminalizes Identity Christians who take a stand to protect their right to live their religious beliefs within their own homes and to teach their children to do the same.

The symbolic power of Ruby Ridge, then, lies in the way it provided proof that "the system" will kill those who resist. Peters illustrates this in a trio of cartoons that restage the primal scene of familial endangerment. The first cartoon is captioned "An Inside Look at the Workings of a White Supremacist Gang (as reported by the media)." The cartoon depicts a band of marauding Indians doing a war dance with weapons held high. Behind them we see a log cabin. Mother and father lie face down in the dust with arrows in their backs while their baby cries. Inside the cartoon frame, printed in reverse, reads the following: "In the 1800's, when savages attacked white Christian settlers and killed mother and child, it was called *A Massacre!*"

The second cartoon repeats the same scene. The house is now a wooden frame house, but the pioneer family remains unchanged: mother and father dead on the ground as their baby wails. The caption reads: "In the 1930's, when the KGB and the Red Guard rounded up and killed Christian dissidents, it was called *A Communist Purge* and *Bolshevik Terror!*"

The third cartoon depicts the same scene: wooden home, pioneer family murdered in the dust. Over their bodies stand two burly men, one wearing a BATF and the other an FBI jacket, who high-five each other as helicopters and tanks dot the mountain landscape. The caption reads: "In 1992, federal marshals and other government agents, in the process of rounding up alleged white supremacist Randy Weaver, killed his wife and son. This is called *Justice, U.S.S.A. Style!*"[92]

Framing Ruby Ridge, the frontier family, and the cold war family within the same visual thematic asserts the transhistorical nature of this duel. Over and over again, the white Christian family finds itself under attack: first Indians, then communists, and now its own government. Peters proclaims this duel as the "hidden" meaning of the nation's history and heritage: white Christian men exercising their right to protect their own, a right they were given by God in the First and Second Amendments.

Reframing Dobson's soft-sell identification of the desire for a Little House on the Prairie as our nation's cultural heritage, Peters seeks to unify the Right by articulating a rural version of the Christian right's politics of homestead exclusivism. Consider, for example, Peters's involvement with the county rule movement, which forms one segment within the overlapping groups and individuals associated with militias.[93] The place most often named as the birthplace of county rule is Catron County, New Mexico. Seventy-five percent of Catron County is federally owned land, including the Gila National Forest, where most of the county's ranchers graze their herds. In 1990, Catron County passed an ordinance that declared it a criminal offence for federal employees to enforce any environmental law that conflicts with land-use plans as devised by the county. Similar ordinances have passed in over one hundred western counties. The ordinance is part of the invented tradition of constitutional fundamentalism (see chapter 5). Advocates cite as precedent the National Environmental Policy Act, which stipulated that the preservation of important aspects of national heritage must be considered when environmental laws are enacted. According to county rule attorney James Catron:

> The feds were managing us out of existence. So we began reading laws and regulations and found that the law protects our local customs and culture and economic base. Our custom is we believe in the value of production. It is our cultural use of the land to mine, timber, hunt, fish, and graze.
>
> Eighty percent of the people in Catron County have Scots-Irish last names. The Scots-Irish were a warrior people, at home on the frontier, a warrior race too wild for the civilized East. So they were pushed to the frontier, where they confronted the Indians, who they understood, because they were another warrior people. They'd kill or marry the Indians, made no difference, any way you could pacify them. That's our customs and our culture.[94]

Such views are not in the minority in Catron County. Of the county's 2,500 inhabitants, 300 came to the first militia meeting. Nancy Brown, age seventy-two, explained why she attended: "We're organizing to defend against all enemies, domestic and foreign. We feel we need to protect our property rights." According to County Commissioner Hugh McKeen: "We're trying to keep our livelihood and our homes here. The federal government wants us out of here in a moment. They want complete authority. . . . My ancestors had to fight Indians, and several of them died to settle this county. You're looking at the same people who settled this place. We're still here, and we're willing to fight."[95]

Reared on a ranch and a former ranch hand himself, Peters endorsed county rule: "They made the U.S. Constitution a county ordinance, forcing the feds to obey it while in their county."[96] In October 1994, Peters delivered the opening address at a United Nations flag-burning held at the Catron County courthouse in which he endorsed militias by setting them in an apocalyptic frame that likened the fire that set the UN flag aflame to the fire in Revelation 20:9 that devours the forces of Satan that surround the camp of the saints and the beloved city: "I say unto you, that little spark that ignited that UN flag was just a little spark. We must not let that fire go out. We must let it grow, turn it into a conflagration that the entire world will know who is God and who His people are. The United States of America must take the lead. . . . The whole world is watching us, waiting to

The Romance of Privatism / 189

see what we, as Christian patriots, are going to do. They are waiting. Patiently. Because how we respond to this entire issue, including the Second Amendment rights, is how they will go. If we go down, they will go down immediately following. It is up to the United States of America to keep the country, to keep the world, free." Once again, Peters practices politics as performance: praying that militias be the spark that catalyzes God's promise in 2 Chronicles 7:14 that if people repent He will heal the land. After invoking this text, he beseeches, "You, Father, please bring about that fire which you promised you would send . . . and return our land to a peaceful Christian Republic."[97]

It's as if Ruby Ridge offers proof that modern society usurps both divine Providence and each man's right to protect his family and assert supremacy in his home—and in so doing fuses the F/father indelibly. All the hierarchies (divine/human, male/female, parent/child, U.S./world) interlock to close the gap between penis and Phallus, men and Real men— and thereby resurrect power as innocent. In this monotheistic imaginary, believing in Christ as King entails enshrining each man's home as his castle and therefore defending one's honor. The sanctity of one is coproduced through, as, and by the sanctity of the other. And both hinge on protecting the sanctity of one's women.

Although Dobson and Peters frame their battle against the government in terms of biblical memories that attack Canaanites and defend monotheistic fidelity, this battle can also be framed in terms of Foucault's insight into the nature of modern power. Rather than being embodied in the king who issues laws backed by the threat of death, power in modern societies takes effect most strongly through bureaucratic governments that regulate the production of life. Foucault called this biopower, "distributing the living in the domain of value and utility."[98] The government still prohibits certain acts as unlawful, but its primary way of exercising power is through promoting norms, practices, and identifications that facilitate economic growth. This promotion requires "a form of surveillance, of control as watchful as that of the head of the family over his household and his goods." As the discursive means through which the West envisioned the specifically modern exercise of power, "the family" is no mere metaphor but a crucial technology by which modern power is produced and exercised.[99]

Earlier, we saw how the California tax revolts galvanized Middle American Radicals from the suburbs by articulating a sensibility that fused protecting private property with protecting the family homestead. Similarly, Christian Constitutionalist movements such as county rule draw on the legacy of privatism to galvanize Middle American Radicals from rural areas by articulating cultural memories regarding a man's sacred duty to protect the family homestead. Although Peters had vainly hoped that the Estes Park meeting would catalyze the Right into a united front (as ancient Israel had been catalyzed in Judges 19–21) by mimetically enacting "the Law" that he finds written in this text, the failure of his performative theology to change the governmental institutions of this country should not blind us to the power of the cultural sensibility being produced here. In other words, although Peters's hopes of performatively catalyzing the kingdom have continually failed to produce the institutional changes of which he dreams, change can also come through a cultural sensibility, especially one that has the potential to bridge the white supremacist and the Christian right through a shared ideology of privatism.

Yet, although Peters is interested in constructing convergences, he must also articulate divergences to appeal to his primary constituency. Dobson glosses privatism with prosperity theology; Peters adopts a different religious idiom. In "White Crime in America," which Peters appended to *America the Conquered* to discuss Ruby Ridge, he proclaims that, without Jesus Christ, the Anglo-Saxon race is "nothing more than ungodly, Baal-worshipping white trash." But with Christ and touched by His Blood, they are "once again free men."[100] His constituents look down the class ladder and see where they will be if they slip: nothing more than white trash. They look up the ladder and see where they want to be but are not: free men. This middling position is simultaneously about reality and phantasms. It is about being perched on an edge where the ground under your feet is actually a rung on a class ladder, where you stand just one small slip from the trash you fear you are. By sacralizing the family, Peters enables people to protest—and thereby retain their reality—yet still identify up the class ladder rather than down. Here, religion "stands in the gap" that Peters's class protest threatened to open. Together, religion and the family speak class fears at the same time that they deny the existence of class as a meaningful division in society by voicing class as original sin. We are none righteous, no, not one. We might have nothing, but with Christ we are not nothing.

The Romance of Privatism / 191

In Peters's narration of militias, the pain of economic embattlement, its deep disappointment, is eased through pride in being "free men," where freedom is made visible and tangible through the bodies of one's family. This pride is about class. It is also about male honor: how class is lived and embodied, performed and acquired, through disciplined behavior— above all, through the "respectability" of one's family, where respectability is put at risk first and foremost through sexuality. This pride is also about religion: how religion offers respectability through identity forged around God, race, sex, and generations. In this imaginary, sexual purity offers the proper issue around which Real men unite and bond.[101] In exchange for not joining hands with those a rung below themselves, men gain a respectability that is secured through the family and a sense of private freedom that is lived as proprietorial desire.

Peters concludes, "LET THIS BE A LESSON TO THE FEW SURVIVING WHITE PEOPLE IN AMERICA. All of you are potential sinners of the same sort as the Weaver gang. Sin can enter anyone's lives but these white sins or crimes that the Weavers thought they could commit and get by with are particularly peculiar to white people. Be honest, white man, haven't you at times fantasized about owning your own little home free and clear, getting your children away from bad influences and haven't you at times wanted to be separate, that is with your own kind?"[102]

"Be honest, white man." With these words, Peters speaks to the coded silences that circulate through and around contemporary discussions of "family values": owning your own home, protecting your children, and living among people like yourself. By appealing to masculinity, both its sacrality and its obviousness, Peters represents white supremacy as simple common sense: no violent abrogation of law but lawful submission to God. Not rebellion but the preservation of a national heritage. In so doing, he represents the desire for white supremacy as the simplest and most natural of desires, one rooted in a man's desire for a family of his own. This is Peters's bridge.

Conclusion

9 The Bowl, the Crossing Point, and the Moment After

Seeing the Bowl

Postcolonial critic Gayatri Spivak compares the margins of society with the margins of an ancient text. In both cases, she says, the margins are where the arguments are.[1] Studying the Right, listening to the argument in these margins, is to hear mainstream America talk to itself, interpellate itself, reproduce itself anew: as white, as male, as middle-class, as Protestant, as straight, as innocent.

Analyzing the countermemories disseminated across these two sociologically diverse sectors of the Right (symptomatized in the ministries of Scriptures for America and Focus on the Family) reveals that the path that leads some to right-wing "extremism" crosses through mainstream America. There it often vanishes, disappearing in and as our highest religious ideals; our notions of national identity and supremacy; our norms for gender and sexuality; our cultural geography of race and class, written in the spatial arrangements of our suburbs and cities; our hope that in America one can be innocent again—and if not us, then our children. Listening to the silences that speak amid these hopes and fears, methinks we, like Virgil Griffin proclaiming "I'm not in this organization for me. I want to win rights for that little boy right there," protest too much.

Noting that such protestations make her wonder just what it is that Americans are so insistently innocent of, Toni Morrison observes that as a result of the nation's historical emergence in such intimate association with race, "American" means white, so that others add hyphen after hyphen in an effort to hear/speak/see themselves in this overtly race-neutral word. As she explains: "Statements to the contrary, insisting on the meaninglessness of race to American identity, are themselves full of meaning. The world does not become raceless and will not become unracialized by assertion. . . . Pouring rhetorical acid on the fingers of the black hand may indeed destroy the prints, but not the hand. *Besides, what happens in that violent, self-serving act of erasure to the hands, the fingers, the fingerprints of the one who does the pouring? Do they remain acid-free?*"[2]

Studying the Right with an eye to its memory-work suggests otherwise. For the silences from which conservative countermemories draw their power are not symptomatic of some monolithic Unspeakable buried deep within contemporary culture. Rather, these silences are ordinary and manifold but mostly unremarked on, a string of everyday unsaids dispersed across the surface of discourse, available to be mobilized by conservative countermemories into an in-your-face ignore-ance that blares and obscures by its very visibility. The power of such silences is structural, but not abstract. Such silences transcend individual intention, yet their power is intimate. Reflecting on the pervasive presence of Africans in American literature, Morrison concludes:

> As a writer reading, I came to realize the obvious: the subject of the dream is the dreamer. . . . It requires hard work *not* to see this. It is as if I had been looking at a fishbowl—the glide and flick of the golden scales, the green tip, the bolt of white careening back from the gills; the castles at the bottom, surrounded by pebbles and tiny, intricate fronds of green; the barely disturbed water, the flecks of waste and food, the tranquil bubbles traveling to the surface—and suddenly I saw the bowl, the structure that transparently (and invisibly) permits the ordered life it contains to exist in the larger world. . . . What became transparent were the self-evident ways that Americans choose to talk about themselves through and within a sometimes allegorical, sometimes metaphorical, but always choked representation of an Africanist presence.[3]

By waging culture war on the terrain of popular memory, the Right seeks to shape the manner in which this not quite not-present absence is articulated. Listen to the Right and you hear mainstream cultural memories construct intelligibility and legitimacy by stigmatizing a domain where people, places, and things can be deemed not worth caring about— abject. You hear a culture reimagine itself into being through memories that ward off loss, insisting on same-as-me-ness as a precondition for intimacy, stipulating the suspension of disbelief as a prerequisite for true belonging—as if faithfulness requires us to idealize the arms in which we rest as innocent, as if trust were an all-or-nothing game. And you can hear this cultural imaginary's unspoken underside: how idealization demands the discipline of normalization, a discipline that requires us to hold others and ourselves at bay: close, but not too close. It takes hard work not to hear this.

In the preface, I suggested that beneath its arguments and evidence and thesis statements, this book circles an empty space: those "unspeakable things unspoken" away from which we strive to move with all our might and that nevertheless remain present at every turn because constitutive of bone, marrow, blood.[4] A different kind of kinship, this, and a different type of family: to be held/contained by a structuring principle that both cannot be named and is yet nevertheless an open secret. Nothing is hidden and we all know what is going on, even as—especially when—we turn our heads away. *Not going there.*

What one learns from going there, or what I learned anyway, is the power of memory—and ignorance—as active constructions. Viewing the Right with the power of memory in mind can help make sense of what at first glance seems incomprehensible. How someone can believe that Anglo-Saxons are the literal descendants of the Ten Tribes of northern Israel who carry the sacred memory of Yahweh's law written in their blood's genetic code. How conservative women find liberation in submitting to male "headship." How someone can insist on not associating with, not renting to or hiring, queer people as a religious right. How someone can claim with a straight face that the nation's security rests on the clear and distinct sexual and gender identifications of its children. How a religious person can believe in a racist God.

For although memory is ephemeral, fragile, and fleeting, memory can also be an iron fist in whose grip the most tender and daily intimacies of familiarity and familiality turn into a right-wing body politics that engenders its populist appeal by projecting an imaginary masculine body. Through this imagined body, people can inhabit the nation as an experience of enjoyment, the pleasure of identifying with an ego-ideal by virtue of which one need not resort to force to get what one wants. The Right's countermemories dream this power fantasy as submission to the Father, burying its pleasure underground where it resurrects—only this time as fear, in the form of apocalyptic narratives that interpellate the nation as parents whose children need protection. In the name of protecting the innocence of children, this submission performs violence as compassion: Lift high the cross.

For me, the shock of this crossing point comes from its reversal, from the sense that this could all go another way. Who has not seen love (be it love of a child, partner, community, idea, God) soften someone's edges, open them outward and expand their heart? And who has not been moved by love, to find oneself in that ambiguous space carved out through connection and power where protections and defenses fall away effortless, unneeded and unheeded as leaves? Love can open people beyond imagining, open worlds so unforeseen they seem (as James Baldwin once wrote) another country.[5] Yet, there's the rub: for movement, especially at the limit, can go both ways.

The Limits of a Politics of Resistance

At its heart, this book has been about exploring Morrison's bowl: the power of the cultural violence out of which arise culture and subjectivity, vulnerability and agency. Listening to the Right, what becomes evident is how cultural memory engenders circuitous vectors of approach/avoidance, hope/fear, self-accusation/righteous judgment, and knowledge/ignorance that wheel us around the empty space of cultural violence, and thereby reinscribe the crossing point where "the territorializing power of the state [becomes] invisible—and effective—as the ideality of conscience."[6]

Yet, if the margins are where the arguments are, then fixating on the Right can be a red herring. As stated in the preface, I started this book mostly because it felt impossible not to. Right-wing initiatives constrain my possibilities: as a daughter; as queer; as a feminist; as a teacher, and especially as a teacher of religious studies; as someone committed to children in a culture whose most "cherished myth of child-centeredness . . . conceals the extent to which adult-centeredness had displaced children to the margins of postindustrial consumer society";[7] as someone who struggles with dismantling the taken-for-granted normativity of white middle-class-ness that cripples the communities in which I live and work.

Although this book began by identifying impossibility, it cannot end there. For conclusions are about making commitments. *Been there, done that: now what?* What stands in stark relief at this stage of the process are the manifold ways in which the subject of this dream, too, is the dreamer. Reflecting on the public controversy that surrounded federal funding for the National Endowment for the Arts in the late 1980s and early 1990s, women's studies scholar Miranda Joseph remarks, "I was initially drawn to explore this controversy because, at the time, it was the main site for a mutual obsession of gays with the Christian right and Christians with gays. It seemed to me a counterproductive obsession, insofar as we (gay people) were creating Christians, giving them power by defining ourselves in relation to them."[8]

I certainly know the energy about which Joseph speaks. This transference is part of why I picked this topic, and I trade on its energy when I present my work; it's why people listen. Yet transference has an undertow. I think about the energy that would crackle through the air when I would be at a party with friends, for example, and the conversation would turn to what I was writing about. Isn't that dangerous, people asked, aren't you scared? By the time I was far enough along to be semicoherent about my topic, I was painfully aware that what I found scary came from someplace else. It felt scary to relinquish the comforts that forgetting brings, especially the space to move on. Why risk reinjury?[9] Scary, too, is something I experienced firsthand while doing interviews in Colorado Springs: the simple fact of my attention could strengthen the Right, inflate their importance in their own eyes and those of others. This is a risk that any teacher knows all too well: I cannot control the effects of my words. I feared that my attempt to understand the Right would be misinterpreted as an apologia that sanctions apathy in the name of "fair play." Yet, although my fears centered less on the Right and more on our response to the Right, the energy released by my friends' question, sparking up as it seemed out of nowhere, would spook me. I could never shake it off completely. For this energy does not arise out of nowhere. It evoked how I first felt when I started attending right-wing gatherings. It is the energy of a cultural position.

As such, it is an energy to which we enact complex and circuitous attachments. There are, after all, pleasures to paranoia: the thrill of playing "spy," the sense of eavesdropping incognito and undercover on a culture charged as inaccessible, "other," even dangerous. And always, there is the ambiguity of "passing," an experience that fuses intimacy and knowledge,

The Moment After / 199

love and sexuality, with power and ignorance, distance and blasphemy. Passing shields the pain of people presuming that what you are is not within the pleasure of a secret knowledge that dreams of unmasking their presumption for the ignorance it is. In this voyeuristic fantasy, the pain of disconnection is also its pleasure, for the distancing implicit in such looking whispers the sweet promise of a connection that will not require you to shed invulnerability at the door.

Yet resistance comes with its own vulnerabilities. This is why, though resisting the Right is necessary, it is insufficient alone. As I learned while interviewing, the gaze through which we see the Right can strengthen it, bestowing a power that the Right did not originally have but that it can exercise by citing the image of itself reflected in our eyes. Pete Peters turns our gaze into his power when he boasts about his inclusion—"by name"— in a report issued by Morris Dees's Southern Poverty Law Center. Or when he proudly cites Ted Koppel's description of his Scriptures for America ministry as "the most extreme group in America": "We rejoice over this new honor that has been bestowed upon us and proudly add it to the list right next to 'One of the World's Most Dangerous Men' [which was attributed to Peters by Radio Peace International]." In 1996 promotional materials, Peters concluded his biography by citing these denunciations as part of his credentials.[10]

Likewise, the power of our gaze helped fuel the direct mail campaigns mounted by the Right to end federal funding of the National Endowment for the Arts. Miranda Joseph observes that these direct mail solicitations "incorporated many gay-themed or authored art critical of Christianity (of which there is certainly a significant corpus, much of it responding to 'Christian' antigay attacks by Jesse Helms)."[11] The Right cites these artworks to prove its claim to be a minority community fighting to protect its First Amendment rights from the encroachments of feminists, gay liberationists, and multiculturalists. At the same time, however, the Right also cites these works to authorize itself as speaking for the national majority, to represent its authoritarianism as populism and thereby portray its politics as innocent, as not "politics" really, simply an attempt to protect those specific folkways, commonsense values, and shared-origin narratives that constitute "Americanness."

More generally, if memory and ignorance constitute acts, then rearticulating the terms of this argument cannot be a formula: resist silence with speech and ignore-ance with visibility. The self-evidence of these identifications only misleads. For whereas silences can be performed by holding one's tongue, silence can also be instituted no less effectively by means of a torrent of words that fill the air space so that no other voices can get a word in edgewise. (Think of the presidential elections or the "debate" regarding welfare reform.) Likewise, ignorance is often performed as a refusal to see (as when the Right closes its eyes to the violence enacted by its exclusionary identification with "America's heritage"). Yet ignore-ance can also be instituted through investing certain figures with hypervisibility. (Is the attention that surrounds the mythic mannish lesbian or the African American crack user really about helping us see them? And what about the success with which Bill Clinton's ability to evoke black styles and cultural responses has obscured the willingness of these New Democrats, time and again, to sacrifice their African American constituency to woo Reagan Democrats "who had fled what renowned funk musician George Clinton termed 'chocolate cities' to seek refuge in what he called 'vanilla suburbs'?")[12]

Nevertheless, when I feel the pressure of a massive silence (enacted with or without words) or the weight of a gaze that refuses to see, it is hard to resist the inside/out dichotomy that identifies silence/invisibility as "bad" and speaking out/visibility as "good." This dichotomy is especially powerful because not resisting, not speaking, and not being visible are not answers either. It's just that, in and of themselves, these answers are not enough. I feel this sense of "not enough" when opening the direct mail solicitations from progressive organizations that turn up in my mailbox, even though I understand the scare rhetoric of the genre and even though I sympathize with the tendency to up the volume in a world where too few seem to hear. Yet I am troubled by the stalemate that arises as both sides become mirror images, representing each other as "Nazis" and "extremists" with equal abandon, each fostering, feeding, and even cocreating what it seeks to oppose. What troubles me about this dynamic is not that it happens; what troubles me is how, from within, this stalemate feels like motion. When we resist the Right, we move like the fish gliding and careening through the water. Yet such movement is not enough. These fish do not swim freely. For what about Morrison's bowl?

Reinterpreting Similarities:
Failure and the Return of the Repressed

In the case studies, I argued that convergences between sociologically distinct sectors of the Right testify to the power of mainstream silences regarding cultural violence. Likewise, this tendency of both Right and Left to cocreate each other testifies to this self-same power: how cultural memory constitutes, and is reconstituted at, the crossing point where hope turns into fear, love into violence, knowledge into ignorance, and idealization into abjectification.

In reading these dynamics in this way, I am arguing against those analysts who point to the presence of these projections to idealize the American "center." These analysts represent We The People as sharing a consensus (nonideological, nonpartisan) middle way between the agendas and interests that are alleged to drive and blind our culture's extremes, both Right and Left.[13] To my mind, these readings miss how the "bowl" determines and enables—nay, locates—this "center."

In contrast, I read the tendency of Right and Left to mirror each other in the culture wars as symptomatic of how agency emerges in the cultural interstices through, and as, a double-cross. Thus, political theorist Wendy Brown argues, "Initial figurations of freedom are inevitably reactionary in the sense of emerging in reaction to perceived injuries or constraints of a regime from within its own terms. Ideals of freedom emerge to vanquish their imagined immediate enemies, but in this move they frequently recycle and reinstate rather than transform the terms of domination that generated them. Consider exploited workers who dream of a world in which work has been abolished, blacks who imagine a world without whites, feminists who conjure a world either without men or without sex, or teenagers who fantasize a world without parents." Brown goes on to suggest that ideals of freedom cross themselves in this way, in their very first impulse, because of "freedom's relation to identity—its promise to address a social injury or marking that is in itself constitutive of identity."[14]

After all, the glance through which we view the Right is not happenstance. Implicit in this gaze are self-images, structured through and as memories of loss. Through this gaze we renegotiate these memories, producing an imaginary ego body for ourselves (and therefore, by default, for the Right as well). And we produce another body, too, one for the relationship itself, the space in which we meet: Morrison's bowl.

It is these multiple bodies and the losses they re-member, this desire for self-assertion and the very promise of freedom, that keep us focused on the fish, the castles, the flecks of waste and food. For even when the vision through which we see the Right empowers us, even when this vision helps us resist by refusing to see ourselves as they do, the way we see the Right can *still* re-create and re-fuse our own identification with and emotional attachment to places of wounding—through the very process of refusing. This is the performative power of memory: how culture embeds possibility and impossibility within one another, as distinct vectors out of whose opposition curvature arises: a sense of being held, a sense of being contained.

The point in calling attention to this crossing point where the desire for freedom vanishes into an attachment to our own subjection is not, as Brown herself notes, the small-minded goal of unmasking hypocrisy by revealing internal contradictions. I assume that no one stands apart and aloof, untouched and untainted, by the cultural violence from which these arguments draw their power. The point in noting these contradictory vectors is to unfix our gaze so that the empty spaces that mark our losses and abjections do not wheel us around quite so much, and we become free to take up their energies toward different ends. When freedom is conceived as this kind of project, the goal is not to get clear of this empty space. Who could? For this empty space is structural. Hence, the task is to use it lest we be used by it.

For example, I think of how much my own identification as queer comes from rejecting the limits that "the traditional family" placed on my mother. For me, being queer is in large part about repudiating heterosexual culture: its ways of loving, and what these meant for women. I wanted to do love and gender differently, and wanted a community that desired such difference. Clearly, in feminist and queer communities of the 1980s these repudiations returned, often in painful and conflicted ways. More than that, though, I seek these repudiations out, shaping relationships that move into the interstices between categories and cite gender back; entering into, disentangling, and reconfiguring its terms; proliferating genders to engender ambiguity, and desiring the ambivalence itself.[15] For identities are formed in this interstice, through negotiating loss. Given that the repressed returns, its return can be seen not as evidence of hypocrisy or political failure, but as the moment of commitment: the moment that moves us past the edge where what we have been fails us and we glimpse another terrain. The return of such repudiations can be the condition of the forward motion we seek—if we take them as such.

Similarly, my friend Kelly Jarrett argues (often, admittedly, to my amazement) that her feminist identifications arise in part out of her rejection of religious fundamentalism, noting with irony how fundamentalism has shaped her cultural feminist ideals and politics in limiting and yet also empowering ways.[16] Miranda Joseph notes a similar pattern of repudiation in gay identity. Reflecting on the many testimonials of conversion from Christian to gay that she heard while interviewing participants in the NEA debates, Joseph writes, "These conversion narratives suggest the mutual incompatibility, if symmetry, of gayness and Christianity, but also an extraordinary intimacy."[17]

Such "conversion" or repudiation/emergence narratives are not to be read only literally. These narratives are also speech acts, technologies by which people produce themselves as a certain sort of subject. Crucial to this production is renarrating loss from the inside/out, becoming somebody. In her analysis of gay coming-out narratives, anthropologist Kath Weston reminds us that, as narratives, these accounts follow genre conventions. There are certain ways you tell a coming-out story that make it recognizable to others and to yourself as a coming-out story. Most notably: out of the country, into the big city.[18] Perhaps: out of a certain sort of "church" religiosity, and into the community. And ultimately: out of the closet, and into pride. Comments cultural critic Sally Munt:

> Coming out into the modern Gay and Lesbian Movement we have celebrated a rubric of pride. Outside, in this context, meant claiming a place in society. Inside carried the connotations of the closet, as a prison of shame. The lesbian inside/outside structure is characterized by this *affect*—the binary opposition of shame/pride. Pride is dependent on shame; pride is predicated on the—sometimes conscious—denial of its own ostracized corollary, shame. . . . Its counterpart of shame is no more (or less) real—it is not a deeper truth—but equally it is a consequence of social locution. . . . Shame is a foundational moment in lesbian identity,

and, I am arguing, in butch/femme identity. Like most psychic structures its pattern is to repeat. We interminably reconstitute our lesbian pride out of shame. (Perhaps we need to reconsider Judith Butler's claim that the origin of gender identity resides in melancholy.) By addressing shame we can reforge the bond, not with the original parent, nor with the symbolic blaming parent—social opprobrium—but with each other. This *is* a survival issue: we can actively learn to forget the pain, panic and apathy of shame. The aim is not to magically commute shame into pride but to revision shame as facilitating a kind of agency or motility.[19]

One alternative to a magical thinking that seeks to get as far from shame as we can—pride being our communal version of not going there—is what I in the preface termed a politics of grief. For if the place of wounding is also the place where we come into social being, then identity (and identity politics) is structured through this two-handed gesture by which we re-narrate loss: haunted by repudiations even as we transform these conditions of impossibility into conditions for possible action. Turning inside/out is, it seems to me, just how identities work—and fail to work. To my mind, that failure is not a bad thing. To the contrary, it is a necessary precondition. Particularly given the formation of our primary identities as consumer and taste preferences through the production of images both in the psychoanalytic sense—fantasy and desire, ego ideals and identifications—as well as in the collective sense: the nation as an imagined community, religious identity, and identity-based politics.

Disjoining a Sense of Home from a Politics of Protectionism

The preceding chapters have argued that the Right's crossing point is children—or more exactly, adult images that idealize children as embodying the very possibility of futurity for both individuals and the nation. The Left's crossing point might well be "community," an ideal that, like children, is also imagined in relation to loss, and thus is "almost always invoked with a halo over it."[20] Much as Munt urges us to revision the traces of shame implicit in narrating lesbian identity through "pride," so Joseph urges the Left, and especially gay people, to examine how our identification with the image of "community" supports the underlying conjunction of forces on which the culture war floats. Analyzing the public debate that surrounded funding the NEA, Joseph concludes that both Right and Left ended up promoting the emerging regime of global capital (a "bowl" if there ever was one)—and did so (despite the fact that both sides also sought to shore up the power of the nation-state) precisely by representing their claims through the image of "community."

Our usual cultural common sense associates capitalism with pulling people away from tight-knit rural communities and into urban work spaces that are characterized by individual alienation rather than communal connection. Joseph draws on geographer David Harvey to argue that capitalism must also manufacture communities and community identification as part and parcel of commodity production. According to Harvey, at the dawn of industrial capitalism, the bourgeoisie had to "invent a tradition of community" simply "to keep the urban pot from boiling over." Later, in Fordist regimes of capital accumulation, which saw the introduction of mass production, communities were necessary not only to subvert class antagonisms but also to consume the goods produced. Henry Ford made this connection quite explicit when he started mass-producing Model Ts on an assembly line and paying white men $5 a day so that they could eventually afford to buy one.[21]

This interest in producing community is accelerated in today's post-Fordist economies, in which service and information dominate as primary sectors of production (and whose strategic, incipient, and emergent character is marked by the "post" prefix: we know not yet where this will go). Such regimes depend on production and consumption being localized, flexible, and niched. Thus, the highest profits are made by producing, not a mass consuming class as in Fordism, but a consuming class segmented into specialized market niches, a.k.a. communities. As a result, Joseph argues:

> Community is the raw material for the narrative machine that churns out American individuals, participants in a national economy and political space. . . . To participate in a community in the United States is to participate in a group with certain standardized features, such as businesses—bars, bookstores, restaurants and foodshops, and small-scale manufacturing—and often more importantly, voluntary associations—churches, schools, arts organizations, lobbying groups, and employee associations—that are frequently organized as governmentally regulated

and state sanctioned not-for-profit corporations. Subjects are produced whose reasonable behavior—such as voluntary cooperation in interest group organizations—marks them for inclusion in the mainstream. If the state can persuade newly emergent and potentially dangerous social forces to constitute themselves as communities, it can also provoke interpellation into an assimilation narrative and thus generate subjects who are not only members of a discrete group but are also or primarily individuals in U.S. society, interested in preserving rather than reforming or deforming the nation and capitalism.[22]

Occurring within a regime that is predicated on the proliferation of communities, the culture wars helped assimilate conservative Christians as well as gays and lesbians—both outsider identities—by fostering organizing practices that produced "communities" whose conflicting identifications and ideologies differentiate diverse markets. In such a regime, pluralism becomes a way for the nation-state to discipline and manage this segmented market, and thus to construct for itself a new legitimation narrative. As I argued in chapter 8, the public good "is now negotiated or partnered in the triangle of government, the corporate sector, and civil society. It makes no sense to speak of public and private, for they have been pried open to each other in this triangulation."[23] In this transitional borderland, governments advance their own claims by citing their ability "to further the growth and strength of global capital."[24]

In chapter 8, I argued that the suburban family was produced as a mechanism of ignorance-power that enables us not to see the multiple and overlapping exclusions that conditioned its prosperity. The same is true of queer family, be it the newer sense of "families we choose" or the older sense in which people identified someone as gay by saying "they're family." Insofar as the communities afforded by new social movements are produced (like other commodities) through and as mechanisms of ignorance-power, our identification with these communities enables us not to see those whom globalization positions as not capable of being assimilated, not worth including, and, ultimately, as not really citizens.

Such ignore-ance requires no small amount of discipline. For post-Fordism produces communities that are sharply polarized along class lines. At one end of the service industry spectrum lie gourmet shoppes, patronized by advanced service workers whose knowledge and information-intensive careers earn high wages. The concentration of these high-wage professionals in cities has led to the resurrection of a postmodern version of "the serving classes": residential block attendants, restaurant workers, preparers of specialty and gourmet foods, child care workers, dogwalkers, errand runners, and apartment cleaners.[25] At the other end of this service industry spectrum lies Goodwill, with Wal-Mart somewhere in the middle. Moreover, according to economist Saskia Sassen, this spectrum is bottom heavy. For example, even in global finance, which includes some of the highest paying positions in the service sector, most of the jobs are low-paying, manual, and part time. This is not our image of financial services, for these jobs are usually deemed irrelevant to an advanced information economy. This disregard is enabled by the fact that these jobs are mostly performed by people of color, immigrants, and women. Sassen argues that despite the essential role that these service workers play, the particular ways in which economic globalization is currently being imagined leave them increasingly unable to buy into the post-Fordist promise according to which citizenship is reimagined as belonging to a community of consumers—because they literally cannot "buy" in.[26]

Once again, the point of noting how our commitments to community facilitate and replicate global geographies of power is not to argue that we must forsake the discourse and practice of community—as if we could somehow stand outside this dynamic. Where would such a place be? And who would one be standing there? I write as someone deeply shaped by these communities: they are my home.[27] Yet studying the Right has been a lesson in the importance of disjoining a sense of home from a politics of protectionism. My life has taught me that I do not keep what I love by refusing to risk it—or even by refusing to lose it. To the contrary, such refusals are why resisting the Right is both something that we must do and something itself that we need to resist. Because paradoxes are easily misunderstood, let me spell out more fully what I mean.

Consider how resisting the Right enables us to position ourselves as "truly belonging," as in People for the American Way, for example, or in arguments (such as the one I just cited) that insist that disparaged service workers play an essential role in an advanced economy. Although arguing for inclusion is necessary, it is difficult to walk the delicate line between articulating your argument in ways that communicate and making yourself acceptable. Take, for example, the current mobilization around gay

208 / Lift High the Cross

marriage, which tends to insist that gay people have families—and family values—"just like yours." The price one pays for that ticket is repeating the exclusions and marginalizations that locate the center as such. What about those who do not share the white middle-class privilege that conditions this likeness? What about people whose class position or form of sex-gender identification leaves them with little to gain from the entitlements that accompany marriage?[28] Arguments for inclusion fail us when they are not coupled with practices that critique what we seek to join.

Or consider how resisting the Right enables us to position ourselves as a victim community that the state is pledged to protect (as in hate speech legislation). Rather than unfixing our gaze from the Right and the wounds that hold us there, this self-image tethers us to the empty space of injury all the more tightly by anchoring identification in victimization. This way of navigating loss, much like the countermemories disseminated by Dobson and Peters, acknowledges loss only to ward it off more fully. This focus on injury leads liberation movements such as feminism to speak a moralistic language of accountability that continually reinvolves us in the fantasy of trying to make power answer to truth/morality. Actively ignoring the multiple ways in which our claims, too, embody a will to power, this fixation on injury limits our political desire and vision to punishment (for them) and protection (for us).[29]

Studying the Right with an eye to its convergences makes the insufficiency of this way of negotiating loss all too clear. For the impossibility with which we must grapple is not only the Right but also and primarily the mainstream investments in diverse forms of cultural violence—racism, sexism, homophobia, and classism—from which the Right's counter-memories, and our resistance, engender their power. This interlocking string of silences generates mobile cultural loops of identity—communities—that articulate in complex ways with larger structural shifts associated with globalization. When resisting the Right is not coupled with practices that foster disidentification from these articulations, we forfeit our ability "to generate futures together rather than merely navigate or survive them."[30]

Ultimately, neither negotiation nor survival, punishment nor protection, are what I long for. These longings are hard to talk about, not least because they evoke in me no small quantity of shame. My touchstone is the concrete, day-to-day struggles in which I am actually engaged. This semester, that has meant working with a handful of students to establish a queer-straight alliance as an officially recognized campus group. At a small southern women's college that, until a few years ago, retained institutional links to the North Carolina Baptist Convention and that has historically drawn its students predominantly from small North Carolina towns, this is no small thing—much as I hate to acknowledge this fact. Working on this issue, I have heard more protectionist discourse—from administrators, faculty, students, *myself*—than I ever want to hear again. It is amazing how quickly we go there, and in how many permutations. Mostly what this experience has brought home to me is how much I want—for students, queer and not, for myself. And conversely, how little the available political language speaks to these desires. For I want much more than protection, much more than an academic community that sees itself as "making it safe" to be gay. This vision is too small. But it is also too big. We don't have the power to make it safe for queer students to love, for anyone to love anything: not a lover, a work, a child, an idea, a community, a geographic locale, the world. But love is not about safety. What I want for my students is the tools to love; to be free to take risks and to take the responsibility for self, others, and world that goes along with loving big. Although I hesitate to admit this (for it sounds so middle class, so *soft*), cultivating this responsiveness is what I need most when facing (in my own, very local fishbowl) the sorts of ambiguous interstices and impasses that I have mapped in this book. I want my students to "choose" loving (of whatever kind) and that means choosing it all: including the risk and responsibility, the trying and the failing. Writes Brown, "The pursuit of political freedom is necessarily ambivalent because it is at odds with security, stability, protection and irresponsibility; because it requires that we surrender the conservative pleasures of familiarity, insularity, and routine for investment in a more open horizon of possibility and sustained willingness to risk identity, both collective and individual."[31] I want us to develop the practices necessary to face, walk through, and work with this deep ambivalence. To embrace ambivalence itself as a key moment in this ongoing practice of freedom.

Identities do indeed fall into disidentification on all sides. The moment for politics is not the moment of failure, but the moment after. What happens next? Do we open into that in-between space where identities are both true and not true, absolutely partial and inextricably implicated with (rather than opposing) power? Or do we close?

If studying the Right teaches anything, it teaches that it matters—so much—how we articulate this edge where hopes and fears meet. For it is at this crossing point that religion becomes so frequently involved with violence. In this book I have argued that when we deny the crossing point where people's love for their children, their highest religious ideals and deepest hopes cross into a politics of aggression, exclusion, and fear, we miss how mainstream investments in cultural violence provide the Right's condition of possibility. Yet, such denial is not even necessary.

Take the Right's favorite book. The Bible locates itself quite squarely in the interstices between Israel's religious identity as a chosen people of God and Israel's geopolitical position as a land bridge between continents. This position meant both that the land promised to Israel was inhabited and also that any inhabitants were continually caught in the crossfire of broader imperial conflicts. As a result, biblical texts are crucially concerned with negotiating contradictions between how things ought to be and how things are in an imperfect world where people end up in the wrong place at the wrong time. Hence, the law is given but forgotten. Moses receives the law but never enters the Promised Land—which is promised but never completely given. Hence, too, the suffering wrought by dreams of empire birthed hopes for an end to this world in favor of another kingdom where justice would roll down like water. Yet this law of love has continually been taught by the sword. And scriptural passages promising that the meek shall inherit the earth are used to justify power, presenting the medieval Pope, for instance, as the meekest of servants. This dialectic of contradictions goes on and on—and that, suggests literary critic Regina Schwartz, might be precisely the point.[32]

Even the Bible itself is continually being lost-then-found. We've seen how the injunctions of Deuteronomy are lost until the Temple is restored during the reign of Josiah, when the law is "found again," along with the injunction to remember. Even the tablets of the law that Moses received on

The Moment After / 211

Mount Sinai are dashed to pieces. And there is no triumph on Easter Sunday without death on the old rugged cross. Much depends on how we articulate these persistent gaps, forgettings, and absences.

Sometimes the Bible dismisses these losses as failures, often through metaphors focusing on gender and sexuality; at other times, the Bible represents these failures as necessary. Schwartz calls our attention to the Joseph story in Genesis. When Joseph's brothers recognize the Egyptian official standing before them as their long-lost brother whom they had sold into slavery years ago, Joseph offers the following counsel: "And now, do not be distressed and do not be angry with yourselves for selling me here [into Egypt], because it was to save lives that God sent me ahead of you" (Genesis 45:5).[33]

Joseph's words might be used to efface past memories of abuse and violence, just as Christians once argued that slavery benefited Africans by making it possible for them to attain eternal life. The preceding chapters have provided ample testimony to the persistence of reading strategies that acknowledge the presence of loss only to ward it off more fully— usually by setting different scenes, stories, and characters within an over- arching master narrative that puts everything in the service of a grand providential design, retrospectively recoding "might" into "right."

Yet one can read differently. If the Bible can avow the loss and violence that run through its (and our) memories as death runs through life, then we can put its texts in the service of commitments that do not require us to disavow its (and our) complex entanglement in relations of power and histories of violence. In making this argument, I seek to counter the no- tion that the popularity of fundamentalist religion in the past few decades means that religion must offer clear and unambiguous answers if it is to speak to people today. As my analysis of the Right's memory-work sug- gests, it is precisely this shifting collusion between biblical texts and histor- ical contexts (past, present, and future) that enables the Bible (or any religious tradition) to "speak" to people today. It takes hard work *not* to hear this. Yet, we get lost, I think, in the tangled texture of texts and contexts, experiencing a kind of historical gridlock. For the same text that portrays God as radically on the side of the poor and disadvantaged (sid- ing, for example, with the enslaved Israelites against their Egyptian op- pressors) constructs the identity of those former slaves by scapegoating others, particularly Canaanites and women, as sexually and morally deviant. The same Bible that was used by white Christians not simply to justify an existing slave system but also actively to construct a slave system that hinged on race, was used by black Christians to mandate freedom.[34] Whereas slaves learned to read the Bible as an act of rebellion, white Protestants later insisted on reading that same King James Bible in public schools as a way to exercise hegemony over Catholics.[35] And both these memories of biblical literacy contrast with secular humanist conspiracy theories which hold that America is being punished for the 1962 and 1963 Supreme Court decisions that removed official Bible reading and prayer from public schools. What a roaring.[36]

Yet, if the celebrated postmodern "world without boundaries" is not to isolate people within the most toxic aspects of our histories, then it is not only possible but necessary to read religious traditions like the Bible as resources for hope without fabricating religion into a place where we can stand innocent, aloof, and untouched by the tangled mass of pain we call history.

The problem, in short, is neither religion, nor identities, nor even ideals. The problem is how we *hold* the beliefs, identities, and ideals to which we commit our lives. Given the power of cultural memory, ideals are constituted through aggression, identities are made through hostility, a sense of inside is produced by holding an outside at bay. What matters is less that these dual gestures happen, and more what we do in the moment that opens next.

Walking through this level of ambivalence requires us to go beyond standard clichés, such as: To be inside requires an outside; To know white one must contrast it with black; To experience happiness one must also be acquainted with unhappiness; To recognize form one must contrast definite lines with empty and unbounded space. For when one watches a particular form emerge through relationship with space (I think of the delicate interactions between leaves and wind), then form is no longer only form: for there is no definite bounded form apart from the space through which it constitutes as form.

More to the point: when loss is neither denied nor decried as failure (as in Virgil Griffin's "They are teaching your children to be ashamed of themselves because of slavery"), the task is not to love as if one had never lost—who would want to do that?—but to love without ignoring, excluding, or opposing loss through practices of protection—why play a game

The Moment After / 213

one cannot win? Rather than living the alternation of love and loss, one lives their indistinguishable interconnection. When love includes loss, love itself alters.

Likewise, through seeing how the inside is produced by holding an outside at bay, how we stand inside changes. For precisely as inside, one is called outside oneself to the margins. When one stands inside, rooted where one is but turned out to where one is not, then intimacy and connection do not require familiarity and same-as-me-ness. At the edge of unfamiliarity, two can truly become a multitude. Such is the hope and the fear—but also the power—of working the interstices.

Notes

Preface

1 Wendy Brown, *States of Freedom* (Princeton, NJ: Princeton University Press, 1995), especially chaps. 1 and 3, pp. 3–29 and 52–76.

2 See Randall Styers, *Magical Theories: Magic, Religion, and Science in Modernity,* Oxford University Press, forthcoming.

3 Eric Santner, *Stranded Objects* (Ithaca, NY: Cornell University Press, 1990).

4 Jeffrey Kaplan and Leonard Weinberg. *The Emergence of a Euro-American Radical Right* (New Brunswick, NJ: Rutgers University Press, 1998), 67.

5 Minnie Bruce Pratt, *Rebellion* (Ithaca, NY: Firebrand, 1991), 71.

6 Toni Morrison, *Beloved* (New York: Plume, 1987). My reading of *Beloved* owes much to Mae Henderson, "Toni Morrison's *Beloved:* Remembering the Body as Historical Text," in *Comparative American Identities: Race, Sex, and Nationality in the Modern Text,* ed. Hortense Spillers (New York: Routledge, 1991), 62–86. Henderson's discussion of the veil separating the speakable from the unspeakable and unspoken occurs on pp. 63–64.

7 Donna Haraway, *Simians, Cyborgs, and Women* (New York: Routledge, 1991), 192–93. The impossibility and dishonesty of such a position became painfully clear as I began to interview. Due to finding limitations as well as the fact that neither of the leaders on whom I focus currently grants interviews, I spoke with only a select number of individuals on the Christian right. A good interview depends on establishing personal relationships, yet in this situation, personal relationships collided with clear communication; even points of agreement were not common ground because we meant different things by the same words. The biggest point of miscommunication involved a standard problem in ethnography: the researcher does not see things the way informants do. As I interviewed people in Colorado Springs, the miscommunications caused by different understandings of academic research became particularly apparent in regard to Amendment 2. (A statewide ballot initiative that declared the inclusion of sexual orienta-

tion in antidiscrimination legislation unconstitutional, Amendment 2 was passed by 53.4 percent of the Colorado electorate in 1992 but overturned as unconstitutional by the Supreme Court. See Did Herman, *The Antigay Agenda* [Chicago: University of Chicago Press, 1997], 147.) Those I interviewed assumed I would either simply present their view of Amendment 2 as not bigotry but truth, or rebut their arguments for Amendment 2. I saw my function as not proving the truth or falsity of Amendment 2, but exploring how a religious countermemory enables people to see Amendment 2 as compassionate and just. This way of framing the problem was interpreted as betrayal by the people I interviewed, for it meant I was not simply describing their views. Yet I interpreted their understanding of objectivity as a betrayal of why I do this work, and dishonest to boot. As Barbara Herrnstein Smith puts it: "The moment the skeptic understood the believer's position exactly as the believer did, or vice versa, then the difference—the dispute—between them would dissolve. . . . There is an alternative, however, to sheer polemics or blithely self-privileging asymmetry, though it is not, to my mind, either transcendentally guaranteed objectivity or a self-conscious (and, I think, inevitably strained) effort at rigorously symmetrical representation. It is, rather, something more familiar and mundane (although perhaps sublime enough in its way) . . . [namely,] accurate citation, representative quotation, nontendentious summary, and forbearance from name-calling and motive-mongering": *Belief and Resistance* (Cambridge, MA: Harvard University Press, 1997), xix.

From my point of view, the problem of neutrality goes both ways. I was not neutral because people often granted me interviews based on the fact that I came from Duke University, which they knew as a bastion of political correctness. Most discussions of ethnography stress giving something back in exchange for the knowledge one receives, yet my association with Duke meant that I could not control what I "gave" back. For many, my identity legitimated their views. I could watch my attention strengthen their conviction. There was no place from which to be a neutral observer. For a quite different way of negotiating this paradox, see Susan Harding, *The Book of Jerry Falwell* (Princeton, NJ: Princeton University Press, 2000), especially 33–60.

1 Countermemory, Children, and Ignorance-Power

1 Virgil Griffin, speech delivered at Christian Knights of the Ku Klux Klan rally, Goldsboro, NC, 13 September 1992.

2 Michel Foucault, "Nietzsche, Genealogy, History," in *Language, Counter-*

memory, Practice, ed. Donald Bouchard, trans. Donald Bouchard and Sherry Simon (Ithaca, NY: Cornell University Press, 1977), 139–64. Foucault developed this term as part of a polemic against traditional notions of history that he accused of masking relations of power, sanctifying might as right by framing the past through narratives that celebrate the unbroken continuity of tradition. In contrast, Foucault declared: "Humanity does not gradually progress from combat to combat until it arrives at universal reciprocity, where the rule of law finally replaces warfare; humanity installs each of its violences in a system of rules and thus proceeds from domination to domination. . . . Rules are empty in themselves, violent and unfinalized; they are impersonal and can be bent to any purpose. The successes of history belong to those who are capable of seizing these rules, to replace those who had used them, to disguise themselves so as to pervert them, invert their meaning, and redirect them against those who had initially imposed them; controlling this complex mechanism, they will make it function so as to overcome the rulers through their own rules" (151). Such overcomings are the work of countermemories.

3 Judith Butler, *Gender Trouble* (New York: Routledge, 1990).

4 This romanticization is rooted in the polemic against traditional notions of history that shaped Foucault's coinage of the term countermemory. Yet this critique of Foucault itself owes much to his later work on power, which implies that countermemories cannot exist outside the hegemonic memories they seek to contest, break open, and cut through. Instead, countermemories take shape within mainstream cultural memories that are not monolithic but heterogeneous. Such memories are counter-, not because they are foreign to the mainstream, but because they draw on mainstream currents in order to redirect their flow. See Ann Burlein, "Counter-memory on the Right: The Case of Focus on the Family," in *Acts of Memory,* ed. Mieke Bal, Jonathan Crewe, and Leo Spitzer (Hanover, NH: University Press of New England, 1999), 215–17.

5 My use of "articulation" as a technical term derives from philosopher Louis Althusser. According to Althusser, economic relations form the social base on which proliferate a host of social and linguistic practices and institutions (the ideological superstructures). Although each superstructure acts with a certain degree of autonomy, it also interacts with and is influenced by—that is, articulates with—other ideological superstructures as well as the economic base. These multiple articulations take place in complex and uneven ways. The idea behind Althusser's theory is that social elements do not necessarily or naturally form a unity. Instead, links among diverse social elements must be continually created and are constantly contested. Once established, these links perpetually shift in response to different kinds

of events: not just economic, but also scientific, social, artistic, and religious. As appropriated in cultural studies, articulation calls attention to the historically contingent and variable links that must be forged among diverse discourses, subject positions, institutions, and practices. Rearticulation denotes the social and material processes by which such links are disorganized, reaccented, and repositioned (as when gay folk reclaim the term "queer" or when African Americans proclaim "Black is beautiful").

Articulation and rearticulation are technical terms denoting abstract processes. I use cultural memory and countermemory as a specific subset of the more general terms articulation and rearticulation. All cultural memories are articulations and all countermemories are rearticulations. Yet not all articulations and rearticulations occur on the level of memory.

For articulation, see Louis Althusser, *For Marx,* trans. Ben Brewster (London: Allen Lane, 1969), and *Reading Capital,* trans. Ben Brewster (London: New Left Books, 1970), as well as Ernesto Laclau and Chantal Mouffe, *Hegemony and Socialist Strategy* (London: Verso, 1985). For rearticulation, see Michael Omi and Howard Winant, *Racial Formation in the U.S.* (New York: Routledge, 1986).

6   Audre Lorde, *Sister Outsider* (Trumansburg, NY: Crossing Press, 1984), 110–14.

7   Lawrence Grossberg, *We Gotta Get Out of this Place* (New York: Routledge, 1992), 282–87.

8   Judith Butler, *Bodies That Matter* (New York: Routledge, 1993), 1–23. The term "abject" is adapted from Julia Kristeva, *Powers of Horror,* trans. Leon Roudiez (New York: Columbia University Press, 1982), 1–2.

9   Hazel Carby, *Reconstructing Womanhood* (New York: Oxford University Press, 1987).

10 Lillian Smith, *Killers of the Dream,* rev. and enlarged (New York: Norton, 1961), 83–84; the Oedipus reference is on p. 131.

11 Hazel Carby, *Race Men* (Cambridge, MA: Harvard University Press, 1998), 1–2.

12 Smith, *Killers of the Dream,* 90.

13 Linda Kintz, *Between Jesus and the Market* (Durham, NC: Duke University Press, 1998), 2, 17.

14 Ibid., 7.

15 Butler, *Bodies That Matter,* 1–23.

16 Edward Steichen, *The Family of Man* (New York: Museum of Modern Art, 1955). My attention was drawn to Steichen's exhibit by the analysis in Marianne Hirsch, *Family Frames* (Cambridge, MA: Harvard University Press, 1997), 16.

17 Kath Weston, *Long Slow Burn* (New York: Routledge, 1998), 59.

18 Jennifer Terry traces the history of this tie in modern medicine from the invention of the "homosexual" through the early sexologists to endocrinologists and family therapists in *An American Obsession* (Chicago: University of Chicago Press, 1999).

19 Butler, *Bodies That Matter*, 1–27, 57–91.

20 Kintz, *Between Jesus and the Market*, 81.

21 Teresa Brennan, *The Interpretation of the Flesh* (New York: Routledge, 1992).

22 Butler, *Bodies That Matter*, 205.

23 Kintz, *Between Jesus and the Market*, 217–36.

24 Ariel Dorfman, *Heading South, Looking North* (New York: Farrar, Straus and Giroux, 1998), 49–50.

25 William Chafe, *The Unfinished Journey* (New York: Oxford University Press, 1986), 33.

26 Anne Higonnet, *Pictures of Innocence* (London: Thames and Hudson, 1998), 27, 30.

27 Patricia Williams, *The Alchemy of Race and Rights* (Cambridge, MA: Harvard University Press, 1991), 222; Eve Kosofsky Sedgwick, *The Epistemology of the Closet* (Berkeley: University of California Press, 1990), 3–8.

28 Judith Butler, *Excitable Speech* (New York: Routledge, 1997), 49.

29 Ibid., 50.

30 Richard Hofstadter, *The Paranoid Style in American Politics and Other Essays* (New York: Vintage, 1967).

31 Cornel West, *Prophesy Deliverance!* (Philadelphia: Westminster, 1983), 48. For a summation of these arguments in relation to the contemporary white supremacist movement in the United States, see Abby Ferber, *White Man Falling* (New York: Rowman and Littlefield, 1998), 10–11.

32 Paul Gilroy, *"There Ain't No Black in the Union Jack": The Cultural Politics of Race and Nation* (Chicago: University of Chicago Press, 1987).

33 Judith Butler, *The Psychic Life of Power* (Stanford, CA: Stanford University Press, 1997), 184, 190–91.

34 *The Hymnal 1982: According to the Use of the Episcopal Church* (New York: Church Hymnal Corporation, 1985), 473.

2 Converging Case Studies
Body Politics as Brand Recognition

1 Two additional qualifiers. First, although both ministries are currently located in Colorado, my focus is not meant to imply that the Rocky Mountain State is the national seat of supremacist organizing. Neither ministry fo-

cuses primarily on Colorado; both are national—indeed, international—in scope. My attention was originally drawn to Colorado due to Amendment 2, which has since been overturned by the U.S. Supreme Court. Likewise, the copy-cat amendments that Colorado's initiative spawned in a dozen other states have subsided. Yet the popularity of Amendment 2 raises deeper questions regarding the ability of the Right's long-range movement building to produce a context wherein Amendment 2 could seem not only constitutional but also necessary and even desirable.

Second, my analysis relies primarily on the words of leaders rather than followers. Some reasons for this limitation were stated in the preface. Perhaps the most powerful argument for this focus comes from anthropologist Susan Harding, who locates the power of fundamentalism in the generativity of its Bible-based language, which is "the medium and the ritual practice through which born-again Christians are formed and reformed." After noting that interviews with followers failed to call forth these Bible-based speech codes, Harding justifies her focus on the language of preachers "because preachers are master-speakers. As they teach their language through sermons, speeches and writings and enact its stories in their lives, they mold their church into the Church, a living sequel to the Bible": *The Book of Jerry Falwell* (Princeton, NJ: Princeton University Press, 2000), xi-xiii. Focusing on leaders does not deny the gaps between what leaders say and what followers believe, for the generativity of the former's speech depends on these gaps. As any teacher knows, teaching is an activity that teacher and student perform together; students can refuse to collude and/or can construct alternative lessons that do not necessarily reinscribe the intentions of their teacher. For an analysis which focuses on "Ordinary Evangelicals," see Christian Smith, *Christian America?* (Berkeley: University of California Press, 2000).

2   Sociologists recognize distinctive racist styles in the United States: a dominative (or supremacist) style and an aversive (or separatist) style. See Joel Kovel, *White Racism* (New York: Pantheon, 1970).

3   For the history behind these distinctions as well as reflections on its recent reconfiguration, see George Marsden, *Fundamentalism and American Culture* (Oxford: Oxford University Press, 1980), and *Reforming Fundamentalism* (Grand Rapids, MI: Eerdmans, 1987); Christian Smith, *American Evangelicalism* (Chicago: University of Chicago Press, 1998); and Harding, *The Book of Jerry Falwell.*

4   Coalition for Human Dignity [CHD], "The Covert Crusade," in *The Covert Crusade: The Christian Right and Politics in the West* (Portland: CHD, 1993), 7. Available from CHD, P.O. Box 40344, Portland OR, 97240.

5   Dennis Searles, *Executive News Service,* 4 December 1987, NEXIS.

6 Michel Foucault, *The History of Sexuality,* trans. Robert Hurley (New York: Vintage, 1978), 1:144.

7 My argument here is greatly indebted to the insights of Lawrence Grossberg in *We Gotta Get Out of This Place* (New York: Routledge, 1992).

8 James Dobson and Gary Bauer, *Children at Risk* (Dallas: Word Publishing, 1990), 42.

9 Ibid., viii.

10 Roberto C. Goizueta, *The Coca-Cola Company 1994 Annual Report* (Atlanta: Coca-Cola Company, 1995), 5. Available from The Coca-Cola Company, P.O. Drawer 1734, Atlanta, GA 30301.

11 Ibid., 17. Historians Martin Marty and R. Scott Appleby generalize this point: "Just when the liberal Christian feels comfortable with the church . . . the fundamentalist comes along stressing the doctrine of the birth of Christ to a virgin. . . . Just when modernist Muslims attempt to present Islam as a religious faith that respects human rights and follows due process of law, along comes a regime calling itself Islamic and stoning adulterers, executing impostates and imprisoning dissenters. . . . Just when Zionists establish the state of Israel on secular principles, radical religious Jews raise a hue and cry that the Zionist state is ultimately religious, that it is, in truth, the land promised to Abraham by God in the Torah. *The just when element in this pattern is not accidental, but intentional*": *The Glory and the Power* (Boston: Beacon, 1992), 22–23; emphasis added. Similarly, in one of the earliest studies to explore the significance of the global resurgence of Protestant, Islamic, and Jewish fundamentalisms, Bruce Lawrence writes: "Fundamentalists do not deny or disregard modernity; they protest as moderns against the modern age": *Defenders of God* (San Francisco: Harper and Row, 1989), ix.

12 For the history of this strategy as the source of the distinctively modern style developed in the 1920s and 1930s by U.S. advertisers as the key to success, see Roland Marchand, *Advertising the American Dream* (Berkeley: University of California Press, 1985), xxi, 9. For the idea that cynicism is fundamental to how people get spliced into ideology more generally, see Slavoj Žižek, *The Sublime Object of Ideology* (London: Verso, 1989), especially 28–30. For historical analysis of the crucial role that religion played in pioneering modern pop culture, see R. Laurence Moore, *Selling God* (Oxford: Oxford University Press, 1994), especially 11.

13 The literature on this shift is obviously quite vast. Texts that I have found helpful include Donna Haraway, *Simians, Cyborgs and Women* (New York: Routledge, 1991); David Harvey, *The Condition of Postmodernity* (Cambridge, England: Blackwell, 1990); Jean Baudrillard, *Simulations,* trans. Paul Foss, Paul Patton, and Philip Beitchman (New York: Semiotext(e),

1983); Neil Postman, *The Disappearance of Childhood* (1982; New York: Vintage, 1994); and Saskia Sassen, *Globalization and Its Discontents* (New York: New Press, 1998).

14 Susan Douglas, *Listening In* (New York: Random House, 1999), 5.

15 Miranda Joseph, "The Performance of Production and Consumption," *Social Text* 16, no. 1 (spring 1998): 25–61.

16 Grossberg, *We Gotta Get Out of This Place,* 79.

17 Ibid., 270–71.

18 Ibid., 284.

19 Jacques Lacan, *Ecrits,* trans. Alan Sheridan (New York: Norton, 1977), 1–7; Jane Gallop, *Reading Lacan* (Ithaca, NY: Cornell University Press, 1985); Ruth Leys, "The Real Miss Beauchamp: Gender and the Subject of Imitation," in *Feminists Theorize the Political,* ed. Judith Butler and Joan Scott (New York: Routledge, 1992), 167–214.

20 Judith Butler, *The Psychic Life of Power* (Stanford, CA: Stanford University Press, 1997), 132–98.

3 Mainstream Roots

1 The academic book is James Aho's *Politics of Righteousness: Idaho Christian Patriotism* (Seattle: University of Washington Press, 1990). Jeffrey Kaplan claims that his article in the issue of *Terrorism and Political Violence* devoted to this topic was the first "on the topic of right-wing millennialism to appear in the academic literature." See Kaplan, *Encyclopedia of White Power* (Lanham, MD: Rowman and Littlefield, 2000), regarding his article "The Context of American Millenarian Revolutionary Theology: The Case of the 'Identity Christian' Church of Israel," *Terrorism and Political Violence* 5, no. 1 (spring 1993): 30–82. Examples of journalistic accounts include Kevin Flynn and Gary Gerhardt, *The Silent Brotherhood* (New York: Free Press, 1989); James Ridgeway, *Blood in the Face* (New York: Thunder's Mouth Press, 1990). See also Leonard Zeskind, *The Christian Identity Movement: Analyzing Its Theological Rationalization for Racist and Anti-Semitic Violence* (The Division of Church and Society of the National Council of Churches of Christ in the U.S.A., October 1987).

2 When the dust settled on the media's "discovery" of the world of the radical right through which Timothy McVeigh and Terry Nichols moved, the only reliable link—albeit still tantalizingly ambiguous—connecting Christian Identity to the Oklahoma City bombing concerned Richard Wayne Snell. Born in 1930 the son of a Church of the Nazarene preacher, Snell converted to Christian Identity at a 1981 meeting of the Christian-Patriots Defense

League (where he seems also to have met Peters's associate Jack Mohr). Also early in the 1980s, Snell joined James Ellison's Covenant, Sword and Arm of the Lord, with whom he was involved in a series of robberies and weapons violations. Snell was also involved in attempting to bomb a natural gas pipeline and an electricity transmission tower; both attempts were unsuccessful. Ultimately, Snell was executed on April 19, 1995—the day of the Oklahoma City bombing—for murdering a pawnbroker, Bill Stomp, whom Snell mistakenly believed was Jewish, and for murdering State Trooper Lewis Bryant, who was black. In the years before Snell's execution, his cause was widely publicized in right-wing circles. For example, the newsletter of the Militia of Montana linked Snell's impending execution on April 19, 1995, with a series of other government crimes alleged to have taken place on April 19: the 1993 bombing of Waco, a foiled 1992 raid by federal authorities on Randy Weaver's home, the 1943 burning of Warsaw, and the 1775 burning of Lexington. After Snell's execution, the political prisoners support group run by Scriptures for America took up the cause of Snell's widow, Mary. (Michael Barkun, *Religion and the Racist Right,* rev. ed. (Chapel Hill: University of North Carolina Press, 1997), 255–68. Pete Peters, enclosure in SFA newsletter, vol. 3 (1995), n.p.)

On April 5, exactly two weeks before he bombed the Federal Building, Timothy McVeigh made two telephone calls, both brief, to a phone in the common room of Elohim City, a communal settlement connected to Ellison's Covenant, Sword and Arm of the Lord; its leader, Robert Millar, was spiritual advisor to Richard Snell. The content of these calls is not known. Concludes analyst Michael Barkun: "The residents of Elohim City live reclusive lives at the end of a six-mile dirt road. Unlike the congregation of Pete Peters, for example, this is not an Identity group known for its aggressive outreach activities. Nor is Timothy McVeigh known to have had prior contacts with Millar or any of the community's residents. . . . It seems unlikely, therefore, that McVeigh phoned Elohim City for some casual reason. It is far more likely that he either wished to reach a specific individual (in which case the brevity of the calls suggests that he failed) or to acquire a specific piece of information, perhaps concerning the fate of Richard Wayne Snell" (268–70).

3 Leo Ribuffo, *The Old Christian Right* (Philadelphia: Temple University Press, 1983), xiii.

4 Raphael Ezekiel, *The Racist Mind: Portraits of Klansmen and Neo-Nazis* (New York: Viking, 1995), xxi.

5 J. Gordon Melton estimates Christian Identity believers to number between 10,000 and 20,000: "The Identity Movement," *Encyclopedic Handbook of Cults in America,* rev. ed. (New York: Garland Publishing, 1992), 77. More

recently, Michael Barkun has estimated that committed Christian Identity believers number 20,000 to 30,000 out of a total 100,000 to 200,000 "hardcore" members of the white supremacist right: "Militias, Christian Identity, and the Radical Right," *Christian Century* (2–9 August 1995): 740.

6 Aho, *Politics of Righteousness.* For similar profiles that are not confined to Idaho (as was Aho's survey), see Ezekiel, *The Racist Mind,* xxviii; Jeffrey Kaplan and Leonard Weinberg, *The Emergence of a Euro-American Radical Right* (New Brunswick, NJ: Rutgers University Press, 1998), 62.

7 James Aho, "Popular Christianity and Political Extremism in the United States," in *Disruptive Religion,* ed. Christian Smith (New York: Routledge, 1996), 192. The rural location of Christian Identity (and other religious supremacist groups, which include Klans) is distinguished from the urban location of most skinhead and neo-Nazi organizations (Kaplan and Weinberg, *Euro-American Radical Right,* 64).

8 Aho, "Popular Christianity," 201.

9 Aho, *Politics of Righteousness,* 180.

10 Michael Barkun, "Racist Apocalypse: Millennialism on the Far Right," in *The Year 2000,* ed. Charles Strozier and Michael Flynn (New York: Free Press, 1997), 190.

11 Pete Peters, "Spiritual Warfare," sermon cassette 697 (LaPorte, CO: SFA, June 1996).

12 Pete Peters, "About the Author," in *Baal Worship* (LaPorte, CO: SFA, 1995).

13 For a history of the Church of Christ, see Richard Hughes, *Reviving the Ancient Faith* (Grand Rapids, MI: Eerdmans, 1996). Peters is not a lone spinoff into Identity from the Church of Christ. For others, see Aho, *Politics of Righteousness,* 52, 201–2.

14 *Denver Post,* 22 January 1984.

15 Sara Diamond, *Roads to Dominion* (New York: Guilford, 1995), 259.

16 Catherine McNichol Stock, *Rural Radicals* (Ithaca, NY: Cornell University Press, 1996), 156–57; David Bennett, *The Party of Fear* (New York: Vintage, 1988), 354–55.

17 Pete Peters, "What It Takes to Make It in 1985," sermon cassette 152 (LaPorte, CO: SFA, n.d.).

18 Pete Peters, "Introductory Tape: Minister's Seminar," unnumbered sermon cassette (LaPorte, CO: SFA, spring 1996).

19 Pete Peters, newsletter (LaPorte, CO: SFA, January 1985), 1. For more information on Sheldon Emry, see the entry on Dave Barley (Emry's successor) in Kaplan, *Encyclopedia of White Power,* 13.

20 Jeffrey Kaplan, *Radical Religion in America* (Syracuse, NY: Syracuse University Press, 1997), 7; Kaplan and Weinberg, *Euro-American Radical Right,* 142.

21 Aho, *The Politics of Righteousness,* 190; Michael Barkun, *Religion and the*

Racist Right (Chapel Hill: University of North Carolina Press, 1994), 203; Kaplan and Weinberg, *Euro-American Radical Right,* 142. The Colorado Springs paper gave Peters's mailing list as 5,000: D'Arcy Fallon, "Controversial Pastor Draws Fire from Critics," *Colorado Springs Gazette Telegraph,* 16 May 1993, sec. B, p. 4. Kaplan notes that most South African Christian Identity believers now follow Peters's ministry (rather than that of Dan Gayman, who first began that branch of the movement; Kaplan, *Radical Religion,* 184, n. 21).

22 Cheri Peters, "For Women Only," newsletter (LaPorte, CO: SFA, January 1995), n.p.

23 Cheri Peters, "For Women Only," newsletter (LaPorte, CO: SFA, February 1985), 5–6.

24 Pete Peters, newsletter (LaPorte, CO: SFA, October–November 1987), 16; and newsletter (LaPorte, CO: SFA, March 1988), 3.

25 Mike O'Keefe, "The Cross and the Skinheads," *Westword,* 29 June 1987.

26 "Phineas Priesthood," in Kaplan, *Encyclopedia of White Power,* 242–44.

27 Enclosure in SFA newsletter, vol. 3 (1995).

28 Barkun, *Racist Right,* 3–45; hereafter cited in text.

29 Stanley Wolpert, *A New History of India,* 5th ed. (New York: Oxford University Press, 1997), 297–328.

30 Robert Anderson details Parham's belief in Anglo-Israelism (which was a minority tradition within Holiness circles) in *Vision of the Disinherited* (1979; Peabody, MA: Hendrickson, 1992), 82–83, 87–89.

31 Antonio Gramsci, *Selections from the Prison Notebooks,* ed. and trans. Quintin Hoare and Geoffrey Nowell Smith (New York: International Publishers, 1971), 286, 303–4.

32 Barkun, "Racist Apocalypse," 192–93.

33 Ford is reputed to have financed Smith's radio broadcasts as well as lent him several investigators with whom Smith compiled the "Ford Company Red File," a set of cards that listed reported communists (Ridgeway, *Blood in the Face,* 50, quoting Glen Jeansonne, *Gerald L. K. Smith: Minister of Hate* [New Haven: Yale University Press, 1988]).

34 Barkun defines survivalism as "an omnibus term for a lifestyle of physical withdrawal and self-sufficiency that has as its aim surviving some imagined future calamity" that is often linked to an alleged communist threat (*Racist Right,* 213).

35 Melton, "The Identity Movement," 72–73; Barkun, *Racist Right,* 215–16; Bennett, *Party of Fear,* 350–51.

36 Jack Mohr, "About the Author," description introducing "Exploding the 'Chosen People' Myth," brochure distributed by SFA (n.d.); Jack Mohr speaking to the Minister's Seminar, excerpted on Peters, "Introductory

Tape: Minister's Seminar"; Barkun, *Racist Right*, 144. As Mohr's health has begun to fail, Peters has assumed aspects of his ministry, such as Mohr's work with prisoners. For an account of Mohr's relation to fundamentalism, see "Jack Mohr," Kaplan, *Encyclopedia of White Power*, 215–16.

37 Journalists Kevin Flynn and Gary Gerhardt, through interviews with surviving Order members and their families, document the web of connections that wove through the LaPorte Church of Christ to link Zillah and Jean Craig, David Lane, Robert and Sharon Merki, and Dennis and Mary Schlueter (*The Silent Brotherhood*, 267–68, 119, 140, 143–44, 202). Peters claims that the extent of "church attendance" was one Order member who attended a special meeting at which the LaPorte Church of Christ brought Jack Mohr to speak: Peters, "Review of *The Far Right Radio Review*," sermon cassette (LaPorte, CO: SFA, June 1994). Order members Robert Mathews and David Lane professed to be Odinists, a reconstructed form of pre-Christian Germanic beliefs, as do many skinheads and National Socialists. See Jeffrey Kaplan, "Odinism and Asatru," in *Radical Religion in America* (Albany, NY: Syracuse University Press, 1997), 69–99. By his own admission, Peters has tried to recruit skinheads, as did Aryan Nation's leader Richard Butler, but without success. In his analysis of the Order, Mattias Gardell cautions against simplistic understandings of the importance of Pierce's novel *The Turner Diaries*. Gardell argues instead that "members differed widely in their perception of what they were doing, ranging from modest hopes of contributing financially to racialist organizations to optimistic expectations of inspiring a chain reaction, thus fomenting an armed Aryan revolution." Mattias Gardell, "The Order," in *Encyclopedia of White Power*, 234.

38 Virginia Culver, "Pastor Focus of Anti-Semitic Uproar," *Denver Post*, 22 January 1984, sec. E, pp. 3–4; "Mohr a 'Strong Patriot' Not a 'White Supremacist,'" *Denver Post*, 22 January 1984, sec. E, p. 3.

39 Barkun, *Racist Right*, 68–70; Melton, "The Identity Movement," 73.

40 Stock, *Rural Radicals*, 148.

4 Biblical Memories and the Erotics of Domination
"Not Politically Correct but Biblically Correct"

1 Regina Schwartz, *The Curse of Cain* (Chicago: University of Chicago Press, 1997), x.

2 Susan Harding, "If I Should Die before I Wake: Jerry Falwell's Pro-life Gospel," in *Uncertain Terms*, ed. Faye Ginsburg and Anna Lowenhaupt Tsing (Boston: Beacon, 1990), 82.

3 Raphael Ezekiel, *The Racist Mind* (New York: Viking, 1995).

4 Marita Sturken makes this argument more generally in *Tangled Memories* (Berkeley: University of California Press, 1997), 6, 20, 25–26, 37.

5 Jacques Derrida, "Signature Event Context," in *Margins of Philosophy,* trans. Alan Bass (Chicago: University of Chicago Press, 1982), 307–30.

6 Neil Postman, *The Disappearance of Childhood* (1982; New York: Vintage, 1994), 82.

7 V. N. Volosinov, *Marxism and the Philosophy of Language,* trans. Ladislav Matejka and I. R. Titunik (Cambridge, MA: Harvard University Press, 1973), 23.

8 Michael Taussig, *Shamanism, Colonialism and the Wild Man* (Chicago: University of Chicago Press, 1987), 121–22.

9 Jean Baudrillard, *Simulations,* trans. Paul Foss, Paul Patton, and Philip Beitchman (New York: Semiotext(e), 1983), 30–37.

10 Peters, "How Much Is That Doggie in the Kingdom?" sermon cassette 263 (LaPorte, CO: SFA, n.d.). Also see his interview with Peter Marshall, sermon cassette 657 (LaPorte, CO: SFA, spring 1995).

11 Eric Hobsbawm, "Introduction: Inventing Traditions," in *The Invention of Tradition,* ed. Eric Hobsbawm and Terence Ranger (Cambridge, England: Cambridge University Press, 1984), 1–14.

12 Wilson Jeremiah Moses, *Black Messiahs and Uncle Toms,* rev. ed. (University Park: Pennsylvania State University Press, 1993).

13 Colleen McDannell, "The Bible in the Victorian Home," in *Material Christianity* (New Haven: Yale University Press, 1995), 67–102.

14 Marianne Hirsch, *Family Frames* (Cambridge, MA: Harvard University Press, 1997).

15 Alice Bach, *Women, Seduction and Betrayal in Biblical Narrative* (New York: Cambridge University Press, 1997), 128–65.

16 Sharon Welch, *A Feminist Ethic of Risk* (Minneapolis: Fortress, 1990), 111–16.

17 Michel Foucault, *The History of Sexuality,* trans. Robert Hurley (New York: Vintage, 1978), 1:92–93.

18 George Mosse, *Nationalism and Sexuality* (Madison: University of Wisconsin Press, 1985), 150–51, 137.

19 Ibid., 133.

20 Zillah Eisenstein, *Hatreds* (New York: Routledge, 1996), 43.

21 For a quick overview of this vast field of research, see Cornel West's essay "A Genealogy of Modern Racism" in *Prophesy Deliverance!* (Philadelphia: Westminster, 1982), 48–65.

22 My discussion of the Church of Christ comes from Richard Hughes, *Reviv-*

ing the Ancient Faith (Grand Rapids, MI: Eerdmans, 1996). For Campbell's Baconian reading of the Bible, see 30–31.

23 Alexander Campbell, *The Christian System*, 5th ed. (1835; reprint Cincinnati: Standard Publishing, 1901), 6; quoted in Hughes, *Reviving the Ancient Faith*, 32.

24 George M. Marsden, *Fundamentalism and American Culture* (Oxford: Oxford University Press, 1980), 120, 57; Sadik Al-Azm, "Islamic Fundamentalism Reconsidered, Part II," *South East Asia Bulletin* 14, no. 1 (1994): 89–90.

25 Pete Peters, "Preparatory for October 1992 Meeting of Men of God," sermon cassette 556 (LaPorte, CO: SFA, n.d.).

26 Peters is more liberal in his literalism than many. He ridicules those who, claiming that its archaic language renders it closer to God, read only the King James Version. Peters acknowledges the mediated nature of translations. He uses multiple translations as well as an interlinear version that refers to the Greek and Hebrew text. He most often uses the North American Standard version because it is the most "relevant" translation, as it uses the language Americans speak. Unless otherwise noted, Bible references in this case study are taken from the North American Standard.

27 Pete Peters, *The Greatest Discovery of Our Age* (LaPorte, CO: SFA, 1985), 15.

28 Denis Wood, *The Power of Maps* (New York: Guilford, 1992), 70, 79.

29 Tracey Eaton, "LaPorte Church Leader Predicts Reports Will Boost Membership," *The Coloradoan*, 11 March 1985, sec. A, p. 1.

30 Ezekiel, *The Racist Mind*, 64–5.

31 Minnie Bruce Pratt, "The Maps in My Bible," in *Rebellion* (Ithaca, NY: Firebrand Books, 1991), 192.

32 J. L. Austin, *How to Do Things with Words* (Cambridge, MA: Harvard University Press, 1962).

33 Barkun traces the intellectual history of pre-Adamism in his *Religion and the Racist Right* (Chapel Hill: University of North Carolina Press, 1994), 150–58. Robert Young identifies America as the primary locus for the debate regarding polygenesis and monogenesis in *Colonial Desire* (New York: Routledge, 1995), 9. Young discusses polygenesis and monogenesis on 46–47, 64–68, 101–9.

34 Pete Peters, shortwave broadcast, 20 May 1996; "By God We Will Get This Country Back," sermon cassette 694 (LaPorte, CO: SFA, April 1996).

35 Young, *Colonial Desire*, 9.

36 Pete Peters, "The True Creation Story: Man and Then Adam," sermon cassette 102 (LaPorte, CO: SFA, n.d.).

37 Pete Peters, "We Want This Country Back by God," sermon cassette 693 (LaPorte, CO: SFA, April 1996).

38 Pete Peters, *America the Conquered* (1991; LaPorte, CO: SFA, 1993), 228–29.

39 Catherine McNichol Stock, *Rural Radicals* (Ithaca, NY: Cornell University Press, 1996).

40 For examples, see ibid., 129–30; Tomas Almaguer, *Racial Faultlines* (Berkeley: University of California Press, 1994). Similarly, early settlers argued that ownership devolved on those who improved the land, where improvement meant development. This notion of improvement developed in the 1800s into a belief in the superior productivity of the white race. See Reginald Horsman, *Race and Manifest Destiny* (Cambridge, MA: Harvard University Press, 1981).

41 Barkun, *Racist Right,* 159–62.

42 In his interviews with Dan Gayman, Jeffrey Kaplan notes that Church of Israel leader also considers the seedline theory to be subject to review: "The Context of American Millenarian Revolutionary Theology," *Terrorism and Political Violence* 5, no. 1 (spring 1993): 56. Peters's rejection of the two-seedlines theory remains consistent through the earliest tapes from the beginning of his ministry.

43 Stephen O'Leary, *Arguing the Apocalypse* (New York: Oxford University Press, 1994), 66–68.

44 Peters, "How Much Is That Doggie in the Kingdom?"

45 Young, *Colonial Desire,* 54, 91.

46 Peters, "How Much Is That Doggie in the Kingdom?"

47 Peters, shortwave broadcast, 20 May 1996.

48 Peters, "How Much Is That Doggie in the Kingdom?"

49 Schwartz, *The Curse of Cain,* 110.

50 Ibid., 111.

51 For the notion of the rivalrous double, see Rene Girard, *Violence and the Sacred,* trans. Patrick Gregory (Baltimore: Johns Hopkins University Press, 1977), 143–68.

52 Peters, newsletter (LaPorte, CO: SFA, March 1987), 11.

53 Peters, "How Much Is That Doggie in the Kingdom?"

54 Marsden, *Fundamentalism and American Culture,* 54.

55 Susan Niditch, *Underdogs and Tricksters* (New York: Harper and Row, 1987), 99–101.

56 Pete Peters, "The Most Confusing Word in Scripture: Jew," sermon cassette 120 (LaPorte, CO: SFA, n.d.). For the history behind Peters's Jewish genealogies, see Barkun, *Racist Right,* 147–96.

57 Peters, *The Greatest Discovery of Our Age,* 9.

58 Pete Peters, "The Greatest Love Story Never Told," Act 1, sermon cassette 563 (LaPorte, CO: SFA, fall 1993). Also see his "Sons of Darkness vs. Sons of Light," sermon cassette (LaPorte, CO: SFA, fall 1993).

59 Pete Peters, *Special Report: Framing Deceit,* newsletter (LaPorte, CO: SFA, spring 1996), 1.

60 Peters, *The Greatest Discovery of Our Age,* 15. The passages are Revelation 2:9, 3:9, and 2 John 1:7.

61 Peters, "How Much Is That Doggie in the Kingdom?" Peters recites 2 John 1:7: "Many deceivers have gone out in the world, those who do not acknowledge Jesus Christ as coming in the flesh. This is the deceiver and the antichrist."

62 Ibid.

63 Ibid.

64 Pete Peters, *A Scriptural Understanding of the Race Issue: God's Call for Repentance* (LaPorte, CO: SFA, n.d.), 18; "Lost Israel in Scripture," sermon cassette 290 (LaPorte, CO: SFA, n.d.).

65 Peters, *The Greatest Discovery of Our Age,* 21.

66 Peters, "We Want This Country Back by God!"

67 Scholars disagree about whether the marriage took place or was a metaphor. Those who agree that the marriage took place disagree about the nature of Gomer's "sexual deviance," some regarding her as a woman with a "loose reputation," others regarding her as a prostitute.

68 Peters, "Greatest Love Story Never Told," Act 1.

69 Pete Peters, "America the Redeemed," part 4, sermon cassette 607 (LaPorte, CO: SFA, winter 1994).

70 Peters, "Greatest Love Story Never Told," Act 1.

71 Literary critic Jan Radway makes a similar argument for the appeal of romance novels in *Reading the Romance* (Chapel Hill: University of North Carolina Press, 1984).

72 Suzanne Kessler, *Lessons from the Intersexed* (New Brunswick, NJ: Rutgers University Press, 1998); Judith Butler, *Gender Trouble* (New York: Routledge, 1992), 6–7, 16–25.

73 The classic text is Benedict Anderson, *Imagined Communities* (New York: Verso, 1983). Drawing on Anderson, media analyst Susan Douglas analyzes the active participation (and accompanying pleasures) stimulated by this kind of multidimensional listening in *Listening In: Radio and the American Imagination* (New York: Times Books, 1999), 4, 199–219.

74 This split—between audience/viewer and projected ideal—is part and parcel of the baggage that constitutes any identification. In Lacanian terms, when we recognize ourselves in an image, we enact a fundamental misrecognition insofar as we erase or disidentify with the one who points the finger at the image and finds himself or herself there: Jacques Lacan, *Ecrits,* trans. Alan Sheridan (New York: Norton, 1977), 1–7.

75 Etienne Balibar, "The Nation Form: History and Ideology," in *Race, Nation,*

Class, ed. Etienne Balibar and Immanuel Wallerstein, trans. Chris Turner (New York: Verso, 1991), 93, 95.

76 This analysis of the gaze comes from Teresa Brennan, who argues that the male subject creates his visible bodily boundaries (and thus forms an ego identity) by projecting any unpleasant affect (fears of vulnerability or the hostility that accompanies love) onto others, who internalize its traces: *The Interpretation of the Flesh* (New York: Routledge, 1992), 132–34.

77 Pete Peters, *Awake, Awake O America! You Are in the Bible!* (LaPorte, CO: SFA, n.d.), 9.

78 Isaiah's unfulfilled promises (along with others in Micah and Hosea) speak of "the last days." Isaiah wrote as ancient Israel's Southern Kingdom was falling apart. Scholars usually read these words as statements of consolation and utopian desire for a world Israel never knew, given its geopolitical location between contending empires. In contrast, a rich tradition in Protestant biblical hermeneutics known as dispensational premillennialism reads these images not as poetic longing or coded expressions for ancient Israel's historical context, but as codes for the future. See Adela Yarbro Collins, "Reading the Book of Revelation in the Twentieth Century," *Interpretation* 40 (1986): 234. Thus, the Scofield Bible decodes Ezekiel's prophesies against Gog, the chief prince of Meschech and Tubal, as a "clear" reference to Moscow and Tobolsk: C. I. Scofield, *The Scofield Reference Bible* (New York: Oxford University Press, 1909), 883. Dispensational premillennialism grew after the Civil War, was codified in the Scofield Bible (published 1909), and was repopularized as a mass market phenomenon by Hal Lindsey's *The Late Great Planet Earth,* which in the 1970s was the nonfiction bestseller. See O'Leary, *Arguing the Apocalypse,* 134–71; Paul Boyer, *When Time Shall Be No More* (Cambridge, MA: Harvard University Press, 1992), 5. Boyer reports that 9 million copies of Lindsey's book were in print by 1978 and 28 million (in all languages) by 1990.

79 Sacvan Bercovitch, *The American Jeremiad* (Madison: University of Wisconsin Press, 1978); Moses, *Black Messiahs and Uncle Toms.*

80 Peters, *America the Conquered,* 196.

81 Ibid., viii.

82 Ibid., 18–19.

83 Pete Peters, "Death to America on the Battleground of Fornication, Part 1," sermon cassette 560 (LaPorte, CO: SFA, n.d.). For analysis of similar prejudices in early biblical scholarship, see Keith Whitelam, *The Invention of Ancient Israel* (New York: Routledge, 1996), 83–84.

84 Peters, "Death to America on the Battleground of Fornication, Part 1."

85 Joseph Unwin, *Sexual Regulations and Cultural Behavior* (London: Oxford University Press, 1935).

86 Pete Peters, "Minister's Seminar: What Difference Does Identity Make?", sermon cassette 700 (LaPorte, CO: SFA, spring 1996).

5 Nichemarketing the Apocalypse
Violence as Hard-Sell

1 Jeffrey Kaplan, "Christian Identity," in *Encyclopedia of White Power,* ed. Jeffrey Kaplan (Lanham, MD: Rowman and Littlefield, 2000), 53, and *Radical Religion in America* (Syracuse: Syracuse University Press, 1997), 54.
2 Philip Lamy, "Secularizing the Millennium," in *Millennium, Messiahs, and Mayhem,* ed. Thomas Robbins and Susan Palmer (New York: Routledge, 1997), 93–117. This gap between the real and the "really" real is why religion is so frequently involved with violence, an involvement that even the most militant believers in nonviolence do not escape. Writes historian R. Scott Appleby: "Both the extremist and the peacemaker are militants. Both types go to extremes of self-sacrifice in devotion to the sacred. . . . In these ways they distinguish themselves from people not motivated by religious commitments—and the vast middle ground of believers": *The Ambivalence of the Sacred* (Lanham, MD: Rowman and Littlefield, 2000), 11.
3 Elizabeth Grosz, *Jacques Lacan: A Feminist Introduction* (New York: Routledge, 1990), 64–67.
4 Jeffrey Kaplan, "The Context of American Millenarian Revolutionary Theology," *Terrorism and Political Violence* 5, no. 1 (spring 1993): 54.
5 SFA, *Remnant Resolves* (LaPorte, CO: SFA, 1989), 1–3; hereafter cited in text as *RR.*
6 The text is Romans 13: "Every person must submit to the supreme authorities. There is no authority but by act of God, and the existing authorities are constituted by him; consequently anyone who rebels against authority is resisting a divine institution, and those who so resist have only themselves to thank for the punishment they receive."
7 Pete Peters, *Authority: Resistance or Obedience? The Door to the Kingdom* (LaPorte, CO: SFA, n.d.), 8.
8 See Jeffrey Kaplan's analysis of Dan Gayman, head of the Church of Israel in Schell City, Missouri, in "The Context of American Millenarian Revolutionary Theology," 53–54, and *Radical Religion in America,* 56–57.
9 Pete Peters, *Sedition and the Old Time Religion* (LaPorte, CO: SFA, n.d.), 19; distributed in pamphlet form with SFA's March 1988 newsletter.
10 Peters's more "radical" message has attracted followers of Dan Gayman who are frustrated by Gayman's increasing withdrawal in the name of Romans 13. See Jeffrey Kaplan and Leonard Weinberg, *The Emergence of a*

Euro-American Radical Right (New Brunswick, NJ: Rutgers University Press, 1998), 140.

11 Sadik Al-Azm, "Islamic Fundamentalism Reconsidered: A Critical Outline, Part II," *South Asia Bulletin* 14, no. 1 (1994): 95; Michael Barkun, *Religion and the Racist Right* (Chapel Hill: University of North Carolina Press, 1994), 284–87.

12 Jeffrey Hadden and Anthony Schupe, *Televangelism* (New York: Holt, 1988), 65.

13 Ibid., citing Martin Marty, *Context* 17, no. 19 (1 November 1985): 1.

14 Ibid.

15 Pete Peters, newsletter, vol. 1, no. 2 (LaPorte, CO: SFA, 1988).

16 Write Kaplan and Weinberg: "Common law courts are pseudo-judicial bodies that issue bogus liens, arrest warrants and various fake judicial rulings. They are intended to harass real judges, county recorders, other public officials and private citizens who stand in the freemen's way in one fashion or another. . . . The most spectacular of these 'courts' was the Freemen/Justus Township in Jordan Montana, a ranch where some 2 dozen freemen claimed immunity to American law and held federal authorities at bay for over a month before surrendering" (*Euro-American Right*, 73, 72). For a brief review of events in Jordan, plus an excerpt from one of the teaching texts the Freemen used, see Ted Daniels, *A Doomsday Reader* (New York: New York University Press, 1999), 176–98. On the Freemen generally, see Catherine Wessinger, *How the Millennium Comes Violently* (Chappaqua, NY: Seven Bridges, 2000), 158–217.

17 Pete Peters, newsletter, vol. 3 (LaPorte, CO: SFA, 1989), 11–12.

18 SFA, *Our Forefathers' Resolves* (LaPorte, CO: SFA, n.d.), 1.

19 Norman Gottwald, *The Hebrew Bible* (Philadelphia: Fortress, 1985), 370.

20 Indeed, some biblical scholars argue that the Bible's account of the monarchic period is itself more pretext than text, a narrative told from the perspective of later political struggles that were retrojected into Israel's past. In this reading, talking about Assyria, the first Temple, and the monarchy are ways of talking about Persia, the second Temple, and the elite ambition to resist Persian imperial domination.

21 Homi Bhabha, ed., *Nation and Narration* (New York: Routledge, 1990).

22 Etienne Balibar, "The Nation Form: History and Ideology," in *Race, Nation, Class*, ed. Etienne Balibar and Immanuel Wallerstein, trans. Chris Turner (New York: Verso, 1991), 93, 95.

23 Peters, newsletter, vol. 3, 13.

24 Pete Peters, *Baal Worship* (LaPorte, CO: SFA, 1995), 23.

25 Peters, newsletter, vol. 3, 14.

26 Matthew Moen, *The Christian Right and Congress* (Tuscaloosa: University

of Alabama Press, 1989), 37–38. This verse plays a key role in the National Day of Prayer headed by James Dobson's wife, Shirley.

27 Pete Peters, newsletter, vol. 2 (LaPorte, CO: SFA, 1992), 4.

28 Pete Peters, newsletter (LaPorte, CO: SFA, February 1988), 2.

29 Barton is Reconstructionism's most well-known popularizer. In September 1992, Dobson interviewed Barton on his radio show and sold his videotape arguing that separation of church and state is a myth disseminated by secular humanists. Dobson rebroadcast the Barton interview on 2 May 1996, the National Day of Prayer: Dobson, "Our Spiritual Heritage (Mr. David Barton)," CS 744/8923 (1992; Colorado Springs: FOF, 1996). Barton's books were highly influential for early versions of Focus on the Family's public policy seminars (see chapter 7).

30 Pete Peters, "Never-Ending Last Days?" newsletter, vol. 3 (LaPorte, CO: SFA, 1995).

31 Pete Peters, "The Spirit of the Lord, Part II, Liberty in America," sermon cassette (LaPorte, CO: SFA, July 1993).

32 Michael Barkun, *Religion and the Racist Right,* rev. ed. (Chapel Hill: University of North Carolina Press, 1997), 281–84.

33 Alisa Solomon, "Nothing Special: The Specious Attack on Civil Rights," in *Dangerous Liaisons,* ed. Eric Brandt (New York: New Press, 1999), 65–66.

34 John Hope Franklin, "The Moral Legacy of the Founding Fathers," in *Race and History* (Baton Rouge: Louisiana State University Press, 1989), 159.

35 Toni Morrison, *Playing in the Dark* (Cambridge, MA: Harvard University Press, 1992), 6, xiii. Also see Gayatri Chakravorty Spivak, "Constitutions and Culture Studies," *Yale Journal of Law and Humanities* 2, no. 1 (winter 1990): 136; Robin Blackburn, *The Overthrow of Colonial Slavery 1776–1848* (London: Verso, 1988), 123–24.

36 Roberto C. Goizueta, *The Coca-Cola Company 1994 Annual Report* (Atlanta: Coca-Cola Company, 1995), 17; available from The Coca-Cola Company, P.O. Drawer 1734, Atlanta, GA 30301.

37 Slavoj Žižek, "Eastern Europe's Republics of Gilead," in *Dimensions of Radical Democracy,* ed. Chantal Mouffe (New York: Verso, 1992), 200, 194–96.

38 Barkun, *Racist Right,* rev. ed., 290.

39 Ibid., 289–90.

40 Susan Douglas, *Listening In* (New York: Random House, 1999), 5.

41 Susan Jeffords, *The Remasculinization of America* (Bloomington: Indiana University Press, 1989).

42 Ibid., 44, referring to Richard Nixon, *No More Vietnams* (New York: Arbor House, 1985).

43 William Gibson, *Warrior Dreams* (New York: Hill and Wang, 1994), 7, 148, 236–40, and "Is the Apocalypse Coming? Paramilitary Culture after the

Cold War," in *The Year 2000,* ed. Charles Strozier and Michael Flynn (New York: Free Press, 1997), 181–82.

44 Gibson, "Is the Apocalypse Coming?" 182.

45 Ibid., 180.

46 Gibson, *Warrior Dreams,* 57.

47 Ibid., 236–40.

48 David Savran, *Taking It Like a Man* (Princeton, NJ: Princeton University Press, 1998), 202, 5, 197–206. Savran sets the New War hero's reinvigoration of masculinity through victimization within a broader context that includes Robert Bly's followers searching for the Wild Man within as well as the spiritual male advancing toward the New Age. For analysis of how these dynamics also limit the vision of Vietnam films whose message is antiwar, see Marita Sturken, *Tangled Memories* (Berkeley: University of California Press, 1997). For the argument that the legacy of rooting male bonding in the shared experience of oppression in South Asia eviscerates the vision of racial reconciliation offered by buddy films such as *Lethal Weapon* and *Grand Canyon,* reiterating racism in ways that work against interracial dialogue and encounter, see Hazel Carby, *Race Men* (Cambridge, MA: Harvard University Press, 1998), 170–83.

49 Louis Beam, "Vietnam: Bringing It on Home," in *Essays of a Klansman* (Hayden Lake, ID: AKIA, 1983), 35–41, cited in James Aho, *This Thing of Darkness* (Seattle: University of Washington Press, 1994), 191, n. 8.

50 James Ridgeway, *Blood in the Face* (New York: Thunder's Mouth, 1990), 87, 102. For an analysis of Beam's white supremacist involvement, see "Louis Beam," in Kaplan, *Encyclopedia of White Power,* 17–23. For a genealogy of Beam's notion of leaderless resistance, see Kaplan, "Leaderless Resistance," in *Encyclopedia of White Power,* 173–85.

51 Aho, *This Thing of Darkness,* 54–58, 60–65.

52 Gibson, *Warrior Dreams,* 160–61.

53 Ibid., 212–13.

54 Paul Boyer, *When Time Shall Be No More* (Cambridge, MA: Harvard University Press, 1992), 258–60.

55 James Dobson, newsletter (Colorado Springs: FOF, August 1993).

56 Peters, newsletter, vol. 3, 22. During the 1960s and 1970s, Gothard's seminars were the most popular source of family advice among fundamentalists. See Susan Harding, *The Book of Jerry Falwell* (Princeton, NJ: Princeton University Press, 2000), 171. At the time of the seminar Peters attended, Gothard was directing the Institute in Basic Youth Conflicts. According to *Christianity Today:* "Essentially, he uses Scriptures to teach that everyone is under authority, and that the chief authority, God, deals with people through various structures and channels of authority: family, church, business and

government" ("Bill Gothard Steps Down During Institute Shakeup," *Christianity Today,* 8 August 1990, 46–47).

57 Peters, newsletter, vol. 3, 23. At SFA's next Family Bible Camp, Peters was filmed addressing biblical teachings on gun control. Individual campers were then filmed speaking directly to their congresspersons, asking them to listen to Peters's message because he represented their views. The constituent's personal message was spliced at the head of Peters's more general message, the constituent signed a letter to the congressperson, and the package was mailed to Washington. See Pete Peters, "Congressional Video Outreach," newsletter, vol. 4 (LaPorte, CO: SFA, 1989), 20.

58 Pete Peters, *Everything You Wanted to Know (and Preachers Were Afraid to Tell You) about Gun Control* (LaPorte, CO: SFA, n.d.), 20.

59 Pete Peters, *Strength of a Hero* (LaPorte, CO: SFA, December 1989), 2–3.

60 Appleby, *The Ambivalence of the Sacred,* 90.

61 Peters, *Everything You Wanted to Know,* 20.

62 Gibson, "Is the Apocalypse Coming?", 185.

63 Peters, newsletter, vol. 3, 2; Pete Peters, newsletter, vol. 2 (LaPorte, CO: SFA, 1990), 2. The theme verse of *America the Conquered,* Isaiah 52:1–2, promises that Israel will shake itself up from the dust and loose the chains around its neck: "It only takes a remnant . . . *for a strange phenomenon* exists in this end time captivity that has never existed before. NEVER HAVE SLAVES BEEN SO WELL ARMED": Peters, *America the Conquered* (1991; LaPorte, CO: SFA 1993), 214; emphasis in original.

64 The militia movement is usually dated several years after this newsletter, for the movement is typically understood as responding to Ruby Ridge (August 1992) and Waco (February 1993). Certainly, it was the latter events, occurring in the media eye, which led to a proliferation of citizen militias.

65 Pete Peters, "The Planting of Spirits: Introduction to 1996 Summer Bible Camp," sermon cassette 787 (LaPorte, CO: SFA, n.d.).

66 Raphael Ezekiel, *The Racist Mind* (New York: Viking, 1995), xxx, 62, xxxi.

67 Appleby, *The Ambivalence of the Sacred,* 94–95.

68 Pete Peters, *The Bible: Handbook for Survivalists, Racists, Tax Protestors, Militants and Right-wing Extremists* (LaPorte, CO: SFA, n.d.), 12.

69 Peters responded in the same way to The Order. Whereas he declared its rank and file innocent (except for charges of racketeering), he denounced Order leader Bob Mathews as a government operative who tricked his followers by claiming to be forming a revolutionary movement: Peters, newsletter (LaPorte, CO: SFA, December–January 1988), 3.

70 Jacqueline Rose, *Why War? Psychoanalysis, Politics and the Return to Melanie Klein* (Cambridge, England: Blackwell, 1993), 64.

71 Judy Harrington, "Gays in Fort Collins Back Anti-Discrimination Law,"

Denver Post, 8 June 1988, sec. B, p. 4; "Votes on Rights for Gays Likely in Fort Collins," *Denver Post,* 1 August 1988, sec. B, p. 5; "Fort Collins Voters to Decide Gay Rights Issue," *Denver Post,* 4 August 1988, sec. B, p. 5.

72 Pete Peters, newsletter, vol. 5 (LaPorte, CO: SFA, 1988), 4. "Opposition to the law was spearheaded by a conservative minister in nearby LaPorte, and the issue was fought largely in the city's churches": "Fort Collins Rights Law Losing," *Denver Post,* 9 November 1988, sec. GAA.

73 Exhibit 1 of *LaPorte Church of Christ's Brief to the Colorado Court of Appeals in "Meyer v. LaPorte Church of Christ,"* distributed with newsletter (La-Porte, CO: SFA, 1991), n.p.

74 Noebel still heads the Summit today. I discuss the Summit in greater detail in chapter 7, for Noebel's influence on Dobson has been quite direct. Whereas in this chapter I focus on gender and sexuality, in chapter 7 I investigate the racial dimensions of the political body imagined by Noebel, as revealed by his attacks on rock music.

75 David Noebel, *The Homosexual Revolution* (Tulsa, OK: American Christian College Press, 1977), 19. Noebel's response of male headship was mirrored by Cheri Peters after the Fort Collins campaign. Moved by the sight of her "sweet shy" teenage daughter speaking at a City Council meeting in contrast to the many outspoken lesbians in attendance, Cheri Peters concluded, "I want to propose to our City Council that we eliminate women from serving in a position God never intended for them to be in, and never allow anyone but a white Christian male to make decisions in our town!": Cheri Peters, newsletter, vol. 5 (LaPorte, CO: SFA, 1988), 24–25.

76 Noebel, *Homosexual Revolution,* 15.

77 William Martin, *With God on Our Side* (New York: Broadway Books, 1996), 345–48; Ward Harkavy "Original Sin," *Westword,* 8–14 September 1988, pp. 13–14, 16–28; Tom Morton "The Summit," *Colorado Springs Telegraph,* 1 July 1990, sec. F, pp. 1, 4–5. For a less abbreviated account of CFV's origins that gives greater room to the role initially played by women, see Stephen Bransford, *Gay Politics vs. Colorado and America: The Inside Story of Amendment Two* (Cascade, CO: Sardis, 1994), 12–27.

78 Noebel, *The Homosexual Revolution,* 36, 54–55, 26, 49.

79 Ibid., 118–19.

80 Ibid., 28, 143–56. For analysis of 1950s antigay campaigns, see Jennifer Terry, *An American Obsession* (Chicago: University of Chicago Press, 1999), 329–52.

81 Noebel, *The Homosexual Revolution,* 27–28.

82 Judith Butler, *The Psychic Life of Power* (Stanford: Stanford University Press, 1997), 27.

83 Ibid., 137–38.

84 Linda Kintz, *Between Jesus and the Market* (Durham, NC: Duke University Press, 1997), 247.

85 Peters, "Sodomites Seduce City Council," sermon cassette tape 280 (LaPorte, CO: SFA, n.d.). Also see Peters, *Baal Worship*, 136. For discussion of the association of homosexuality with narcissism more generally, see Kath Weston, *Families We Choose* (New York: Columbia University Press, 1991), 156.

86 Peters, "Sodomites Seduce City Council."

87 Noebel, *The Homosexual Revolution*, 63.

88 Ibid., 20.

89 Ibid., 134.

90 Within CFV, there was considerable debate about the degree of distance desirable. For an account of the controversy regarding this particular strategy, see John Gallagher and Chris Bull, *Perfect Enemies* (New York: Crown, 1996), 109–11; Michael Booth, "Amendment Two Architect Hits CFV for Tactics," *Denver Post*, 9 March 1993, sec. A, pp. 1, 10. DoveTail ministries was founded by Joyce Marco, wife of CFV cofounder Tony Marco; she has a lesbian daughter. Tony Marco claims to have left CFV due to the organization's willingness to use materials that defamed and degraded gays and lesbians (personal letter from Tony Marco to Tony Ogden, head of Equal Protection Only Coalition, 25 November 1991, in possession of the author).

91 CFV campaign materials in possession of the author.

92 CFV, model notebook, tape 6.

93 CFV, model notebook, tape 3. Likewise, in the special message delivered at this seminar by James Ryle, pastor of the Boulder Valley Vineyard Church, Ryle declared: "Satan was the original homosexual in that he was created for the express purpose of taking all the praise and worship of creation and giving it unto God through his incredible endowments. . . . Somewhere in there he took it [the worship of creation] and turned it onto himself and began making love to himself and he became in that act homosexual. That is why he takes the musicians, the artists, the craftsmen, the entertainers." Ryle goes on to dream of a world where creativity was not "perverted": "Can you imagine the music that would fill the air? Can you imagine the art that would adorn our houses? Can you imagine the movies that we would see? Can you imagine the books that we would read? Can you imagine the plays that would be put on, the unfolding drama of redemption?" (CFV, model notebook, tape 6).

94 Mark Olsen, *Refuge* (Cascade, CO: Sardis Press, 1996), 120, 165, 191.

95 Kintz, *Between Jesus and the Market*, 235.

96 Peters, "Sodomites Seduce City Council." The church is thought to have

spent about $1,000 on the campaign: "LaPorte Church Ordeal with the Law Over," *Colorado Christian News,* June 1993, p. 4.

97 UPI, 9 November 1988, NEXIS, accessed 29 July 1993.

98 Exhibit 4 in *LaPorte Church of Christ's Brief* (booklet distributed by SFA in lieu of a newsletter, 1991), n.p. This booklet collects the various legal documents produced during this process.

99 Exhibit 7, *LaPorte Church of Christ's Brief,* n.p.

100 Peters, "Our TV Debut," cassette tape (LaPorte, CO: SFA, n.d.).

101 Peters, *LaPorte Church of Christ's Brief,* n.p.

102 Peters, Exhibit 10, *LaPorte Church of Christ's Brief,* n.p. Garry Wills argues against the myth that the Founding Fathers' distrust of strong central government led them to institute a government of "checks and balances" in *A Necessary Evil* (New York: Simon and Schuster, 1999), especially the chapters "Checking Efficiency" and "Co-equal Branches," 71–90.

103 "LaPorte Church Ordeal with Law Over," p. 4.

104 For this authoritarian personality reading, see Kaplan, *Radical Religion in America,* 7.

105 D. James Kennedy, "Taking Liberty: The Betrayal of Our Heritage," videotape in possession of the author.

106 Peters, "Our TV Debut."

107 Butler, *The Psychic Life of Power,* 142, 183.

108 Associated Press, "Gays See Pamphlet as Threat: Pastor Defends Flier as His Response to Fine," *Rocky Mountain News,* 6 May 1992, regional ed., local sec., p. 7, NEXIS, accessed 29 July 1993.

109 Pete Peters, *Intolerance of, Discrimination against, and the Death Penalty for Homosexuals Is Prescribed in the Bible* (LaPorte, CO: SFA, April 1992), iii–iv; hereafter cited in text as *Death Penalty.*

110 For Cameron, see Jean Hardisty, *Mobilizing Resentment* (Boston: Beacon, 1999), 102.

111 Peters recounts his first—failed—proposal in "Sodomites Seduce City Council." Arguing with the clergy coalition that if Christians continue fighting (as they usually do) in a defensive posture they will lose to homosexuals "step after step, city after city, state after state, child after child. We've got to start taking aggressive action with as much guts as they have." Peters tried to persuade them to propose a counterordinance—"I'm not talking about vigilante action, I don't believe in it"—according to which if a court of law found someone guilty of sodomy, that person would be treated as a murderer subject to a felony charge and execution if convicted. The clergy coalition did not bite.

112 North Carolinians Against Racist and Religious Violence [NCARRV], "White Patriots Indicted for Shelby Mass Murder," newsletter, vol. 7 (Dur-

ham: NCARRV, spring 1988), 1–4; Center for Democratic Renewal [CDR], update (Atlanta, GA: CDR, 29 May 1989).

113 Appleby, *The Ambivalence of the Sacred,* 15, quoting David Little, "Religious Militancy" in *Managing Global Chaos,* ed. Chester Crocker and Fen Hampson (Washington, DC: U.S. Institute of Peace, 1996), 79–81.

114 Begun in 1984 by Willis Carto, head of the Liberty Lobby, the Populist Party sought to mainstream white supremacy through electoral campaigns (including running David Duke for president in 1988). See Sara Diamond, *Roads to Dominion* (New York: Guilford, 1995), 260–65.

115 The dedication begins "To politicians running for office or attempting to stay in office who are more concerned for God's vote than man's and His Laws than man's" and goes on to pray that "my Colonel friend . . . and all Christian soldiers be mindful of the need to be obedient to our Great Commander and Master, the Lord Jesus Christ, and uphold His orders concerning homosexuality" (Peters, *Death Penalty,* n.p.).

116 Peters, *Baal Worship,* 26.

117 Kaplan, *Radical Religion,* 6–7, and "Pete Peters," in *The Encyclopedia of White Power,* 241.

118 Peters, *Baal Worship,* 68–69; hereafter cited in text as *Baal.*

119 Wessinger, *How the Millennium Comes Violently,* 169, 160.

120 Barkun, *Racist Right,* 252.

121 Pete Peters, newsletter, vol. 2 (LaPorte, CO: SFA, 1990), 2.

6 The Power of Soft-Sell Style

Building a Multimillion-Dollar Ministry by Subverting Feminism

1 Focus on the Family [FOF], *Annual Report* (Colorado Springs: FOF, 1993), 13; "A Day in the Life of Focus," *Focus on the Family Magazine,* November 1993, 2; "Focus on the Family Distribution Overview," handout to tour participants, revised 16 February 1994.

2 *Focus on the Family,* March 1994, 6. Also see the 1993 edition of *The Encyclopedia of Associations;* Paul J. Weber and W. Landis Jones, *U.S. Religious Interest Groups* (Westport, CT: Greenwood, 1994), 79–80.

3 Gustav Niebuhr, "Advice for Parents, and for Politicians," *New York Times,* 30 May 1995.

4 FOF, *Annual Report,* 13; "A Day in the Life of Focus," 2; and "Meeting Future Needs," *Focus on the Family Magazine,* December 1999, 19; "Focus on the Family Distribution Overview," revised 16 February 1994.

5 *Focus on the Family Magazine,* January 1996, 6–7; and March 1997, 14–15; James Dobson, newsletter (Colorado Springs: FOF, May 2001), 1–3.

6   James Dobson, newsletter (Colorado Springs: FOF, June 1994). A fourth building was begun in 1998.

7   James Dobson, newsletter (May 2001), 2.

8   James Dobson, newsletter (Colorado Springs: FOF, November 1995), 2.

9   FOF Web site (*www.family.org*), accessed 27 June 2000.

10 Eithne Johnson, "The Emergence of Christian Video and the Cultivation of Videovangelism," in *Media, Culture and the Religious Right*, ed. Linda Kintz and Julia Lesage (Minneapolis: University of Minnesota Press, 1998), 195.

11 FOF Web site.

12 *Christianity Today*, 22 April 1988, 18.

13 FOF Web site; Marc Fisher, "The GOP, Facing a Dobson's Choice," *Washington Post*, 2 July 1996, sec. D, pp. 1–2. The annual budget allots $1.9 million for grants to be given to constituents in financial need.

14 FOF Web site; Julia Lesage, "Christian Media," in *Media, Culture and the Religious Right*, ed. Kintz and Lesage, 31.

15 Russell Chandler, "Evangelical Broadcaster Seeks 'Pro-Family' Lobby," *Los Angeles Times*, 4 March 1989, p. 6, NEXIS; FOF radio broadcast, 9 February 1994; *Family Research Council*, rev. April 1993, 15. In 1999 there were thirty-four local Family Policy Councils. See Frederick Clarkson, "Takin' It to the States," *Public Eye* 13, nos. 2, 3 (summer–fall 1999): 8.

16 The three million figure includes both editions (interview with Theresa Spevazek-Walsh of Tyndale House Publishers, 14 May 1996).

17 Rolf Zettersten, *Dr. Dobson: Turning Hearts toward Home* (Dallas: Word Publishing, 1989), 90.

18 Elaine Tyler May, *Homeward Bound* (New York: Basic Books, 1988). On fundamentalist distrust of democracy, see Paul Boyer, *When Time Shall Be No More* (Cambridge, MA: Belknap), 247–49.

19 For similar accounts by conservative women activists, see Rebecca Klatch, *Women of the New Right* (Philadelphia: Temple University Press, 1987), 123.

20 Zettersten, *Turning Hearts toward Home*, 149.

21 Judith Stacey, *Brave New Families: Stories of Domestic Upheaval in Late Twentieth-Century America* (New York: Basic Books, 1990); "Sexism By a Subtler Name? Post-industrial Conditions and Post-feminist Consciousness in the Silicon Valley" in *Women, Class, and the Feminist Imagination: A Socialist-Feminist Reader*, ed. Karen Hansen and Ilene J. Philipson (Philadelphia: Temple University, 1990), 338–56; and with Elizabeth Gerard, " 'We Are Not Doormats': The Influence of Feminism on Contemporary Evangelicals in the United States," in *Uncertain Terms*, ed. Faye Ginsburg and Anna Lowenhaupt Tsing (Boston: Beacon, 1990), 59–77. Susan Rose recounts a similar pattern in "Women Warriors: The Negotiation of Gen-

der in a Charismatic Community," *Sociological Analysis* 48, no. 3 (1987): 245–58.

22 Laura Sessions Stepp, "The Empire Built on Family and Faith: Psychologist James Dobson, Bringing His Evangelical Focus to Politics," *Washington Post*, 8 August 1990, sec. C, p. 1. The *Washington Post* cites FOF surveys that identify the typical Dobson listener as a woman, age twenty-five to forty, with a year or two of college and at least two children (Fisher, "The GOP, Facing a Dobson's Choice," 2). FOF confirmed these statistics. They see themselves as speaking to a representative slice of the nation that is no different from the statistical profile of the general population (phone interview with FOF representative Dick Travis, 9 August 1996).

23 Margaret Lamberts Bendroth, *Fundamentalism and Gender, 1875 to the Present* (New Haven: Yale University Press, 1993), 3; Betty DeBerg, *Ungodly Women: Gender and the First Wave of American Fundamentalism* (Minneapolis: Fortress, 1990).

24 James Dobson, *What Wives Wish Their Husbands Knew about Women* (Wheaton, IL: Tyndale House, 1975), 68.

25 Susan Harding, *The Book of Jerry Falwell* (Princeton, NJ: Princeton University Press, 2000), 172, 180.

26 "Focus on the Family: Who We Are and What We Stand For," *Focus on the Family Magazine*, August 1993, 11.

27 James Dobson, "A New Look at Masculinity and Femininity," pamphlet produced by FOF, 1992, excerpting Dobson's *Straight Talk* (Dallas: Word, 1991). For a feminist refutation of the claim that cultural gender roles are rooted in biological sex differences, see Anne Fausto-Sterling, *Myths of Gender*, rev. ed. (New York: Basic, 1985). Whereas early feminist scholarship sought to distinguish anatomical or physiological sex from cultural gender roles, more recent feminist scholarship has called into question the notion of sex itself. These scholars have not denied the existence of chromosomes and hormones, or penises and vaginas; they have, however, questioned our taken-for-granted understandings of the connections between anatomical/physiological sex and gender and sexuality: "The more we look for a simple physical basis for 'sex,' the more it becomes clear that 'sex' is not a pure physical category. What bodily signals and functions we define as male or female come already entangled in our ideas about gender" (Anne Fausto-Sterling, *Sexing the Body* [New York: Basic, 2000], 4).

28 James Dobson, newsletter (Colorado Springs: FOF, September 1995), 4.

29 "Focus on the Family: Who We Are and What We Stand For," 11.

30 Eithne Johnson, "Dr. Dobson's Advice to Christian Women: The Story of Strategic Motherhood," *Social Text* 16, no. 4 (winter 1998): 68.

31 After interviewing anti-ERA activists in North Carolina, historians Jane

Sherron de Hart and Donald Mathews found that the primary motivation driving these activists was a desire to "protect" gender, which they invested with the aura of the sacred: *Sex, Gender, and the Politics of ERA* (New York: Oxford University Press, 1990), 163. And see Sherron de Hart, "Gender on the Right: Meanings behind the Existential Scream," *Gender and History* 3, no. 3 (1991): 255–56.

32 For an extended analysis of the way the social position of the white middle class tends toward disengagement from structural issues, see Sharon Welch, *A Feminist Ethic of Risk* (Minneapolis: Fortress, 1990), 101–80. Historian Nancy MacLean notes that the 1920s Klan built itself into a mass movement by representing itself as upholding proper manhood, womanhood, and parenting. She cites letters from women who wrote to local Klan leaders asking that nightriders be sent to discipline husbands who were abusive or neglectful: *Behind the Mask of Chivalry* (New York: Oxford University Press, 1994).

33 Zettersten, *Turning Hearts toward Home,* 150; T. Stafford, "His Father's Son," *Christianity Today* 22, April 1988, 21.

34 FOF Web sit; Zettersten, *Turning Hearts toward Home,* 182, 152–53.

35 Zettersten, *Turning Hearts toward Home,* 151–52.

36 According to the 1993 *Encyclopedia of Associations,* the Family Research Council (FRC) has fifty thousand members. Weber and Jones report that the FRC has a staff of over twenty-five, plus volunteers and interns (*U.S. Religious Interest Groups,* 77). Because the FRC is an educational organization (incorporated as a 501(c)(3)), in 1992 Gary Bauer founded American Renewal (incorporated as a 501(c)(4)) as an affiliate of FRC (Gary Bauer, fundraising letter for American Renewal, 15 June 1995, 1). Frustrated with the 1996 elections, in 1997 Bauer founded a political action committee called the Campaign for Working Families "to elect pro-family, pro-life, pro–free enterprise candidates" (Bauer, fundraising letter, 6 February 1997, 2). In 1999, Bauer left FRC to run in the Republican presidential primaries.

37 "Western Empire," *Denver Post,* 15 February 1998; Ralph Hallow, "GOP Ally's Threat Seen Cause for Party Concern: Dobson Vows to Pull Out 2.1 Million Members," *Washington Times,* 17 February 1998, sec. A, p. 4; "Dobson Hears Appeals of House Conservatives; Angry Moralist Cancels Interviews after Session," *Washington Times,* 20 March 1998, sec. A, p. 4; Muriel Dobbin, "GOP Promises Right Wing It Will Try Harder," *Rocky Mountain News,* 9 May 1998, sec. A, p. 42; Jim VandeHei, "GOP Leaders Craft Agenda to Please Conservatives," *Roll Call,* 23 April 1998, NEXIS, accessed 15 June 1998.

38 "Arrington Gets Backing from Dobson," *Bulletin Frontrunner,* 23 April 1998, quoting Brown, *Denver Post,* 22 April 1998; "Terry Fundraising Tops

$500,000; Endorsed by Dobson," *Bulletin Frontrunner,* 19 May 1998, quoting Gavin, *Syracuse Herald American,* 17 May 1998, NEXIS, accessed 15 June 1998.

39 *Coming Home: A Family Album,* VHS (Colorado Springs: FOF, 1993).

40 *Focus on the Family: Our Faith, Values, Mission and Guiding Principles,* n.d., received with the November 1995 newsletter, 5.

41 James Dobson, newsletter (Colorado Springs: FOF, April 1996), 3.

42 Phone interview, 25 January 1996.

43 *Focus on the Family: Our Faith, Values, Mission and Guiding Principles,* 6–7.

44 Jose Casanova, *Public Religions in the Modern World* (Chicago: University of Chicago Press, 1994).

45 These ideas come from many conversations with Kelly Jarrett.

46 Steve Bruce, "The Inevitable Failure of the Christian Right," *Sociology of Religion* 55, no. 3 (1994): 240–41.

7 Remembering the Sixties as Pop Cultural Conspiracy

"Everyone's Best Interest Group"

1 Charles B. Strozier, *Apocalypse: On the Psychology of Fundamentalism in America* (Boston: Beacon, 1994), 3, 46–55. For similar views, see Timothy Weber, *Living in the Shadow of the Second Coming,* rev. ed. (Chicago: University of Chicago Press, 1987), 229; Ernest Sandeen, *The Roots of Fundamentalism* (Chicago: University of Chicago Press, 1970), 211.

2 Sigmund Freud, "Mourning and Melancholia," in *Standard Edition,* trans. James Strachey (London: Hogarth, 1964), 14:243–58.

3 Mark Juergensmeyer, *Terror in the Mind of God* (Berkeley: University of California Press, 2000), 159.

4 Billy Graham, *Approaching Hoofbeats* (Waco, TX: Word Books, 1983), 203, quoted in Susan Harding, *The Book of Jerry Falwell* (Princeton, NJ: Princeton University Press, 2000), 49.

5 Stephanie Coontz, *The Way We Never Were* (New York: Basic, 1992).

6 This evaluative shift characterizes the Christian right in general. See Didi Herman, *The Antigay Agenda* (Chicago: University of Chicago Press, 1997), 29.

7 James Dobson, newsletter (Colorado Springs: FOF, June 1994), 7.

8 James Dobson, newsletter (Colorado Springs: FOF, May 1993), 3.

9 Steven Tipton analyzes how some 1960s hippies became born again in the 1970s in *Getting Saved from the Sixties* (Berkeley: University of California Press, 1982).

10 James Dobson, *1968 Re-visited: Baby Boomers Look Back,* cassette recording 793 (Colorado Springs: FOF, 1993).

11 James Dobson, *Dare to Discipline* (Wheaton, IL: Tyndale House, 1970), 22.

12 Dobson, newsletter (May 1993).

13 James Dobson, *Dare to Discipline*, 2d ed. (Wheaton, IL: Tyndale, 1992), 127–28.

14 Dobson, newsletter (May 1993), 2, citing "According to John," *Time*, 12 August 1966, 38.

15 David Noebel, *The Marxist Minstrels: A Handbook on Communist Subversion of Music* (Tulsa, OK: American Christian College, 1974), and *Communism, Hypnotism and the Beatles* (Tulsa, OK: Christian Crusade, 1965). The Summit graduated three hundred teenagers a year until Noebel appeared on Dobson's radio program, after which it has graduated about one thousand a year (*A Summit Experience for Leaders*, cassette 752 [Colorado Springs: FOF, 1992]). Dobson became connected to Noebel when Dobson's son attended Noebel's Summit Ministries. Noebel describes his mission: "Christian teens who have graduated from high school and are heading off to our institutions of higher humanistic education . . . need to hear exactly what they will be facing in their freshman English classes, their politically correct classes, their feminoids, evolutionistic, world government brainwash!! And the Summit is just the right antidote for such an educational experience" (*Summit Journal*, April 1993, 6).

16 Noebel, *Marxist Minstrels*, 53–54.

17 James Dobson and Gary Bauer, *Children at Risk* (Dallas: Word, 1990), 5–12; hereafter cited in text as *Children*.

18 Lawrence Grossberg, *We Gotta Get Out of This Place* (New York: Routledge, 1992), 80, 85. Far from being a newcomer to pop culture, religion played a crucial role in pioneering its forms. See R. Laurence Moore, *Selling God* (Oxford: Oxford University Press, 1994).

19 Grossberg, *We Gotta Get Out of This Place*, 83–84.

20 James Hunter interprets the culture war as competing systems of authority in *Culture Wars* (New York: Basic Books, 1992).

21 Grossberg, *We Gotta Get Out of This Place*, 282.

22 Stuart Hall, *The Hard Road to Renewal* (London: Verso, 1988), 34–35.

23 Alan Wolfe, "Politics by Other Means," *New Republic*, 11 November 1991, 39, 40, cited in Grossberg, *We Gotta Get Out of This Place*, 15.

24 Dobson specifically refutes the idea that these cultural changes result from a casual and random drift in mores over time (*Children at Risk*, 2d ed., 37–38). "The family is not simply disintegrating from natural forces and pressures. Its demise is being orchestrated at the highest levels of government and by radical special interest groups" (James Dobson, newsletter [Colorado Springs: FOF, January 1994], 6).

25 Stephen O'Leary, *Arguing the Apocalypse* (New York: Oxford University Press, 1994), 180.

26 David W. Blight, " 'For Something beyond the Battlefield': Frederick Douglass and the Struggle for the Memory of the Civil War," *Journal of American History* 75 (March 1989): 1167.

27 Rolf Zettersten, *Dr. Dobson: Turning Hearts toward Home* (Dallas: Word, 1989), 143.

28 Larry Burtoft, *Setting the Record Straight: What Research Really Says about the Social Consequences of Homosexuality* (Colorado Springs: FOF, 1994), 4.

29 James Dobson, newsletter (Colorado Springs: FOF, January 1995).

30 Anna Marie Smith makes a similar argument for the British Right in *New Right Discourse on Race and Sexuality* (Cambridge, England: Cambridge University Press, 1994).

31 Greg R. Jesson and Joan Eldredge, *Community Impact Seminar* (Colorado Springs: FOF, 1993), 30; hereafter cited in text as *CIS*.

32 Seminars are usually held in cooperation with a local organization affiliated with Focus on the Family. The Community Impact Seminar I attended in spring 1994 was held in Asheville and cosponsored by the North Carolina Family Policy Council. Over five hundred people attended. In June 1995, the North Carolina Family Policy Council hired a community impact director to work full time with the committees that formed in churches across the state as a result of the Community Impact Seminar (Bill Brooks, letter inserted into the *North Carolina Family Policy News*, December 1995, n.p.).

33 Not all Dobson's statements are consistent with the Seminar's rejection of America as a Christian nation in favor of recognizing religious pluralism as a "sociological fact." Perhaps Dobson and younger members of his organization do not always see eye-to-eye on this issue. It is possible that his followers push the soft-sell approach that he pioneered further than Dobson himself is prepared to go.

34 Matthew Moen, *The Transformation of the Christian Right* (Tuscaloosa: University of Alabama Press, 1992), 133, 34.

35 Linda Kintz, *Between Jesus and the Market* (Durham, NC: Duke University Press, 1997), 121; George Marsden, *Fundamentalism and American Culture* (New York: Oxford University Press, 1980), 14–19, and "Preachers of Paradox: The Religious New Right in Historical Perspective," in *Religion and America*, ed. Mary Douglas and Steven Tipton (1982; Boston: Beacon, 1983), 162–65.

36 Josh McDowell and Bob Hostetler, *The New Tolerance: How a Cultural Movement Threatens to Destroy You, Your Faith and Your Children* (Wheaton, IL: Tyndale House, 1998).

37 Writes Grossberg: "This shift to the Right cannot be described in purely ideological terms; it does not necessarily signal a transformation in the ideological positions of the population. For example, the vast majority of the population have consistently opposed the use of military force in inter-

national relations (another reason for Reagan's creation of a second administrative apparatus to supply the Contras) and they have consistently supported taxing the rich to fund more social programs and greater ecological incentives. In fact, it seems that people need not agree with the ideology or the specific programs of the ascending conservative alliance to find themselves drawn into its discourses or its positions" (*We Gotta Get Out of This Place,* 161). Likewise, political scientist Jerome L. Himmelstein notes that polls indicate that Americans' views on social issues remained liberal during the 1980s: *To the Right: The Transformation of American Conservatism* (Berkeley: University of California Press, 1990), 105.

38 George Marsden, *Fundamentalism and American Culture* (New York: Oxford University Press, 1980), 85.

39 *Focus on the Family: Our Faith, Values, Mission and Guiding Principles,* n.d., received with the November 1995 newsletter, 5.

40 Historians John D'Emilio and Estelle Freedman argue that what distinguishes the purity crusades currently waged by the Christian right from similar crusades waged earlier in the century is this focus on youth sexuality: *Intimate Matters* (New York: Harper and Row, 1988), 353.

41 Martin Reisebrodt, *Pious Passion,* trans. Don Reneau (Berkeley: University of California Press, 1993), 9, 94, 192.

42 James Dobson, preface to "Let's Make a Memory" (Colorado Springs: FOF, 1992), pamphlet excerpting Shirley Dobson and Gloria Gaither, *Let's Make a Memory* (Dallas: Word, 1983).

43 Dobson, *Dare to Discipline* (1970), 27, 35.

44 James Dobson, *The New Dare to Discipline* (Wheaton, IL: Tyndale House, 1992), 19; second and third ellipses in original.

45 Ibid.

46 Phillip Greven, *The Protestant Temperament* (New York: New American Library, 1977); Kintz, *Between Jesus and the Market,* 43.

47 For analysis of this change, see Lionel Lewis and Dennis Brissett, "Sex as God's Work," *Society* 23 (March–April 1986): 67–75; Barbara Ehrenreich, Elizabeth Hess, and Gloria Jacobs, *Re-making Love* (Garden City, NJ: Anchor, 1986).

48 Dobson, *Dare to Discipline* (1970, 1992), 16–17.

49 Kintz, *Between Jesus and the Market,* 44.

50 Joseph Daniel Unwin, *Sexual Regulations and Cultural Behavior: An Address Delivered before the Medical Section of the British Psychological Society on 25 March 1935* (London: Oxford University Press, 1935; U.S. reprint 1969).

51 James Dobson, "A New Look at Masculinity and Femininity" (Colorado Springs: FOF, 1992), pamphlet excerpting Dobson's *Straight Talk* (Dallas: Word, 1991).

52 Randall Bailey, "They're Nothing but Incestuous Bastards: The Polemical Use of Sex and Sexuality in Hebrew Canon Narratives," unpublished paper presented at Duke University, Durham, NC, January 1993.

53 Regina Schwartz, "The Histories of David: Biblical Scholarship and Biblical Stories," in *Not in Heaven,* ed. Jason P. Rosenblatt and Joseph F. Sitterson (Bloomington: Indiana University Press, 1991), 192–210; Mieke Bal, *Death and Dissymmetry* (Chicago: University of Chicago Press, 1988).

54 Michel Foucault, *Discipline and Punish,* trans. Alan Sheridan (New York: Vintage, 1977), 29–30.

8 Nichemarketing the Family Homestead
Rearticulating Mainstream Silences in the Romance of Privatism

1 Lawrence Grossberg, *We Gotta Get Out of This Place* (New York: Routledge, 1994), 82–83. See his definitions of disciplined mobilization and structured mobility, 398.

2 Ibid., 294.

3 This argument builds on the insight advanced by historian Rosalind Pollack Petchesky in her analysis of the antiabortion movement. Noting that the Christian right's pro-family program "invokes deep fears of loss of control over what is considered most private, most personal," Petchesky concludes: "Historically, the concept of 'privacy' for American conservatives has included not only 'free enterprise' and 'property rights,' but also the right of the white male property owner to control his wife and his wife's body, his children and their bodies, his slaves and their bodies. . . . Thus what appear to be attacks on federalism are simultaneously attacks on movements by women, blacks and young people to assert their right to resources, services, and a viable existence outside the family and the ghetto": "Antiabortion, Antifeminism, and the Rise of the New Right," *Feminist Studies* 7, no. 2 (summer 1981): 222.

4 Ibid., 223–24.

5 One could put this question differently. For at the heart of this chapter lies an interpretive conundrum: the Christian right ignores collective entities, yet one of the most salient features of fundamentalist religion is its ability to offer community. In this chapter, I show how framing the culture wars as an opposition between "community or no community" misses the heart of the matter, namely, the kind of community being imagined. Which social spheres can a community see as worth caring about and which social spheres does a community feel it must ignore?

6 Quoted in Marc Cooper, "God and Man in Colorado Springs: Salvation City," *The Nation,* 2 January 1995, 9, NEXIS.

7 James Dobson, newsletter (Colorado Springs: FOF, June 1995), 8.

8 FOF, *Annual Report* (Colorado Springs: FOF, 1993), 2a.

9 Although Focus relocated to Colorado Springs in 1991, it took up temporary residence in two buildings downtown until its new Briargate campus was finished in 1993.

10 Stephanie Coontz, *The Way We Never Were* (New York: Basic Books, 1992), 68–92.

11 Linda Kerber, "Women and Individualism in American History," *Massachusetts Review* (winter 1989): 604–5; quoted in ibid., 73.

12 Coontz, *The Way We Never Were,* 73.

13 Ibid., 78.

14 Ibid., 79.

15 Jeffrey A. Roberts, "Colorado Growth Spurt Highest Since '70s: State's Increase in Population 3rd Fastest in Nation," *Denver Post,* 29 December 1993, sec. A, pp. 1, 16. In 1993, Colorado ranked third in the nation in population growth, fourth in employment growth, and ninth in personal income growth. In 1993, over seventy thousand more people moved into Colorado than moved away, a figure that marks the highest in-migration in twenty years. See Palmer McAllister, *Colorado Springs Economic Review and Outlook,* 1994, Palmer Collection, Penrose Public Library, Colorado Springs, 3.

16 Robert Loevy, quoted in *Colorado Business Magazine,* February 1993, 25. The Colorado Springs Economic Development Council estimated that in 1993 the city was home to over three hundred thousand people, 81.5 percent of whom are white, 6.9 percent black, 8.4 percent Hispanic, and 3.2 percent "other": Greater Colorado Springs Economic Development Council, *Colorado Springs Fact Sheet,* 1.

17 Mike Davis, *City of Quartz* (New York: Vintage, 1990), 161–62; David Chalmers, *Hooded Americanism* (1965, 1968; New York: Franklin Watts, 1981), 118.

18 Davis, *City of Quartz,* 165–66.

19 Gary Miller, *Cities by Contract* (Cambridge, MA: MIT Press, 1981), 176; quoted in ibid., 166.

20 Davis, *City of Quartz,* 182. Davis documents multiple connections among homeowners associations, antibusing movements, and tax-payers associations. For similar connections, see Y. H. Lo, *Small Property versus Big Business* (Berkeley: University of California Press, 1990).

21 Davis, *City of Quartz,* 180, 215 n. 62, 183.

22 Samuel Francis, "Message from MARS: The Social Politics of the New

Right," in *Beautiful Losers: Essays on the Failure of American Conservatism* (Columbia: University of Missouri Press, 1993), 60–78. Francis appropriated the designation "Middle American Radicals" from sociologist Donald Warren's study of George Wallace.

23 Mike Davis, *Prisoners of the American Dream* (New York: Verso, 1986).

24 See Mike Davis, "Who Killed LA? A Political Autopsy," *New Left Review* 197 (1993): 17; Thomas Byrne Edsall and Mary D. Edsall, *Chain Reaction* (1991; New York: Norton, 1992).

25 Karen de Witt, "Burbs Have Pull at Polls," *Denver Post*, 25 December 1994, sec. A, pp. 1, 20.

26 My analysis of this mythic geography draws on anthropologist Michael Taussig's claim that a moral topography/poetics of control informed how white Europeans saw and colonized the landscape of the Andes: *Shamanism, Colonialism, and the Wild Man* (Chicago: University of Chicago Press, 1987), 287–335.

27 Hazel Carby, *Race Men* (Cambridge, MA: Harvard University Press, 1998), 170.

28 Ibid., 169.

29 Alan Wolfe, *One Nation After All* (New York: Viking, 1998), 191.

30 Ibid., 193–94. Wolfe notes that the percentage of African Americans living in the suburbs has increased from 21 in 1980 to 27 in 1990 to 30 in 1994. Their average income in 1990 was 55 percent higher than the average income of African Americans living in the inner city (185–86). Wolfe's reading of the suburbs is quite different from the one I develop. See Wolfe's chapter "Suburbia's Changing Moral Story," 180–228.

31 James Dobson and Gary Bauer, *Children at Risk* (Dallas: Word, 1990), 31.

32 Ibid., 182–83.

33 "The only dependable route from poverty is always work, family and faith. The first principle is that in order to move up, the poor must not only work, they must work harder than the classes above them. Every previous generation of the lower class has made such efforts. But the current poor, white even more than black, are refusing to work hard": George Gilder, *Wealth and Poverty* (San Francisco: Institute for Contemporary Studies Press, 1993), 79.

34 Ibid., 82.

35 Ibid.

36 James Dobson, *Straight Talk to Men and Their Wives* (Waco, TX: Word, 1980), 32–33.

37 Kaja Silverman, *Male Subjectivity at the Margins* (New York: Routledge, 1992).

38 Elaine Tyler May, *Homeward Bound* (New York: Basic, 1988), 16, 19–20.

39 David Savran, *Taking It Like a Man: White Masculinity, Masochism, and*

Contemporary American Culture (Princeton, NJ: Princeton University Press, 1998), 46–48.

40 John D'Emilio, "Homosexual Menace," in *Making Trouble* (New York: Routledge, 1992), 57–73, and *Sexual Politics, Sexual Communities* (Chicago: University of Chicago Press, 1983). For an oral history of the effects that antigay and antilesbian campaigns in the Florida University system during the 1950s had on the lives of gay men and lesbians, see James Sears, *Lonely Hunters* (Boulder, CO: Westview, 1997), 48–107.

41 William Chafe, *The Unfinished Journey* (New York: Oxford University Press, 1986), 148–68.

42 Judith Butler, *Gender Trouble* (New York: Routledge, 1990); John Fiske, "Popular Culture," *Critical Term for Literary Study*, 2d ed., ed. Frank Lentricchia and Thomas McLaughlin (1990; Chicago: University of Chicago Press, 1995), 321–35.

43 Angela Davis, *Blues Legacies and Black Feminism* (New York: Pantheon, 1998), 46.

44 John D'Emilio, "Capitalism and Gay Identity," in *Making Trouble* (New York: Routledge, 1992), 3–16. Julie Matthaei points out that it took the post–World War II breakdown of the sexual division of labor and the resulting increase in women's economic independence to make it easier for women to create identities and communities organized around erotic/ emotional connection with other women: "The Sexual Division of Labor, Sexuality, and Lesbian/Gay Liberation: Towards a Marxist-Feminist Analysis of Sexuality in U.S. Capitalism," in *Homo Economics*, ed. Amy Gluckman and Betsy Reed (New York: Routledge, 1998), 135–64.

45 D'Emilio, "Capitalism and Gay Identity," 11, 13.

46 David Harvey, *The Condition of Postmodernity* (Cambridge, England: Blackwell, 1990), 101.

47 Quoted in "God and Man in Colorado Springs: Salvation City," *The Nation*, 2 January 1995, p. 9, NEXIS.

48 Sam Bass Warner Jr., *The Private City*, 2d ed. (Philadelphia: University of Pennsylvania Press, 1987), 3–4; quoted in Timothy Barnekov, Robin Boyle, and Daniel Rich, *Privatism and Urban Policy in Britain and the United States* (Oxford: Oxford University Press, 1989), 1.

49 Barnekov, Boyle and Rich, *Privatism*, 15.

50 Marshall Sprague, *Newport in the Rockies*, rev. ed. (Athens: Ohio University Press, 1987), 5–7, 9, 15–16, 20. Palmer's vision of building a town as a way to integrate his entrepreneurial ambitions with his need for love proved to be a house bought on borrowed time. Queen never did get over her fear of the Wild West and its Indian inhabitants, eventually moving to Newport, Rhode Island, before finally settling in London (the real one this time).

51 McAllister, *Colorado Springs Economic Outlook,* 9.

52 Sprague, *Newport in the Rockies,* xviii, 303.

53 Ibid., xvii. The Chamber of Commerce claims that the military provided one out of every five jobs (totaling 58 percent of the local economic base), listing the city's three top employers in the metropolitan area as Fort Carson (20,000), Peterson Air Force Base (7,800), and the Air Force Academy (4,000): Chamber of Commerce, *Introduction to Colorado Springs* (received in 1994), 13. For related figures, see McAllister, *Colorado Springs Economic Review,* 14, 16; Colorado Springs Economic Development Council, *Colorado Springs Fact Sheet.*

54 Sprague, *Newport in the Rockies,* 303.

55 Chamber of Commerce, *Introduction to Colorado Springs,* 17.

56 Economist John M. Levy estimates that by 1980 there were fifteen thousand such organizations operating in U.S. communities: *Economic Development Programs for Cities, Counties, and Towns* (New York: Praeger, 1981), 1; quoted in Barnekov, Boyle, and Rich, *Privatism,* 75.

57 Barnekov, Boyle, and Rich, *Privatism,* 74.

58 Ibid., 65–74.

59 Ibid., 75–76.

60 Ibid., 85, citing Robert Goodman, *The Last Entrepreneurs* (New York: Simon and Schuster, 1979), 4.

61 Fantus Corporation, "An Economic Base Analysis of the Greater Colorado Springs Metropolitan Area: Final Report," December 1987, Palmer Collection, Penrose Public Library, Colorado Springs, 20.

62 McAllister, *Colorado Springs Economic Review,* 19. According to the Fantus report, the Springs lost over twenty-four hundred high-tech jobs to mass marketing in Mexico and Asia, where labor was even cheaper. Moreover, the report noted that most high-tech industries move from prototype to mass production to obsolescence in just two to four years (Fantus, "Economic Base Analysis," 35).

63 Sandi Dolbee, "Religious War Turns Rocky in Colorado," *San Diego Union Tribune,* 28 July 1995, sec. E, p. 1, NEXIS; Steve Rabey, "Area Christian Groups Continue to Grow in Size, Number," *Colorado Springs Gazette Telegraph,* 27 February 1994, sec. FF, pp. 11–12; Religious News Service, "Churches, Religious Groups Don't Mix in Colorado Springs," *Orlando Sentinel,* 21 November 1992, sec. D, p. 5; Steve Rabey, "Ministries Flocking to Springs," *Colorado Springs Gazette Telegraph,* 20 December 1992, sec. F, pp. 1–3; Pam Zubeck, "City Becomes Evangelical Center," *Colorado Springs Gazette Telegraph,* 28 February 1993, sec. FF, p. 11.

64 FOF, *Annual Report* (Colorado Springs: FOF, 1991), 1; Steve Rabey, "Evangelical Groups Reach Out to World from Springs Home: City Gaining

Reputation as a Center for Religion," *Colorado Springs Gazette Telegraph,* 24 November 1991, sec. A, p. 12.

65 Jim Gibney, "Pomar Grant Nets Ministry for Springs," *Colorado Springs Gazette Telegraph,* 15 June 1990, sec. A, p. 19; "El Pomar Recipients," *Colorado Springs Business Journal,* 15 December 1992, 8. Founded in 1937 with money made in the mining boom of the 1800s, the El Pomar Foundation represents old, established Colorado Springs money, with Colorado College and Denver University receiving many grants from the institution.

66 For example, see the account of a forum sponsored by an organization of nonprofits in Colorado Springs reported by Steve Rabey, "Panelists See Good and Bad in Religious Groups Impact," *Colorado Gazette Telegraph,* 19 November 1992.

67 Dolbee, "Religious War Gets Rocky in Colorado."

68 Tyler Sage Cordingley Stevens, "The Economic Impact of Nonprofit Organizations on El Paso County" (Master's thesis, Colorado College, 1993), 60.

69 Marc Cooper, "God and Man in Colorado Springs: Salvation City," *The Nation,* 260, no. 1 (2 January 1995): 9, NEXIS; Peggy James, "Religious Organizations a Small but Important Part of Local Economy," *Colorado Springs Business Journal,* 15 June 1992, 22; "Religious Exemption Bill Advances," UPI, 9 May 1989, sec. regional, NEXIS; "Bill Easing Religious Exemptions Standard Moves Ahead," *Daily Report for Executives,* 17 March 1989, NEXIS; "Tax Break for Religious Organizations," *Daily Report for Executives,* 19 May 1989, NEXIS; "Property Tax Exemption for Religious Organizations," *Daily Report for Executives,* 31 March 1989, NEXIS.

70 Interview with author, June 1994.

71 Michael Meyer and Kenneth Woodward, "Onward Muscular Christians," *Newsweek,* 1 March 1993, 68; Dirk Johnson, "Rise in Christian Right Divides a City," *New York Times,* 14 February 1993, 10; Peggy Lowe, "The Epicenter of the Family Values Movement," AP, 20 December 1992; Nancy Cleeland, Alan Gottlieb, and Virginia Culver, "A House Divided? Influx of Religious Groups Rattles Springs," *Denver Post,* 15 November 1992, sec. C, p. 1.

72 Citizens' Project [CP], *Freedom Watch,* newsletter (Colorado Springs: CP, May 1997), 3.

73 Interview with author, Colorado Springs, June 1994.

74 Quoted in Marc Cooper, "God and Man in Colorado Springs: Salvation City," *The Nation,* 2 January 1995, 9, NEXIS.

75 James Dobson, *What Wives Wish Their Husbands Knew about Women* (Wheaton, IL: Tyndale House, 1975), reprinted as the pamphlet *Materialism: Enemy of the Family* (Colorado Springs: FOF, 1993), 4–5.

76 Stephanie Coontz, *The Social Origins of Private Life* (New York: Verso, 1988), 210, 193–94, 212.

77 James Dobson, *When God Doesn't Make Sense* (Wheaton, IL: Tyndale, 1993).

78 Rolf Zettersten, *Turning Hearts toward Home,* 12–13, 26–27.

79 Ibid., 102.

80 Ibid., 101–3. *Coming Home: A Family Home* (Colorado Springs: FOF, 1993), VHS.

81 Regina Schwartz, *The Curse of Cain: The Violent Legacy of Monotheism* (Chicago: University of Chicago Press, 1997), 11.

82 Eithne Johnson, "The Emergence of Christian Video and the Cultivation of Videovangelism" in *Media, Culture and the Religious Right,* ed. Linda Kintz and Julia Lesage (Minneapolis: University of Minnesota Press, 1998), 200, 202.

83 Paul Boyer, *When Time Shall Be No More* (Cambridge, MA: Harvard University Press, 1992), 258–60.

84 Robert Bradley, *Citizen Soldier: A Manual of Community Based Defense* (Reliance Publications, 1994).

85 SFA, *Special Report on the Meeting of Christian Men Held in Estes Park Colorado October 23, 24, 25 1992 Concerning the Killing of Vickie [sic] and Samuel Weaver by the United States Government* (LaPorte, CO: SFA, 1992), 4.

86 Pete Peters, "Preparation for the October 1992 Meeting of the Men of God," cassette tape 556 (LaPorte, CO: SFA, n.d.).

87 Mieke Bal, *Death and Dissymetry* (Chicago: University of Chicago Press, 1988).

88 The Hebrew term used to denote the woman in this text, usually translated as concubine, is contested as to its meaning.

89 Peters, Preparation for October 1992 Meeting of the Men of God. In the biblical book of Judges, it is unclear whether the woman dies at the hands of her rapists or at the hands of her husband when he dismembers her.

90 Ibid.

91 SFA, *Special Report,* 11.

92 Pete Peters, *America the Conquered* (LaPorte, CO: SFA, 1991, 1993), 218–22.

93 County rule is an offshoot of the Wise Use movement, which opposes federal environmental regulation, claiming that the ranchers and private businesspeople who make their living off the land know best how to preserve public land. See David Helvarg, *The War against the Greens* (San Francisco: Sierra Club, 1994).

94 Ibid., 235.

95 Ibid., 123.

96 Pete Peters, newsletter, vol. 5 (LaPorte, CO: SFA, 1994), 10.

97 Pete Peters, "Report on a Flag Burning," sermon cassette 633 (LaPorte, CO: SFA, speech delivered on 22 October 1994).

98 Michel Foucault, *The History of Sexuality,* trans. Robert Hurley (New York: Vintage, 1978), 1:144.

99 Michel Foucault, "Governmentality," ed. and trans. Pasquale Pasquino, *Ideology and Consciousness* 6 (1979): 10, 20.

100 Peters, *America the Conquered,* 229.

101 This reading is heavily influenced by Nancy MacLean's analysis of the 1920s Klan in *Behind the Mask of Chivalry* (New York: Oxford University Press, 1994), especially p. 97.

102 Peters, *America the Conquered,* 224.

9 The Bowl, the Crossing Point, and The Moment After

1 Gayatri Chakravorty Spivak, "The New Historicism: Political Commitment and the Postmodern Critic," in *The New Historicism,* ed. Aram Veeser (New York: Routledge, 1989), 281.

2 Toni Morrison, *Playing in the Dark* (Cambridge, MA: Harvard University Press, 1992), 45–47; emphasis added.

3 Ibid., 17.

4 Toni Morrison, *Beloved* (New York: Plume, 1987), 199.

5 James Baldwin, *Another Country* (1962, 1988; New York: Vantage, 1990).

6 Judith Butler, *The Psychic Life of Power* (Stanford: Stanford University Press, 1997), 191.

7 Nancy Scheper-Hughes and Carolyn Sargent, "Introduction: The Cultural Politics of Childhood," in *Small Wars,* ed. Scheper-Hughes and Sargent (Berkeley: University of California Press, 1998), 10.

8 Miranda Joseph, "The Perfect Moment: Christians, Gays, and the NEA," *Socialist Review* 3–4 (1996): 111.

9 In an insightful analysis of the different kinds of amnesia that afflict the nation's collective memory of Martin Luther King Jr., Michael Eric Dyson speaks of resistant amnesia: "The deliberate repression of painful memory is intended to give the injured person or group the need to mend and to fashion an existence that depends less on the past and more on the present. The danger of such an approach, of course, is that the injured party fails to grasp the important lessons of one's suffering for one's group but also for the nation": *I May Not Get There with You: The True Martin Luther King, Jr.* (New York: Free Press, 2000), 292.

10 Pete Peters, *Special Report: Framing Deceit* (LaPorte, CO: SFA, 1996), 6; and newsletter, vol. 2 (LaPorte, CO: SFA, 1996), 2.

11 Joseph, "The Perfect Moment," 121.

12 Dyson, *I May Not Get There with You,* 170–73.

13 For examples, see Jeffrey Kaplan, "The Context of American Millenarian Revolutionary Theology: The Case of 'Identity Christian' Church of Israel," *Terrorism and Political Violence* 5, no. 1 (spring 1993): 30–82, and "The Anti-Cult Movement in America: A History of Culture Perspective," *Syzygy* 2, nos. 3–4 (1993): 267–96; James Hunter, *Culture Wars* (New York: Basic, 1992), 170 and passim; Alan Wolfe, *One Nation After All* (New York: Viking, 1998).

14 Wendy Brown, *States of Freedom* (Princeton, NJ: Princeton University Press, 1995), 7.

15 I offer this example as a place where I work with these dynamics in my own life in a concrete way, not as a universal definition of lesbian identification. In *Render Me, Gender Me,* Weston suggests that those of us whose gender and sexual identifications focus on ambivalence and ambiguity might share an experience of other sorts of mobility—most notably, the class mobility that comes with education. Elsewhere, Weston has noted that a stock episode in many coming-out narratives is "the book": going to the dictionary or the library to look up "homosexuality" and learn who you are. Superimposing these two tropes has formed a powerful articulation in my life. See Kath Weston, *Render Me, Gender Me* (New York: Columbia University, 1996), 88, and *Long Slow Burn* (New York: Routledge, 1998), 35.

16 Kelly Jarrett, "Strange Bedfellows: Religion, Feminism and Fundamentalism in the Satanic Panic" (Ph.D. diss., Duke University, 2000), 201–10. In her dissertation, Jarrett analyzes the satanic ritual abuse panics that arose in the early 1980s, arguing that these repudiated investments returned, effectively silencing what Jarrett calls "the common horrible" of violence in women's lives.

17 Joseph, "The Perfect Moment," 121. For exploration of the complexity of this repudiation/connection, see the essays collected by Gary Comstock and Susan Henking in *Que(e)rying Religion* (New York: Continuum, 1997). This "incompatibility" is also under review in a new way, one different from the Metropolitan Community Church. A recent article in the *Chronicle of Higher Education* profiled a controversy sparked by gay and lesbian evangelical students who, believing it is ok for themselves to be actively gay or lesbian, ran for a leadership role in their campus evangelical group, where they were banned from occupying leadership positions on the grounds that their beliefs run counter to the group's religious beliefs: Beth McMurtie, "A Christian Fellowship's Ban on Gay Leader Splits Two Campuses," *Chronicle of Higher Education,* 12 May 2000, sec. A, pp. 51–52.

18 Weston, "Get Thee to a Big City," in *Long Slow Burn,* 29–56.

19 Sally R. Munt, introduction to *Butch/Femme: Inside Lesbian Gender,* ed. Sally R. Munt (London: Cassell, 1998), 4–7. Munt formulates her com-

ments with reference to lesbian identity, and specifically with reference to butch/femme identities (which plunges this issue into a discussion of class as well, given the working-class origin of butch/femme roles). If and how these comments apply to other social markings will take further reflection.

20 Joseph, "The Perfect Moment," 114.

21 David Harvey, *The Urban Experience* (Baltimore: Johns Hopkins University Press, 1989), 31, 35.

22 Joseph, "The Perfect Moment," 116. Joseph outlines the theoretical apparatus undergirding her analysis at greater length in "The Performance of Production and Consumption" *Social Text* 16, no. 1 (spring 1998): 25–61.

23 George Yudice, "The Privatization of Culture," *Social Text* 59 (summer 1999): 10.

24 Saskia Sassen, *Losing Control? Sovereignty in an Age of Globalization* (New York: Columbia University Press, 1996), 22. Hence the declining profile of government agencies devoted to domestic equity and the ascent of government agencies concerned with the market. See Sassen, *Globalization and Its Discontents* (New York: New Press, 1998), xxvii. In following Sassen's argument regarding the shifting and declining—but not completely disappearing—significance of the nation-state, I am diverging somewhat from Joseph's reading.

25 Sassen, *Globalization and Its Discontents,* 48, 90.

26 Ibid., xiii, 87; Sassen, *Losing Control,* 37.

27 In this connection, I note that this dynamic of performing community is present in my text as well, in the form of this ambiguous "we" I keep using: this pesky plural pronoun keeps reappearing as quickly as I keep trying to excise it. This "we" seems to hold the space of a condition of this writing, as if I cannot write without fabricating allies, a community that does not really exist, I know. There is a lot of slippage in this "we": slippage that I tried to mark before we began by situating the different dimensions of my life from which this work comes. But as the writing has proceeded, these audiences fall asunder. For this "bowl" does not hold all of us equally. Nor does it make us equally possible. Nor are the existences that it permits all equal. The whiteness that makes my life and this writing possible—my education, my job, my house—holds impossibility for others. And as African American slave narratives sought to make clear, being white holds impossibility for myself as well, albeit impossibility of a different kind. So I interrupt to name these differences here, even though there is no justice in a noun. Nouns cannot but fall short of conveying the dynamics through which identities are inhabited and refused, complicated and cross-cut by other loves.

28 For a thoughtful analysis of the issues at stake here, see Valerie Lehr, *Queer Family Values* (Philadelphia: Temple University Press, 1999).

29 Brown, *States of Injury,* 43–45. Brown notes that this focus has arisen as a response to the Right's attack on the welfare state, along with "the stark abandonment of freedom as an element of the communist project long before its 1989 fall" (10).

30 Ibid., 4.

31 Ibid.

32 Regina Schwartz, "Joseph's Bones and the Resurrection of the Text," in *The Book and the Text,* ed. Regina Schwartz (Cambridge, MA: Basil Blackwell, 1990), 40–59.

33 Ibid., 49.

34 Jon Butler, "Slavery and the African Spiritual Holocaust," in *Awash in a Sea of Faith: Christianizing the American People* (Cambridge, MA: Harvard University Press, 1990), 129–63.

35 Janet Duitsman Cornelius, *When I Can Read My Title Clear: Literacy, Slavery, and Religion in the Antebellum South* (Columbia: University of South Carolina Press, 1991), especially 13, 16–17.

36 Morrison, *Beloved,* 181.

Select Bibliography of Secondary Sources

Aho, James A. *The Politics of Righteousness: Idaho Christian Patriotism.* Seattle: University of Washington Press, 1990.

——. *This Thing of Darkness: A Sociology of the Enemy.* Seattle: University of Washington Press, 1994.

——. "Popular Christianity and Political Extremism in the United States." In *Disruptive Religion: The Force of Faith in Social-Movement Activism,* Christian Smith, 189–204. New York: Routledge, 1996.

Al-Azm, Sadik. "Islamic Fundamentalism Reconsidered: A Critical Outline, Part I." *South Asia Bulletin* 13, nos. 1–2 (1993): 93–121.

——. "Islamic Fundamentalism Reconsidered: A Critical Outline, Part II." *South Asia Bulletin* 14, no. 1 (1994): 73–98.

Almaguer, Tomas. *Racial Faultlines: The Historical Origins of White Supremacy in California.* Berkeley: University of California Press, 1994.

Althusser, Louis. *For Marx.* Trans. Ben Brewster. London: Allen Lane, 1969.

Althusser, Louis, and Etienne Balibar. *Reading Capital.* Trans. Ben Brewster. London: New Left Books, 1970.

Ammerman, Nancy Tatum. *Bible Believers: Fundamentalists in the Modern World.* New Brunswick, NJ: Rutgers University Press, 1987.

——. "North American Protestant Fundamentalism." In *Fundamentalisms Observed,* ed. Martin E. Marty and R. Scott Appleby, 1–65. Chicago: University of Chicago Press, 1991.

Anderson, Benedict. *Imagined Communities: Reflections on the Origin and Spread of Nationalism.* 1983; New York: Verso, 1991.

Anderson, Robert. *Vision of the Disinherited: The Making of American Pentecostalism.* Peabody, MA: Hendrickson, 1992.

Appleby, Scott R. *The Ambivalence of the Sacred: Religion, Violence and Reconciliation.* New York: Rowman and Littlefield, 2000.

Asad, Talal. *Genealogies of Religion: Discipline and Reasons of Power in Christianity and Islam.* Baltimore: Johns Hopkins University Press, 1993.

Austin, J. L. *How to Do Things with Words.* Cambridge, MA: Harvard University Press, 1962.

Bach, Alice. *Women, Seduction and Betrayal in Biblical Narrative.* New York: Cambridge University Press, 1997.

Bailey, Randall. "They're Nothing but Incestuous Bastards: The Polemical Use of Sex and Sexuality in Hebrew Canon Narratives." Unpublished paper, presented at Duke University, Durham, NC, January 1993.

Bal, Mieke. *Death and Dissymetry: The Politics of Coherence in the Book of Judges.* Chicago: University of Chicago Press, 1988.

Balibar, Etienne. "The Nation Form: History and Ideology." In *Race, Nation, Class,* ed. Etienne Balibar and Immanuel Wallerstein, trans. Chris Turner, 86–106. New York: Verso, 1991.

Barkun, Michael. *Religion and the Racist Right: The Origins of the Christian Identity Movement.* Chapel Hill: University of North Carolina Press, 1994.

——. "Militias, Christian Identity and the Radical Right." *Christian Century,* 2–9 August 1995, 738–40.

——. "Racist Apocalypse: Millennialism on the Far Right." In *The Year 2000,* ed. Charles Strozier and Michael Flynn, 190–205. New York: Free Press, 1997.

——. *Religion and the Racist Right: The Origins of the Christian Identity Movement.* Rev. ed. with preface and epilogue. Chapel Hill: University of North Carolina Press, 1997.

Barnekov, Timothy, Robin Boyle, and Daniel Rich. *Privatism and Urban Policy in Britain and the United States.* New York: Oxford University Press, 1989.

Baudrillard, Jean. *Simulations.* Trans. Paul Foss, Paul Patton, and Philip Beitchman. New York: Columbia Semiotexte, 1983.

Bendroth, Margaret Lamberts. *Fundamentalism and Gender, 1875 to the Present.* New Haven: Yale University Press, 1993.

Bennett, David. *The Party of Fear: From Nativist Movements to the New Right in American History.* New York: Vintage, 1988.

Bercovitch, Sacvan. *The Puritan Origins of the American Self.* New Haven: Yale University Press, 1975.

——. *The American Jeremiad.* Madison: University of Wisconsin Press, 1978.

Bhabha, Homi, ed. *Nation and Narration.* New York: Routledge, 1990.

Blackburn, Robin. *The Overthrow of Colonial Slavery, 1776–1848.* London: Verso, 1988.

Blight, David. "'For Something beyond the Battlefield': Frederick Douglass and the Struggle for the Memory of the Civil War." *Journal of American History* 75 (March 1989): 1156–178.

Boyer, Paul. *When Time Shall Be No More: Prophecy Belief in American Culture.* Cambridge, MA: Harvard University Press, 1992.

Brennan, Teresa. *The Interpretation of the Flesh: Freud and Femininity.* New York: Routledge, 1992.

Brown, Wendy. *States of Freedom: Power and Freedom in Late Modernity.* Princeton, NJ: Princeton University Press, 1995.

Bruce, Steve. *The Rise and Fall of the Christian Right: Conservative Protestant Politics in America 1978–1988.* Oxford: Clarendon, 1988.

——. *Pray TV: Televangelism in America.* New York: Routledge, 1990.

——. "The Inevitable Failure of the Christian Right." *Sociology of Religion* 55, no. 3 (1994): 229–42.

Burlein, Ann. "Counter-memory on the Right: The Case of Focus on the Family." In *Acts of Memory: Cultural Recall in the Present,* ed. Mieke Bal, Jonathan Crewe, and Leo Spitzer, 215–17. Hanover, NH: University Press of New England, 1999.

Butler, Judith. *Gender Trouble.* New York: Routledge, 1990.

——. *Bodies That Matter: On the Discursive Limits of Sex.* New York: Routledge, 1993.

——. *Excitable Speech: A Politics of the Performative.* New York: Routledge, 1997.

——. *The Psychic Life of Power: Theories in Subjection.* Stanford: Stanford University Press, 1997.

Carby, Hazel. *Reconstructing Womanhood.* New York: Oxford University Press, 1987.

——. *Race Men: (W. E. B. Du Bois Lectures).* Cambridge, MA: Harvard University Press, 1998.

Carter, Dan. *The Politics of Rage: George Wallace, the Origins of the New Conservatism and the Transformation of American Politics.* Baton Rouge: Louisiana State University Press, 1995.

Casanova, Jose. *Public Religion in the Modern World.* Chicago: University of Chicago Press, 1994.

Chafe, William. *The Unfinished Journey: America since World War II.* New York: Oxford University Press, 1986.

Cherry, Conrad. *God's New Israel: Religious Interpretations of American Destiny.* Englewood Cliffs, NJ: Prentice Hall, 1971.

Collins, Adela Yarbro. "Reading the Book of Revelation in the 20th Century." *Interpretation* 40 (1986): 229–42.

Comstock, Gary, and Susan Henking, eds. *Que(e)rying Religion: A Critical Anthology.* New York: Continuum, 1997.

Coontz, Stephanie. *The Social Origins of Private Life: A History of American Families, 1600–1900.* New York: Verso, 1988.

——. *The Way We Never Were: American Families and the Nostalgia Trap.* New York: Basic Books, 1992.

Daniels, Ted. *A Doomsday Reader: Prophets, Predictors, and Hucksters of Salvation.* New York: New York University Press, 1999.

Davis, Angela. *Blues Legacies and Black Feminism: Gertrude "Ma" Rainey, Bessie Smith, and Billie Holiday.* New York: Pantheon, 1998.

Davis, Mike. *Prisoners of the American Dream: Politics and Economy in the History of the U.S. Working Class.* New York: Verso, 1986.

———. *City of Quartz: Excavating the Future in Los Angeles.* New York: Vintage, 1990.

———. "Who Killed LA? A Political Autopsy." *New Left Review* 197 (1993): 3–28.

Dees, Morris, with James Corocoran. *Gathering Storm: America's Militia Threat.* New York: Harper Collins, 1996.

Derrida, Jacques. "Signature Event Context." In *Margins of Philosophy,* trans. Alan Bass, 307–30. Chicago: University of Chicago Press, 1982.

Diamond, Sara. *Spiritual Warfare: The Politics of the Christian Right.* Boston: South End, 1989.

———. *Roads to Dominion: Right-wing Movements and Political Power in the United States.* New York: Guilford, 1995.

DeBerg, Betty. *Ungodly Women: Gender and the First Wave of American Fundamentalism.* Minneapolis: Fortress, 1990.

de Hart, Jane Sherron. "Gender on the Right: Meanings behind the Existential Scream." *Gender and History* 3, no. 3 (autumn 1991): 246–67.

de Hart, Jane Sherron, with Donald Mathews. *Sex, Gender and the Politics of ERA: A State and a Nation.* New York: Oxford University Press, 1990.

D'Emilio, John. *Sexual Politics, Sexual Communities: The Making of a Homosexual Minority in the United States, 1940–1970.* Chicago: University of Chicago Press, 1983.

———. "Capitalism and Gay Identity." In *Making Trouble: Essays on Gay History, Politics and the University,* 3–16. New York: Routledge, 1992.

D'Emilio, John, and Estelle Freedman. *Intimate Matters: A History of Sexuality in America.* New York: Harper and Row, 1988.

Dorfman, Ariel. *Heading South, Looking North.* New York: Farrar, Straus and Giroux, 1998.

Douglas, Susan. *Listening In: Radio and the American Imagination, from Amos 'n' Andy and Edward R. Murrow to Wolfman Jack and Howard Stern.* New York: Random House, 1999.

Dyson, Michael Eric. *I May Not Get There with You: The True Martin Luther King, Jr.* New York: Free Press, 2000.

Edsall, Thomas Byrne, and Mary D. Edsall. *Chain Reaction: The Impact of Race, Rights and Taxes on American Politics.* 1991; New York: Norton, 1992.

Ehrenreich, Barbara, Elizabeth Hess, and Gloria Jacobs. *Re-making Love: The Feminization of Sex.* Garden City, NJ: Anchor/Doubleday, 1986.

Eisenstein, Zillah. *Hatreds: Racialized and Sexualized Conflicts in the 21st Century.* New York: Routledge, 1996.

Ezekiel, Raphael. *The Racist Mind: Portraits of American Neo-Nazis and Klansmen.* New York: Viking, 1995.

Fausto-Sterling, Anne. *Myths of Gender: Biological Theories about Men and Women.* Rev. ed. New York: Basic Books, 1985.

———. *Sexing the Body: Gender Politics and the Construction of Sexuality.* New York: Basic Books, 2000.

Ferber, Abby. *White Man Falling: Race, Gender, and White Supremacy.* New York: Rowman and Littlefield, 1998.

Fiske, John. "Popular Culture." In *Critical Terms for Literary Study,* 2nd ed., ed. Frank Lentricchia and Thomas McLaughlin. 1990; Chicago: University of Chicago Press, 1995.

Flynn, Kevin, and Gary Gerhardt. *The Silent Brotherhood: Inside America's Racist Underground.* New York: Macmillan, 1989.

Foucault, Michel. *Discipline and Punish: The Birth of the Prison.* Trans. Alan Sheridan. New York: Vintage, 1977.

———. *Language, Counter-memory, Practice.* Ed. Donald F. Bouchard. Trans. Donald F. Bouchard and Sherry Simon. Ithaca, NY: Cornell University Press, 1977.

———. *The History of Sexuality: An Introduction.* Vol. 1. Trans. Robert Hurley. New York: Vintage, 1978.

Franklin, John Hope. *Race and History: Selected Essays 1938–1988.* Baton Rouge: Louisiana State University Press, 1989.

Freud, Sigmund. "Mourning and Melancholia." In *Standard Edition,* 14: 243–58. Trans. James Strachey. London: Hogarth, 1964.

Gallagher, John, and Chris Bull. *Perfect Enemies: The Religious Right, the Gay Movement, and the Politics of the 1990s.* New York: Crown, 1996.

Gallop, Jane. *Reading Lacan.* Ithaca, NY: Cornell University Press, 1985.

Gardell, Mattias. "The Order." In *Encyclopedia of White Power,* ed. Jeffrey Kaplan, 233–35. Lanham, MD: Rowman and Littlefield, 2000.

Gibson, James William. *Warrior Dreams: Paramilitary Culture in Post-Vietnam America.* New York: Hill and Wang, 1994.

———. "Is the Apocalypse Coming? Paramilitary Culture after the Cold War." In *The Year 2000,* ed. Charles Strozier and Michael Flynn, 180–89. New York: Free Press, 1997.

Gilroy, Paul. *"There Ain't No Black in the Union Jack": The Cultural Politics of Race and Nation.* Chicago: University of Chicago Press, 1987.

Girard, Rene. *Violence and the Sacred.* Trans. Patrick Gregory. Baltimore: Johns Hopkins University Press, 1977.

Gluckman, Amy, and Betsy Reed, eds. *Homo Economics: Capitalism, Community, and Lesbian and Gay Life.* New York: Routledge, 1997.

Gramsci, Antonio. *Selections from the Prison Notebooks of Antonia Gramsci.* Ed. and trans. Quinti Hoare and Geoffrey Nowell Smith. New York: International, 1971.

Greven, Phillip. *The Protestant Temperament: Patterns of Child-Rearing, Religious Experience, and the Self in Early America.* New York: New American Library, 1977.

Grossberg, Lawrence. *We Gotta Get Out of This Place: Popular Conservatism and Postmodern Culture.* New York: Routledge, 1992.

Hadden, Jeffrey, and Anthony Schupe. *Televangelism: Power and Politics on God's Frontier.* New York: Holt, 1988.

Hall, Stuart. *The Hard Road to Renewal: Thatcherism and the Crisis of the Left.* London: Verso, 1988.

Hall, Stuart, with Chas Critcher, Tony Jefferson, John Clarke, and Brian Roberts. *Policing the Crisis: Mugging, the State, and Law and Order.* London: Macmillan, 1979.

Haraway, Donna. *Simians, Cyborgs and Women: The Reinvention of Nature.* New York: Routledge, 1991.

Harding, Susan. "If I Should Die before I Wake: Jerry Falwell's Pro-Life Gospel." In *Uncertain Terms: Negotiating Gender in American Culture,* ed. Faye Ginsburg and Anna Lowenhaupt Tsing, 76–97. Boston: Beacon, 1990.

——. *The Book of Jerry Falwell.* Princeton, NJ: Princeton University Press, 2000.

Hardisty, Jean. *Mobilizing Resentment.* Boston: Beacon, 1999.

Harvey, David. *The Condition of Postmodernity: An Enquiry into the Origins of Cultural Change.* Cambridge, England: Blackwell, 1990.

Helvarg, David. *The War against the Greens: The "Wise Use" Movement, the New Right and Anti-Environmental Violence.* San Francisco: Sierra Club Books, 1994.

Henderson, Mae. "Toni Morrison's *Beloved:* Re-membering the Body as Historical Text." In *Comparative American Identities: Race, Sex, and Nationality in the Modern Text,* ed. Hortense Spillers, 62–86. New York: Routledge, 1991.

Herman, Didi. *The Antigay Agenda: Orthodox Vision and the Christian Right.* Chicago: University of Chicago Press, 1997.

Higonnet, Anne. *Pictures of Innocence: The History and Crisis of Ideal Childhood.* London: Thames and Hudson, 1998.

Himmelstein, Jerome. *To the Right: The Transformation of American Conservatism.* Berkeley: University of California Press, 1990.

Hirsch, Marianne. *Family Frames: Photography in the Postmodern.* Cambridge, MA: Harvard University Press, 1997.

Hobsbawm, Eric. "Introduction: Inventing Traditions." In *The Invention of Tradition,* ed. Eric Hobsbawm and Terence Ranger, 1–14. Cambridge, England: Cambridge University Press, 1984.

Hofstadter, Richard. *The Paranoid Style in American Politics and Other Essays.* New York: Knopf, 1965.

Horsman, Reginald. *Race and Manifest Destiny: The Origins of American Racial Anglo-Saxonism.* Cambridge, MA: Harvard University Press, 1981.

Hughes, Richard. *Reviving the Ancient Faith: The Story of Churches of Christ in America.* Grand Rapids, MI: Eerdmans, 1996.

Hunter, James Davison. *American Evangelicalism: Conservative Religion and the Quandary of Modernity.* New Brunswick, NJ: Rutgers University Press, 1983.

——. *Culture Wars: The Struggle to Define America.* New York: Basic Books, 1992.

Huyssen, Andreas. *Twilight Memories: Marking Time in a Culture of Amnesia.* New York: Routledge, 1995.

Jeffords, Susan. *The Remasculinization of America: Gender and the Vietnam War.* Bloomington: Indiana University Press, 1989.

——. *Hard Bodies: Hollywood Masculinity in the Reagan Era.* New Brunswick, NJ: Rutgers University Press, 1994.

Johnson, Eithne. "Dr. Dobson's Advice to Christian Women: The Story of Strategic Motherhood." *Social Text* 16, no. 4 (winter 1998): 55–82.

——. "The Emergence of Christian Video and the Cultivation of Videovangelism." In *Media, Culture and the Religious Right,* ed. Linda Kintz and Julia Lesage, 191–210. Minneapolis: University of Minnesota Press, 1998.

Joseph, Miranda. "The Perfect Moment: Christians, Gays, and the NEA." *Socialist Review.* 3–4 (1996): 111–44.

——. "The Performance of Production and Consumption." *Social Text* 16, no. 1 (spring 1998): 25–61.

Juergensmeyer, Mark. *Terror in the Mind of God: The Global Rise of Religious Violence.* Berkeley: University of California Press, 2000.

Kaplan, Jeffrey. "The Context of American Millenarian Revolutionary Theology: The Case of the 'Identity Christian' Church of Israel." *Terrorism and Political Violence* 5, no. 1 (spring 1993): 30–82.

——. *Radical Religion in America: Millenarian Movements from the Far Right to the Children of Noah.* Syracuse: State University of New York Press, 1997.

——. ed. *Encyclopedia of White Power.* Lanham, MD: Rowman and Littlefield, 2000.

Kaplan, Jeffrey, with Leonard Weinberg. *The Emergence of a Euro-American Radical Right.* New Brunswick, NJ: Rutgers University Press, 1998.

Kessler, Suzanne. *Lessons from the Intersexed.* New Brunswick, NJ: Rutgers University Press, 1998.

Kintz, Linda. *Between Jesus and the Market: The Emotions That Matter in Right-Wing America.* Durham, NC: Duke University Press, 1998.

Klatch, Rebecca. *Women of the New Right.* Philadelphia: Temple University Press, 1987.

Kovel, Joel. *White Racism: A Psychohistory.* New York: Pantheon, 1970.

Kristeva, Julia. *Powers of Horror: An Essay on Abjection.* Trans. Leon Roudiez. New York: Columbia University Press, 1982.

Lacan, Jacques. *Ecrits.* Trans. Alan Sheridan. New York: Norton, 1977.

Laclau, Ernesto, and Chantal Mouffe. *Hegemony and Socialist Strategy.* London: Verso, 1985.

Lawrence, Bruce. *Defenders of God: The Fundamentalist Revolt against the Modern Age.* New York: Harper and Row, 1989.

Lehr, Valerie. *Queer Family Values: Debunking the Myth of the Nuclear Family.* Philadelphia: Temple University Press, 1999.

Lesage, Julia. "Christian Media." In *Media, Culture and the Religious Right,* ed. Linda Kintz and Julia Lesage, 21–50. Minneapolis: University of Minnesota Press, 1998.

Lewis, Lionel, and Dennis Brissett. "Sex as God's Work." *Society* 23 (March–April 1986): 67–75.

Leys, Ruth. "The Real Miss Beauchamp: Gender and the Subject of Imitation." In *Feminists Theorize the Political,* ed. Judith Butler and Joan Scott, 167–214. New York: Routledge, 1992.

Lo, Y. H. Clarence. *Small Property versus Big Business: Social Origins of the Property Tax Revolt.* Berkeley: University of California Press, 1990.

Lopez, Donald. *Prisoners of Shangri-la: Tibetan Buddhism and the West.* Chicago: University of Chicago Press, 1998.

Lorde, Audre. *Sister Outsider: Essays and Speeches.* Trumansburg, NY: Crossing Press, 1984.

Luker, Kristin. *Abortion and the Politics of Motherhood.* Berkeley: University of California Press, 1984.

MacLean, Nancy. *Behind the Mask of Chivalry: The Making of the Second Ku Klux Klan.* New York: Oxford University Press, 1994.

Marchand, Roland. *Advertising the American Dream: Making Way for Modernity, 1920–1940.* Berkeley: University of California Press, 1985.

Marsden, George. *Fundamentalism and American Culture: The Shaping of Twentieth Century Evangelicalism 1870–1925.* New York: Oxford University Press, 1980.

———. "Preachers of Paradox: The Religious New Right in Historical Perspective." In *Religion and America,* ed. Mary Douglas and Steve Tipton, 150–68. Boston: Beacon, 1983.

——. *Reforming Fundamentalism.* Grand Rapids, MI: Eerdmans, 1987.

Martin, William. *With God on Our Side.* New York: Broadway Books, 1996.

Matthaei, Julie. "The Sexual Division of Labor, Sexuality, and Lesbian/Gay Liberation: Towards a Marxist-Feminist Analysis of Sexuality in U.S. Capitalism." In *Homo Economics: Capitalism, Community, and Lesbian and Gay Life,* ed. Amy Gluckman and Betsy Reed, 135–64. New York: Routledge, 1998.

Marty, Martin E., and R. Scott Appleby, eds. *The Glory and the Power: The Fundamentalist Challenge to the Modern World.* Boston: Beacon, 1992.

May, Elaine Tyler. *Homeward Bound: American Families in the Cold War Era.* New York: Basic Books, 1988.

McDannell, Colleen. *Material Christianity: Religion and Popular Culture in America.* New Haven: Yale University Press, 1995.

Melton, Gordon. "The Identity Movement." In *Encyclopedic Handbook of Cults in America.* Rev. ed., 68–80. New York: Garland Publishing, 1992.

——. "British Israelism." In *Encyclopedia of American Religions,* 4th ed., 121. Washington, DC: Gale Research Inc., 1993.

Moen, Matthew. *The Christian Right and Congress.* Tuscaloosa: University of Alabama Press, 1989.

——. *The Transformation of the Christian Right.* Tuscaloosa: University of Alabama Press, 1992.

Moore, R. Laurence. *Selling God: American Religion in the Marketplace of Culture.* New York: Oxford University Press, 1994.

Morrison, Toni. *Beloved.* New York: Plume, 1987.

——. *Playing in the Dark: Whiteness and the Literary Imagination.* Cambridge, MA: Harvard University Press, 1992.

Moses, Wilson Jeremiah. *Black Messiahs and Uncle Toms: Social and Literary Manipulations of a Religious Myth.* Rev. ed. University Park: Pennsylvania State University Press, 1993.

Mosse, George. *Nationalism and Sexuality: Middle-Class Morality and Sexual Norms in Modern Europe.* Madison: University of Wisconsin Press, 1985.

Munt, Sally R., ed. *Butch/Femme: Inside Lesbian Gender.* London: Cassell, 1998.

Niditch, Susan. *Underdogs and Tricksters: A Prelude to Biblical Folklore.* New York: Harper and Row, 1987.

O'Leary, Stephen D. *Arguing the Apocalypse: A Theory of Millennial Rhetoric.* New York: Oxford University Press, 1994.

Omi, Michael, and Howard Winant. *Racial Formation in the United States: From the 1960s to the 1980s.* New York: Routledge, 1986.

Petchesky, Rosalind Pollack. "Antiabortion, Antifeminism and the Rise of the New Right." *Feminist Studies* 7, no. 2 (summer 1981): 206–46.

——. *Abortion and Woman's Choice: The State, Sexuality and Reproductive Freedom.* 2d ed. Boston: Northeastern University Press, 1990.

Pharr, Suzanne. *In the Time of the Right: Reflections on Liberation.* Berkeley, CA: Chardon, 1996.

Postman, Neil. *The Disappearance of Childhood.* 1982; New York: Vintage, 1994.

Pratt, Minnie Bruce. *Rebellion: Essays 1980–1991.* Ithaca, NY: Firebrand, 1991.

Radway, Jan. *Reading the Romance: Women, Patriarchy and Popular Literature.* Chapel Hill: University of North Carolina Press, 1984.

Reisebrodt, Martin. *Pious Passion: The Emergence of Modern Fundamentalism in the United States and Iran.* Trans. Don Reneau. Berkeley: University of California Press, 1993.

Ribuffo, Leo. *The Old Christian Right: The Protestant Far Right from the Great Depression to the Cold War.* Philadelphia: Temple University Press, 1983.

Rich, Evelyn. "Ku Klux Klan Ideology (1954–1988)." Ph.D. diss., Boston University, 1988.

Ridgeway, James. *Blood in the Face: The Ku Klux Klan, Aryan Nations, Nazi Skinheads and the Rise of the New White Culture.* New York: Thunder's Mouth, 1990.

Rose, Jacqueline. *Why War? Psychoanalysis, Politics and the Return to Melanie Klein.* Cambridge, England: Blackwell, 1993.

Rose, Susan. "Women Warriers: The Negotiation of Gender in a Charismatic Community." *Sociological Analysis* 48, no. 3 (1987): 245–58.

——. *Keeping Them Out of the Hands of Satan: Evangelical Schooling in America.* New York: Routledge, 1988.

——. "Christian Fundamentalism and Education in the United States." In *Fundamentalisms and Society: Reclaiming the Sciences, the Family and Education,* 452–89. Chicago: University of Chicago Press, 1993.

Sandeen, Ernest. *The Roots of Fundamentalism: British and American Millenarianism 1800–1930.* Chicago: University of Chicago Press, 1970.

Santner, Eric. *Stranded Objects: Mourning, Memory and Film in Postwar Germany.* Ithaca, NY: Cornell University Press, 1990.

Sassen, Saskia. *Globalization and Its Discontents: Essays on the New Mobility of People and Money.* New York: Random House, 1995.

——. *Losing Control? Sovereignty in an Age of Globalization.* New York: Columbia University Press, 1996.

Savran, David. *Taking It Like a Man: White Masculinity, Masochism and Contemporary American Culture.* Princeton, NJ: Princeton University Press, 1998.

Scheper-Hughes, Nancy, and Carolyn Sargent, eds. *Small Wars: The Cultural Politics of Childhood.* Berkeley: University of California Press, 1998.

Schupe, Anson. "The Reconstructionist Movement on the New Christian Right." *Christian Century* (4 October 1989): 880–82.

Schupe, Anson, and Bruce Barron. "Reasons for the Growing Popularity of Christian Reconstructionism: The Determination to Attain Dominion." In *Religion and Politics in Comparative Perspective: Revival of Religious Fundamentalism in East and West,* ed. Bronislaw Misztal and Anson Schupe, 83–96. Westport, CT: Praeger, 1992.

Schwartz, Regina. "Joseph's Bones and the Resurrection of the Text." In *The Book and the Text: The Bible and Literary Theory,* ed. Regina Schwartz, 40–59. Cambridge, MA: Basil Blackwell, 1990.

——. "The Histories of David: Biblical Scholarship and Biblical Stories." In *Not in Heaven: Coherence and Complexity in Biblical Narrative,* ed. Jason P. Rosenblatt and Joseph F. Sitterson, 192–210. Bloomington: Indiana University Press, 1991.

——. *The Curse of Cain: The Violent Legacy of Monotheism.* Chicago: University of Chicago Press, 1997.

Sears, James. *Lonely Hunters: An Oral History of Lesbian and Gay Southern Life, 1948–1968.* Boulder, CO: Westview, 1997.

Sedgwick, Eve Kosofsky. "Privilege of Unknowing." *Genders* 1 (spring 1988): 102–24.

——. *Epistemology of the Closet.* Berkeley: University of California Press, 1990.

Silvermann, Kaja. *Male Subjectivity at the Margins.* New York: Routledge, 1992.

Smith, Anna Marie. *New Right Discourse on Race and Sexuality in Britain, 1968–1990.* Cambridge, England: Cambridge University Press, 1994.

Smith, Barbara Herrnstein. *Belief and Resistance: Dynamics of Contemporary Intellectual Controversy.* Cambridge, MA: Harvard University Press, 1997.

Smith, Christian. *American Evangelicalism.* Chicago: University of Chicago Press, 1998.

——. *Christian America? What Evangelicals Really Want.* Berkeley: University of California Press, 2000.

Smith, Jonathan Z. *Imagining Religion: From Babylon to Jonestown.* Chicago: University of Chicago Press, 1982.

Smith, Lillian. *Killers of the Dream.* Revised and enlarged. 1949; New York: Norton, 1961.

Spivak, Gayatri Chakravorty. "The New Historicism: Political Commitment and the Postmodern Critic." In *The New Historicism,* ed. H. Aram Veeser, 277–92. New York: Routledge, 1989.

——. *The Post-Colonial Critic: Interviews, Strategies, Dialogues.* Ed. Sarah Harasym. New York: Routledge, 1990.

——. "Constitutions and Culture Studies." *Yale Journal of Law and Humanities* 2, no. 1 (winter 1990): 133–47.

Sprague, Marshall. *Newport in the Rockies: The Life and Times of Colorado Springs.* Rev. ed. Athens: Ohio University Press, 1987.

Stacey, Judith. *Brave New Families: Stories of Domestic Upheaval in Late Twentieth Century America.* New York: Basic Books, 1990.

———. "Sexism by a Subtler Name? Post-Industrial Conditions and Post-Feminist Consciousness in the Silicon Valley." In *Women, Class and the Feminist Imagination: A Socialist-Feminist Reader,* ed. Karen Hansen and Ilene J. Philipson, 338–56. Philadelphia: Temple University Press, 1990.

———. "Scents, Scholars and Stigma: "The Revisionist Campaign for Family Values." *Social Text* 40 (fall 1994): 51–74.

Stacey, Judith, and Susan Elizabeth Gerard. " 'We Are not Doormats': The Influence of Feminism on Contemporary Evangelicals in the United States." In *Uncertain Terms: Negotiating Gender in American Culture,* ed. Faye Ginsburg and Anna Lowenhaupt Tsing, 98–117. Boston: Beacon, 1990.

Stern, Kenneth. *A Force upon the Plain: The American Militia Movement and the Politics of Hate.* New York: Simon and Schuster, 1996.

Stock, Catherine McNichol. *Rural Radicals: Righteous Rage in the American Grain.* Ithaca, NY: Cornell University Press, 1996.

Strozier, Charles. *Apocalypse: On the Psychology of Fundamentalism in America.* Boston: Beacon, 1994.

Sturken, Marita. *Tangled Memories: The Vietnam War, The AIDS Epidemic, and the Politics of Remembering.* Berkeley: University of California Press, 1997.

Tabor, James. *Why Waco? Cults and the Battle for Religious Freedom in America.* Berkeley: University of California Press, 1995.

Taussig, Michael. *Shamanism, Colonialism, and the Wild Man: A Study in Terror and Healing.* Chicago: University of Chicago Press, 1987.

Terry, Jennifer. *An American Obsession: Science, Medicine, and Homosexuality in Modern Society.* Chicago: University of Chicago Press, 1999.

Tipton, Steven M. *Getting Saved from the Sixties: Moral Meaning in Conversion and Cultural Change.* Berkeley: University of California Press, 1982.

Volosinov, V. N. *Marxism and the Philosophy of Language.* Trans. Ladislav Matejka and I. R. Titunik. Cambridge, MA: Harvard University Press, 1973.

Walter, Jess. *Every Knee Shall Bow: The Truth and Tragedy of Ruby Ridge and the Randy Weaver Family.* New York: Regan Books, 1995.

Watt, David Harrington. *A Transforming Faith: Explorations of Twentieth-Century American Evangelicalism.* New Brunswick, NJ: Rutgers University Press, 1991.

Weber, Timothy. *Living in the Shadow of the Second Coming.* Chicago: University of Chicago Press, 1987.

Welch, Sharon. *A Feminist Ethic of Risk.* Minneapolis: Fortress, 1990.

Wessinger, Catherine. *How the Millennium Comes Violently: From Jonestown to Heaven's Gate*. New York: Seven Bridges, 2000.

West, Cornel. *Prophesy Deliverance! An Afro-American Revolutionary Christianity*. Philadelphia: Westminster, 1982.

Weston, Kath. *Families We Choose*. New York: Columbia University Press, 1991.

——. *Render Me, Gender Me: Lesbians Talk Sex, Class, Color, Nation, Studmuffins . . .* New York: Columbia University Press, 1996.

——. *Long Slow Burn: Sexuality and Social Science*. New York: Routledge, 1998.

Whitelam, Keith. *The Invention of Ancient Israel: The Silencing of Palestinian History*. New York: Routledge, 1996.

Williams, Patricia. *The Alchemy of Race and Rights*. Cambridge, MA: Harvard University Press, 1991.

Wills, Garry. *A Necessary Evil: A History of American Distrust of Government*. New York: Simon and Schuster, 1999.

Wolfe, Alan. *One Nation, After All: What Americans Really Think about God, Country, Family, Racism, Welfare, Immigration, Homosexuality, Work, the Right, the Left and Each Other*. New York: Viking, 1998.

Wood, Denis. *The Power of Maps*. New York: Guilford, 1992.

Young, James. *The Texture of Memory: Holocaust Memorials and Meaning*. New Haven: Yale University Press, 1993.

Young, Robert. *Colonial Desire: Hybridity in Theory, Culture and Race*. New York: Routledge, 1995.

Yudice, George. "The Privatization of Culture," *Social Text* 59, no. 2 (summer 1999): 17–35.

Žižek, Slavoj. *The Sublime Object of Ideology*. London: Verso, 1989.

——. "Eastern Europe's Republics of Gilead." In *Dimensions of Radical Democracy*, ed. Chantal Mouffe, 193–207. New York: Verso, 1992.

Index

Ann Burlein is Assistant Professor of Religion
at Meredith College.

Library of Congress Cataloging-in-Publication Data
Burlein, Ann
Lift high the cross : where white supremacy and the
Christian right converge / Ann Burlein.
p. cm.
Includes bibliographical references and index.
ISBN 0-8223-2837-2 (alk. paper)—
ISBN 0-8223-2864-x (pbk. : alk. paper)
1. White supremacy movements—United States.
2. Christianity and politics—United States. 3. Right-
wing extremists—United States. 4. Christian Right
(Organization) 5. Christian Coalition. I. Title.
E184.A1 B899 2002
322.4'4'097309045—dc21   2001040716